Messiah

UNVEILING THE
MYSTERY
OF THE AGES

CHARLES CRISMIER

All Scripture quotations are taken from the King James Version of the Bible.

The choice of the King James Version was based upon its continued prominence as the most quoted, read, remembered and published version in the historical life of the Western world. Emphasis is indicated by bold-faced type to highlight portions of the text for particular focus throughout.

Messiah: Unveiling the Mystery of the Ages
Copyright ©2022 by Charles Crismier

Carpenter's Son Publishing
Franklin, TN
and
Elijah Books
P.O. Box 70879
Richmond, VA 23255

Interior design by Pine Hill Graphics
Cover design by Fresh Air Media

Publisher's Cataloging-in-Publication Data
(Provided by Cassidy Cataloguing Services, Inc.)
Crismier, Charles.

   Messiah: Unveiling the Mystery of the Ages
   / Charles Crismier - - Richmond, Va : Elijah Books,
   2022.
         ISBN: 978-1-954437-55-5
         Includes bibliographical references.
         Summary: The apex of human history and the
   culmination of biblical prophecy now loom ominously.
   What, then, should the inhabitants of this mortal sphere
   anticipate as history and prophecy become congruent? In
   order to comprehend the pattern and progress of history,
   it is necessary to understand Messiah: Unveiling
   the Mystery of the Ages. - - Publisher.

         1. History - - Biblical teaching.
   2. History - - Religious aspects - - Christianity.
   3. End of the world. 4. Bible - - Prophecies - -
   Temple of Jerusalem. 5. Eschatology. 6. Kingdom
   of God - - Biblical teaching. 7. Temple Mount
   (Jerusalem) - - Religious aspects - - Christianity.
   8. Antichrist. I. Title.

Table of Contents

PART 5—THE CORRUPTION OF CERTAINTY

PART 6—THE FAKE-REAL MESSIAH

PART 7—THE UNVEILING OF MESSIAH

PART 1

A Preface and Promise

THE MYSTERY OF HISTORY

"The time for extracting a lesson from history is ever at hand for those who are wise."

~Demosthenes

HISTORY HIDES ITS MYSTERIES. While the facts and occurrences, places and events of the footsteps of our human forebears are fixed in time and place, recitation of these details, however knowledgeable and seemingly perceptive, reveals little of their individual or collective implication.

On the other hand, we are continually reminded that "the only thing we learn from history is that we don't learn from history." And we are further warned that "those who don't learn from history are doomed to repeat it." What, then, are we to do? How are we to "learn" from history? Are we inevitably "doomed" to repeat it despite persistent warning? And is it the facts of history we are destined to repeat, or is it the patterns driven by underlying mysterious forces?

HISTORICAL INTERPRETATION LACKS CERTAINTY. The most insightful efforts to discover and define the driving forces and direction of history, in the final analysis, become little more than informed opinion that becomes de-formed by viewpoints, both individual and cultural, that spin the reality of facts and occurrences into a tapestry portraying the predilections of the philosopher, historian or politician. In our current age, where the doctrines and dogmas of political correctness, multiculturalism and religious pluralism have been granted near absolute authority as the screen through which all reality must be filtered, the task of interpreting history with any measure of intellectual integrity has been rendered nearly impossible. The question then remains, therefore, whether there exists any more hopeful, reliable and even more objective way to study and interpret the last six thousand years of the record of mankind upon our plant. And if so, would it make a shred of difference in the direction, disposition and destiny of the nations and of the world's individual inhabitants? Is there a well-defined and perceptible tapestry of historical truth emerging that might guide us all in this most dangerous time?

A TAPESTRY OF TRUTH IS EMERGING. Indeed, the threads of time and the colorful times and events woven therein over sixty centuries last passed are even now revealing an emerging pattern that has been discerned and described by prophets for at least thirty-five centuries. These patterns and their prophetic significance have largely escaped the attention or have been blindly ignored by both the poor and the powerful and by prognosticators even as we teeter on the precipice of global conflagration.

IS THIS OUR MOMENT OF TRUTH? The leaders of the nations are trembling. The peoples of our planet are terrified. Nothing seems certain, except chaos. The lust for power and petroleum have catapulted the planet to the precipice of a chasm so sheer as to shake the confidence of the most courageous. Is there any perspective that might shed a ray of hopeful light in the encroaching darkness?

Indeed, this is our moment of truth. We are languishing in the valley of decision without genuine direction. Destiny rides in the balance. Please, then, join us on this fascinating journey back through time so as to grasp more effectively the solemnity of our time. Time is short so we must proceed quickly. The prophets of times past will point the way even as we grope in darkness. The picture that will soon emerge will either leave you awash in unprecedented hope or in unfathomable horror. Let us be on our way to "Unveil History's Greatest Mystery"—the haunting, yet persistent, mystery of MESSIAH.

Chapter 1

MYSTERIOUS TIMES

"It was the best of times! It was the worst of times."
~Charles Dickens

THE HEADLINES SCREAM the unprecedented seriousness of our times. Europe is on the verge of collapse. The "Arab Spring" that promised the hopeful rise of democracy in the Middle East developed into the growing horror of the dictatorial rule of fundamental Islam. Turkey and Iran vie for dominance over the Islamic world—more than a billion people that have no unifying leadership. Will there be a new Ottoman empire or a resurrected Persian empire? They pursue an Islamic "New World Order" as declared by the former "Persian" president, Mahmoud Ahmadinejad. But Islam is not alone. China also intends to rule the world with well over a billion people—a declared goal now within a mere 25 years.

Pursuit of a New Order

Leaders of the western world increasingly clamor for clarity and courage to implement a "New World Order," claiming it to be the only hope and salvation for our planet. John Kerry, former U.S. Presidential candidate, declared Joe Biden, as president, will "open the door" to the long-sought New World Order and global government. Russia, China, Britain, Canada… indeed most of our world, including

American leaders, have called for the full implementation of such a new global world order, as did U.S. President George Herbert Walker Bush. His address to Congress in 1991 was the first time any American president had ever publicly voiced this global goal.

Even the Vatican, under three successive popes, Pope John Paul II, Pope Benedict XVI and Pope Francis, has issued a call to implement a new global world and economic order with a new global currency. Britain's former prime minister, Gordon Brown, former U.S. Secretary of State Henry Kissinger and other leaders strongly suggested Barack Obama, the 44th president of the United States, was the "anointed one" to lead the way into this new "world of the ages," promising peace and prosperity to a world seemingly in hopeless tumult. Even Germany's respected news magazine, *Der Spiegel*, titled its cover page "THE MESSIAH FACTOR," in reference to the secularly promised peacemaker. Are these not mysterious times?

Planet Earth is not a particularly friendly place at this moment, if indeed it ever was. Perhaps never a more apt description could be given than that of Charles Dickens in his *Tale of Two Cities*… "It was the best of times, it was the worst of times." And who would ultimately rule such a utopian New World Order for the collective peace, prosperity and justice of all humanity? Will a New Age version of the French Revolution present a "Robespierre" to lead into a horror-filled hope of Liberty, Equality and Fraternity?

Hope and Change

"Hope and change" became an increasingly universal cry through-out the nations. There is an intuitive sense among peoples everywhere that the world cannot continue on with even a remote air of confidence in its current state. Hence the promise of "Change You Can BELIEVE IN" carried immense motivational weight whether or not it was rooted in any meaningful reality. The world thus clamors for a deliverer—a "messianic" leader.

Is there any hope? Is there anyone we can truly trust? Who can restore order? What promises will tickle our itching ears to promote participation at the ballot box? What good is freedom in the face of enveloping fear? And is there, in reality, any genuine set of principles…

or even prophecy… that might shed the light of hope amid the encroaching darkness and enveloping global horror?

Is real hope merely a figment of the imagination? And where does change lead? Change *from* what *to* what? If we are truly living in such a modern and enlightened world and society, why the devastating evidence of rapid deterioration even in the face of exploding technology? Is chaos destined to be the new norm?

Haunting Questions

Is there any real answer to our dilemma or are we left only with unending and unanswered questions? Must we grope blindly, hoping upon hope that an exit might be found, that genuine direction be discovered, or that some political savior might appear to usher in a golden age of peace and prosperity?

The answer to these haunting questions lies in an understanding of history—of man's story—from God's viewpoint. History, from a Divine perspective, has a beginning and an end, and He understands the end from the beginning. The trouble is that we do not, or at least refuse to agree with the plan and purposes of our Creator that are clearly expressed in the Bible, often referred to as "the Scriptures" or "the Word of God." And if we have no Creator, are we abandoned to ourselves to provide our own messianic hope?

In the pages that follow, the panoply of history from God's viewpoint as revealed in the Bible will be unfolded in such a way that you will be able to not only capture the grandeur of God's purpose but be able to choose, for yourself, to embrace the only change you will ever be able to totally believe in. A new hope and vision will arise, enabling you to see what lies ahead in this tumultuous time, yet have genuine peace without the terrifying fear that will increasingly grip our planet. The seemingly illusive mystery of the ages—the mystery of messiah—must be unveiled.

Chapter 2

REVEALING MYSTERIES

"If science cannot solve the
mystery of messiah, who can?"

MYSTERIES DEMAND TO BE REVEALED! There is a reason why the publishing genre of *Mystery* is one of the top three year after year. People almost universally, regardless of age or culture, are drawn to seek out the solution to those things hidden or not easily discernable.

Yet mysteries, by their very nature, inherently demand to be understood—to be figured out—to be revealed. And when that moment of revelation happens, a surge of satisfaction issues in our minds—even in our spirits. The resolution of that which had defied understanding brings a peace that cannot clearly be described—seemingly beyond understanding.

Mysteries Are Created

The mere fact that a mystery can be uncovered, revealed or unveiled implies that somewhere, somehow and by someone outside of ourselves, a story, either written by a human author or the *Author of the Ages*, has been "written" such that it can be discerned. It is for that reason that scientists, pursuing understanding of the natural order, are able to come to conclusions that are prefaced by theories as to how certain events or conditions have occurred.

In other words, all mysteries have an author, whether natural or supernatural. Unravelling a crime or other mystery drafted by a human author does not require supernatural or spiritual insight, revelation or discernment. But the ultimate mysteries of the ages sought out for millennia passed require a different level of insight or understanding so as to comprehend the creative mind and heart of the Author. For this reason, the world of science and faith often seem to be at odds. As Richard Lewontin, a renowned Harvard evolutionist, declared:

> We take the side of science in spite of the patent absurdity of some of its constructs…in spite of the tolerance of the scientific community for unsubstantiated commitment to materialism…. We are forced by our *a priori* adherence to material causes to create an apparatus of investigation and set of concepts that produce material explanations, no matter how counterintuitive, no matter how mystifying to the uninitiated. Moreover, that materialism is absolute, for we cannot allow a Divine foot in the door.[1]

Clearly, the refusal to "allow a Divine foot in the door" creates the necessity to devise a counterfeit or alternative explanation for the existence of the universe, the natural order and of life itself. Therefore, that very mode of supposed "scientific thinking" rejecting a spiritual or supernatural creation becomes a self-imposed blindness or inability—yes even unwillingness—to recognize a messiah or to embrace a messianic hope. The very concept of modern science denying Divine creation thus prevents vast numbers of modern man from unravelling, or even contemplating, the mystery of the ages culminating in a messiah.

Who Can Solve Mysteries?

If science cannot solve the mystery of messiah, who can? Are there mysteries that are discernable by the natural mind of man and others that cannot be deciphered by the natural mind, thus requiring infusion of spiritual insight?

Throughout history, many have relied upon cultural traditions interwoven with religious practices to pierce the veil of the mystery of messiah and of the spiritual world. Others have placed great trust in religious training, delegating discernment of spiritual mysteries to mystics, rabbis, imams, priests and pastors or New Age gurus. The result is a plethora of opinions embraced by hundreds of religions and thousands of camps or virtual tribes within those religions, each claiming either the knowledge of the mystery of the ages culminating in a coming messiah, or the means to ultimately obtain that perceptive ability.

Yet, if the Bible, whether Old or New Covenants [Testaments] is correct, the overwhelming majority of humankind will ultimately embrace a counterfeit. The Jewish Tanakh [Old Covenant] explicitly warns of a disastrous embrace of such a counterfeit *messiah* in whom Israel will place ultimate trust, identified in Isaiah 28:14-15 as "a covenant with death," because "under falsehood have we hid ourselves." Rabbi Shaul, otherwise known by Christians as the Apostle Paul, warned of a "great falling away" of believers immediately preceding the manifestation of Satan's counterfeit messiah, the "son of perdition" (II Thess. 2:2-8). He also warned those who by virtue of their perceived human wisdom think they are capable of always "figuring things out." In a clear rebuke, even perhaps to many professing Christians, Paul wrote in I Cor. 2:14:

> But the natural man receiveth not the things of the Spirit of God: for they are foolishness unto him: neither can he know them, because they are spiritually discerned.

The prophet Daniel, in the Tanakh, makes clear the coming of a mystery messiah figure "in the latter time" of human history. This counterfeit messiah personage, invested with the deceptive and demonic power of the Deceiver himself, shall "speak great things" (Dan. 7:8), shall pompously "speak great words against the most High" and shall "wear out the saints of the most High" (Dan. 7:25).

So great was the impact of the revelation of this demonically-empowered imposter that Daniel, one of the most righteous men of Scripture, "fainted and was sick," confessing: "I was astonished at the vision, but none understood it" (Dan. 8:27). While demonstrably real to Daniel's discerning mind and senses, the exact timing and true implications remained undiscerned—a mystery yet to be revealed.

So the question then remains: "Who can solve mysteries?" The prophet provides the one and only answer when challenged by King Nebuchadnezzar to interpret his mysterious dream foretelling the progression of world empires to the end of the age. Daniel answered the king: "There is a God in heaven that revealeth secrets" (Dan. 2:28). After the king's mysterious dream was interpreted, he declared, "Of a truth it is, that your God is a God of gods, and a Lord of kings, and a revealer of secrets, seeing thou couldest reveal this secret" (Dan. 2:47).

Of Secrets and Mysteries

The word *mystery* or *mysteries* occurs 27 times in the New Covenant/Testament. Instead, we find the word *secret* used in the Psalms and Proverbs and in the Prophets, meaning that which is a mystery or an intimate revelation of the mind and heart of God.

A mystery is that which cannot be known but for divine insight or revelation. Similarly, a secret is hidden from the natural view or understanding without the access door being opened by the Spirit of God, thus making understandable or discernable that which is otherwise veiled from view.

An interesting, yet non-specifically prophetic but profound use of the word *secret*, is found in Psalm 25:14. The implication of the truth of this seemingly simple Psalm is of such magnitude that this author has written an entire book unveiling its vast significance for all sincere seekers (*The SECRET of the LORD*, Charles Crismier, ELIJAH BOOKS, ©2011). Soberly consider this use of the word *secret*.

The secret of the LORD is with them that fear him; and he will show them his covenant.

The Mystery of the Ages

If, as the prophet Daniel declared, "there is a God in heaven that revealeth secrets" (Dan. 2:28), "He revealeth the deep and secret things [mysteries]: he knoweth what is in the darkness…" [what is otherwise hidden from His human creation] (Dan. 2:22), how then are we, in our time, to discern history's greatest mystery, the ultimate mystery of the ages… the mystery of Messiah?

The answer may be, at least partially, lurking in a further mystery for which we have many and multiplying clues nearly screaming at those who have eyes to see. The looming question prerequisite to unveiling the "Mystery of the Ages" is to determine, within discernable parameters, the actual age in which we are living. It is to that question we now turn.

Chapter 3

THE MYSTERY OF THE AGES

"Messianic fervor is growing worldwide."

THE VERY CONCEPT OF AGES, or epochs of time, is inherently mysterious. This is most likely true for several reasons.

1. Time itself seems somewhat mysterious to most. Even though we purport to measure it with exactitude, we can neither see it nor fully grasp either the reality of its passing or its true implications. It remains somewhat of an abstraction.

2. The very use of the word *ages*, or as often stated as *epochs*, defies accurate or exact definition, leaving a very nebulous sense of a very significant or vast period of time past, present or future—in which we purport to describe events thought to have occurred but which we do not fully comprehend.

3. If time exists as a reality, is or was it created to assist finite human beings to exist and conduct themselves with a sense of meaning and purpose that is measurable? Is time, therefore, earthbound?

4. And finally, if the very concept of *time* is created relative primarily to earthbound humanity, is there a creative person, force or God who exists outside of time in a realm broadly described by finite beings as *eternity*?

Ages Past, Present and Future

Why do you suppose authors, songwriters and scientists refer to "ages past" or a "future age"? Why do historians, astronomers and astrologers talk of epochs of time? Is it not because there is awareness of events that lie well beyond our current understanding that we yearn to either investigate or embrace with some level of present acknowledgement even though we well know we are "looking through a glass darkly"?

Clearly, notwithstanding the glorious advances of modern technology and other investigative technologies, there remains something every elusive when considering ages, epochs, time and eternity or existence without time.

Amazingly, however, some of the greatest interests, concerns and explorations of homo sapiens throughout time have reached into those realms of the elusive "unknown" that seem to dance perpetually beyond our defining grasp. This is true particularly for those who seek spiritual, or as some would say *esoteric* insight so as to better understand present and future developments on our planet.

Are There Spiritual Ages?

The concept of *ages* now takes on a new dimension—a dimension of consummate significance superseding all other applications and implications of the word. If indeed there are truly "spiritual ages," the mystery of ages deepens as to what is to be understood by inhabitants of planet Earth. Are there, in actuality, spiritual ages encompassing ever-greater implications for the life, purpose and destiny of humankind? If so, what are they? And what might they mean for us as mere mortals living in a world that seems increasingly to be heading inexorably in a direction we cannot seem to "put our finger on" with precise certainty?

The famed Martin Luther, historic symbol of the Protestant Reformation, penned memorable words in his great hymn *A Might Fortress is Our God* that echo down to our time. In describing Messiah as "God's own choosing," he wrote that he is "from **age** to **age** the same."

Another hymnist wrote passionately of faith in a coming messiah: "O God our help from **ages** past, our hope for years to come." Yet another linked the God of history past with a messianic hope to come in the famous lyrics "Rock of **Ages** cleft for me, let me hide myself in thee." Here, the *Rock* of Israel, i.e., HaShem, Jehovah or God is ultimately manifested as Messiah; the Anointed One as redeemer and reconciler of all things, the Hope of Israel, and all who will put their trust in Him (Deut. 32:4; II Sam. 23:3; Matt. 16:18; I Cor. 10:4).

While these are largely expressions of the Christian's hope of a coming age, so also the Hebrew Bible, the Tanakh or "Old Testament" weaves a similar hope and theme throughout Jewish history pointing expectantly toward an age of messianic fulfillment through the line of King David. Belief of the future advent of the Messiah is one of the fundamental requisites of the Jewish faith, as confirmed by the famed Maimonides: "Anyone who does not believe in him or one who does not anticipate his [Messiah's] coming, not only denies the prophets, but also the Torah and Moses our Rabbi."[1]

During the Second Temple period (516BC-70CE), after return from Babylonian captivity, Jewish messianic conceptions developed, ranging from this-worldly, political expectations to apocalyptic anticipation of an endtime in which the dead would be resurrected and the Kingdom of Heaven would be established on earth, ushering in an age of peace and justice. Publications issuing from Israel over the quarter century last passed confirm an ever-intensifying belief that the world has now entered the final messianic age and is rapidly moving toward the "desire of the ages"—the long-expected King Messiah.

Many throughout the Muslim world are also convinced we are living in the messianic age, rapidly approaching an apocalyptic moment. Muslims anticipate the Mahdi—the twelfth imam, who will lead them in the final, glorious conquest of earth, ushering in a global Caliphate. It is the Islamic "apocalypse" or unveiling to be soon revealed as we enter the end of this age or end times.

Messianic fervor is growing worldwide. A flurry of self-proclaimed messiahs is manifesting throughout the nations, some political, some solely spiritual, and some (as with Islam) an ultimate entanglement of politics, religion, law and culture.

And making the messianic moment even more mysterious comes the so-called Age of Aquarius, broadly defining New Age spirituality.

By self-proclamation of the astrological prophets of New Age spirituality, what began to spread through music and culture in the 1960s reached its fulfillment of the true coming of the age with the December 2020 planetary congruency of Jupiter and Saturn.

Thus, this is now the age of spiritual consummation, redefining the world in a spiritual unity of messianic globalization and long-anticipated utopia. Although not easily defined with particularity, this "New Age" spirituality promising a vague utopia and "global consciousness" is a stew of astrology, Hinduism, Buddhism, Judaism and Christianity redefining God as individually desired or felt so as to achieve a sense of personal peace with the promise of global unity as the long-expected "messianic" hope.

The Mystery of Messiah Persists

Most secular Jews do not embrace the concept of Messiah being an actual person. Rather, they embrace what they refer to as the *messianic age* in which *tikkun olam* will be fulfilled in the final restoration or redemption of the world in peace and justice. Most Orthodox Jews, however, anticipate a human, yet not divine "messiah." Thus the mind and heart of the Jewish people is deeply divided over what is to be expected, yet two-thirds of Israel's Jewish population currently believe we are in "the messianic age."

Likewise, many Muslims believe we are in this amorphous "messianic age," yet are looking for the Mahdi or "twelfth imam" who must be ushered in through global conflagration.

Professing Christians, perhaps surprisingly, are uniquely divided in their expectations of a messiah. Many popular pastors preach "Your best life now" rather than a messianic redemption to come. Their focus is seemingly on people-pleasing in the moment rather than on preparation for a soon-coming Messiah who will "judge the world with righteousness" (Psa. 96:13). Many others believe theologically in a coming Messiah but seem to be unconvinced that we are living in the age foretold throughout the Scriptures to expect Him, therefore their lives do not reflect such an anticipation anytime soon. A growing number are increasingly convinced that the Messiah will soon be unveiled in great power and glory, resolving for time and eternity the "Mystery of the Ages."

By contrast, the globalists and New Agers are busy building their self-defined utopias, having dismissed the God of creation from both their mind and spiritual imagination, intent on rebuilding spiritually and politically a post-modern Tower of Babel.

Since the Mystery of the Ages remains unresolved for most, perhaps we should more deeply explore the thinking of these various viewpoints, because without exception, VIEWPOINT DEFINES DESTINY.

PART 2

OUR MYSTERIOUS MESSIANIC HISTORY

THE SEARCH FOR A SAVIOR, A Deliverer, a figure in whom we can repose our hopes for security, prosperity and unity amid chaos, whether temporal or eternal, is deeply stamped on the pages of history.

A Trajectory of Terror and Triumph

With virtually every messianic hope can be found an inevitable trajectory of both terror and triumph. Terror or fear births the cry or yearning for a "savior"—a messianic figure—to deliver us from chaos into a time of utopian expectation of peace, security and prosperity, well encapsulated in the Hebrew word *shalom*. Perhaps shockingly, however, the promised hope soon devolves into a new era of terror as the true nature of the trusted deliverer becomes evident, revealed as unrestrained lust for power and betrayal, the latter terror often more severe than what precipitated the advent of the deliverer.

From "Messiah" to "Messiah"

It might be said that one of the great mysteries of the ages is that humans trustingly and repeatedly repose their hopes for "salvation" in men and women of flesh and blood who "put their pants on one leg at a time" just as the rest of the people, yet are envisioned as the *ONE* to enlighten the world amid its ever-increasing darkness.

In the chapters following in Part 2, we will trace back this somewhat mysterious propensity to seek peace and prosperity, thus achieving an ever-illusory unity amid chaos to save the world. This journey is of profound significance to each of us, since this mysterious messianic history is near, even as we speak, repeating itself with promised glory only to devolve into global destruction.

Climb into your chariot, harness up, for the journey ahead is dangerous and will, for most, determine destiny.

Chapter 4

FROM NIMROD TO THE NEW WORLD ORDER

*"He who rules the Temple Mount
rules the world."*

HIS NAME MEANS "WE SHALL REBEL." Nimrod, Son of Cush, was a hunter and builder of the kingdom of Babel, who inspired the disobedient sons of Noah to build a tower "whose top may reach unto heaven" and "let us make us a name, lest we should be scattered over the earth" (Gen. 10:8-10; 11:1-9).

From Babel to Babylon

We are told in the Hebrew Scriptures that the God of Creation and of History was not at all happy with their building and unifying enterprise and confounded their language so that their purported self-salvation in a religious/political unity could not proceed. But what was the underlying problem from God's viewpoint? To understand the heart motivation of this ungodly enterprise is to gain great insight into the great messianic mystery of the ages that echoes now to this ultimate mystery moment of human history advancing breathtakingly toward its dramatic culmination.

The bricks of that infamous Tower of Babel became the meta-phorical bricks for mankind's repeated efforts to save himself while rebelling in unity against the God who saves. The Creator had instructed Noah, his sons and their families to "go forth of the ark," to "be fruitful and multiply and replenish the earth" (Gen. 8:15-16; 9:1), yet from the very beginning, the "beginning of his [Nimrod's] kingdom", the very first kingdom after the flood, the people determined to defy God's instructions. Rather than to disperse to form the God-designed and intended nations (Gen. 10:1-10), they decided collectively under Nimrod's "messianic" leadership to trust in a false or counterfeit unity.

This would have frustrated God's design to save and protect the people who He protected from the rebellion-destroying flood. And so, "the LORD scattered them abroad from thence upon the face of all the earth." "The LORD did there confound the language of all the earth" and the Lord did "scatter them abroad upon the face of all the earth" (Gen. 11:6-9).

Babel was a monument of human ingenuity but was also a monument of human pride, thus exalting created mankind over the Creator God. And that has become the terrifying trajectory of history, soon to reach the pinnacle of human pride in a One World Order.

Beware Babylonian Betrayal

Babel became Babylon. It was founded in southern Mesopotamia on the Euphrates River sometime around 2000 BC, gaining prominence by ebb and flow over many centuries, overcome by the Assyrians and challenged by Egypt.

Nebuchadnezzar assumed power as king around 610 BC, defeated the Assyrians and routed the Egyptians at the Battle of Carchemish in 605 BC (Jer. 46:2-12). He soon marched on Jerusalem. Many of Judah were killed and later many others were taken captive as a 70-year corrective discipline from the God of Israel for their own rebellion. It is this same Nebuchadnezzar, recorded in the Hebrew Scriptures by Daniel the prophet, who was afforded two or three opportunities to embrace and recognized the God of Israel as Creator, who alone reveals secrets or mysteries.

But Nebuchadnezzar, the greatest king of the Neo-Babylonian period, referred to in Daniel's revelation of the kings' mysterious colossal vision as the "head of gold" (Dan. 2:38), was trapped in the pride of his power.

The king spake, and said, Is not this great Babylon, what I have built…by the might of my power, and for the honour of my majesty?

But while the word was in the king's mouth, there fell a voice from heaven, saying… "The kingdom is departed from thee" (Dan. 4:30-31). God graciously gave Nebuchadnezzar seven years to come to grips with his paralyzing pride, after which time he humbly repented, declaring:

Now I Nebuchadnezzar praise and extol and honour the King of heaven, all whose works are truth, and his ways judgment: and those that walk in pride he is able to abase (Dan. 4:37).

But Nebuchadnezzar was infected with the spirit of Babel. He engaged in what, for that time, was a massive globalized city with a palace and huge throne room fit for a god. He built many temples, the greatest of which was for the city's patron god, Marduk, devilishly decorated with gold. Just north he erected the huge stepped tower of Babylon, a ziggurat, seven stories tall, towering some 300 feet above the city.

Yet in the Jewish mind as well as that of the Christian world, Babylon became symbolic of man's prideful decadence and of God's judgment. As God warned through Jeremiah, "Thus shall Babylon sink, and shall not rise from the evil that I will bring upon her…" (Jer. 51:64).

The world has, in God's eyes, become "Babylon." The very spirit of Babel and Babylon has systemically, as a spiritual virus, invaded the entire earth, "With whom the kings of the earth have committed fornication" and with whom "the inhabitants of the earth have been made drunk with the wine of her fornication." This *Babylon* is described as "the great whore," and "upon her forehead was a name written, MYSTERY, BABYLON THE GREAT, THE MOTHER OF HARLOTS AND ABOMINATIONS OF THE EARTH" (Rev. 17:1-5).

And so it is written, "Babylon the great is fallen…." "Come out of her, my people, that ye be not partakers of her sins, and that ye receive not of her plagues. For her sins have reached unto heaven, and God hath remembered her iniquities."

> How much she hath glorified herself, and lived deliciously, so much torment and sorrow give her: for she saith in her heart, I sit a queen, and am no widow, and shall see no sorrow (Rev. 18:1-7).

Babylon, "by thy sorceries were all nations deceived. And in her was found the blood of prophets, and of saints, and of all that were slain upon the earth" (Rev. 18:23-24).

The Global "Messianic" Kingdoms

Babel and Babylon were the seeds of spiritual *messianic* rebellion that have preceded multiple rebellious messianic supplanters over the twenty-five centuries last passed. These will soon culminate in a mysterious false messianic hope that will sweep the earth through deception so great that few will survive its devastation.

The geo-political expression of this phenomena is best portrayed and understood as the end-time battle for King of the Mountain. But its underlying motivational force is the desire to rule and reign over the planet from the very mount—the Temple Mount in Jerusalem—where the God of Israel chose to place His name (II Chron. 6:6).

The ancient psalmist prophetically revealed the heart of the matter, declaring: "The kings of the earth set themselves, and the rulers take counsel together, against the LORD, and against his anointed…," yet God responds, "Yet have I set my king upon my holy hill of Zion," making clear He speaks of the Messiah to come, declaring "Thou art my Son; this day have I begotten thee." HaShem, Jehovah, the God of

Israel and creation then warns the purportedly *wise* leaders of the world to "Serve the LORD with fear, and rejoice with trembling" and "Kiss the Son" meaning to embrace God's true King-Messiah, for they only will be blessed who "put their trust in him" (Psa. 2:1-12).

Yet the Eternal, Epic and End-time Battle rages, and the people "imagine a vain thing" (Psa. 2:1). It should then be obvious that the real issue or motivation underlying this seemingly geo-political battle for King of the Mountain is actually a spiritually-driven battle against God's authority and against His soon-coming Messiah. For that reason, it has been said that "He who rules the Temple Mount rules the world." To better understand the depth of this drama of the ages, you should seriously consider the author's book, *KING of the MOUNTAIN*, Elijah Books, 2013.

What exactly is it about the 37-acre site known as the Temple Mount that makes it so desirable? What would cause the power brokers of this world to invest their highest hopes in controlling, and therefore governing, the globe from this historic plot of land?

The Temple Institute in Jerusalem described the Temple Mount as "THE HOLIEST PLACE IN THE WORLD." Yet the same mount has been called "the most volatile acreage on earth." It should be increasingly clear that its draw is not primarily political but spiritual—the place of ultimate spiritual power, thus empowering one who rules it to have global dominion, both politically and spiritually. The mount therefore becomes the loadstone of the world, magnetically luring would-be competitors to pre-emptively compete against the soon-to-be revealed Messiah.

This has been the pattern of ancient history, now culminating in a final *messianic* effort to rule the world—to rule all inhabitants of earth—with massively deceptive magnetism unprecedented in history.

After Babylon came Medo-Persia which ruled the then-known world, governing even the Temple Mount. Alexander the Great, in a military blitz, then grasped power over the earth mandating a secular Hellenism over the world and Israel. Then came Rome, polytheistically imposing its dominion over Israel and the world, ultimately destroying the Temple. While Rome lost the power of her legions, Rome never truly died but its spirit has metastasized throughout the western world.

And "Rome" is, and has been, in the process of being reborn, now emerging as the New World Order or One World Government, sometimes referred to as *The New World Order of the Ages*.

This reborn or resurrected *Rome* is being carefully choreographed by godless politicians, financial theorists and business moguls under a great global *RESET* to completely re-form the governments of our planet, compelling every man, woman and child to conform. Unsuspectingly to most, however, is that this new globalization goal is being driven by a *cabal* of spiritual forces each seeking to convince the masses of their respective *messianic* message that presents as false hope, luring the majority of human kind to reject, again, God's Anointed One, The Messiah.

This will necessitate a counterfeit messiah in whom the increasing fearful world will repose trust. We must, therefore, briefly explore this mysterious man known as the Antichrist or Imposter Messiah, but not until we have taken a closer look at the historic and intensifying views portending the perceived imminence of a messiah or messianic age. Consider the deepening passion of these perceptions among their respective religious followers.

Chapter 5

ISRAEL'S HOPE

"The world today is in a state described by sages
as Labor that precedes the coming of a Messiah."
~Russian Chief Rabbi Berel Lazar

TIKVAT ISRAEL means "the hope of Israel." That hope, reduced to its simplest and most fundamental expression, is the hope of a redeemer, the Messiah, who will restore Israel and the Jewish people to the fulness of their biblically prophesied purpose, and thereby also restore the world for HaShem's (God's) glory. This messianic moment in history will then bring global SHALOM—world justice, security and prosperity.

The Messianic Age

The Messiah factor is an embedded article of Jewish faith. And over the years since the 1970s, messianic expectation has exploded to almost fever pitch. The anticipation, particularly in Israel, is of such intensity as to be almost palpable. There is a deep-seated certainty that the world is now in the messianic age, however that may be defined.

Interestingly, a campaign began in the late 1970s with the slogan "We Want Moshiah Now." Of further interest is that the call for Messiah among the more fundamentalist Jewish groups corresponded in time with the publication of the phenomenally best-seller, *The Late Great Planet Earth* by Hal Lindsey, which enjoyed distribution primarily within the greater gentile Christian world. At the same time, the soul-gripping, heart-stirring film *A Thief in the Night* made its striking debut within the gentile Christian world. By 1992, as both the western world began to unravel at the seams and Israel and Islam emerged with increasing prominence, the Messiah movement among Jews also picked up steam declaring, "Prepare for the Coming of the Messiah."[1] At the same time, a series of dramatic full-size billboards appeared along a busy Southern California freeway announcing, "SWORD of the LORD coming Soon," followed by another… "PREPARE TO MEET THY GOD." These were placed, not by a church or religious group, but by Tom Bickers, a simple and unassuming man in his early 30s, who invested his life savings to shout out a message that he said "the Lord burned on my heart."

The Messiah Factor has since mushroomed amazingly across the planet. By 2005, Russian Chief Rabbi Berel Lazar publicly announced his conviction that the earth will soon see the coming of a Messiah to judge all mankind. "We know that he is very near at hand," he said. In explaining his assumptions, Rabbi Lazar noted: "The world today is in a state described by our sages as 'hevley mashiah', that is labor that precedes the coming of a Messiah." "We are living on the verge of history," he said. "It can be felt everywhere."[2]

Many purported messiahs have appeared and disappeared over the course of history. Several such have died within the generation last passed. But it is indeed fascinating that messianic expectations should weave their way into even the secular world. The world is primed for a purported savior, whoever that might be.

Two Messiahs?

Many believe the late Rabbi Schneerson of the Chabad Lubavitch movement, although now dead, would be resurrected as the Messiah, and that his resurrection as "the coming Messiah" is imminent.

Many more believe, perhaps surprisingly, that there are or will be actually two messiahs, a "Suffering Messiah" and a "Ruling Messiah." Many rabbis have formed the viewpoint or conclusion that the Messiah would be someone who would die for the people and also someone who would rule victoriously over a Messianic Kingdom. The *suffering* Messiah is titled Mashiach ben Yosef or Messiah son of Joseph based upon rabbinical interpretation of Isaiah 53 depicting who would suffer. The victorious or *kingly* Messiah is seen as Mashiach ben David or Messiah son of David, who will rule as King of kings referenced in Isaiah 9:6 and Daniel 7:13-14.[3]

The Mystical Messiah

Kabbalah is an ancient Jewish belief system rooted in a mystical interpretation of the Bible. It has been transmitted orally, using esoteric methods, and became prominent in the Middle Ages. However, it remains of particular significance today among the Hasidic Jews, defining their messianic expectations. As of 2016, there were over 130,000 Hasidic households worldwide, about 5% of the global Jewish population.[4]

It is a challenge to distill the depths of Hasidism, but we must make our honest attempt so as to comprehend their mystical view of the Messiah or messianic age. The term *hasid* actually means *pietist*. Hasidic Jews therefore perceive themselves as the most pious of all Jews, though a kind of fundamentalist Orthodox Jew. They envision their sect as "One who wishes to tap the hidden wisdom, and must conduct himself in the manner of the Pious."[5]

The fundamental theme underlying all Hasidic theory is the immanence of God in the universe, believing that "no site is devoid of Him."[6] In essence, it is a pantheistic view—all is God and God is in all. A true Hasidic Jew believes, therefore, that all things of this world must be transcended as but illusory, and that in reality, there is nothing but God. This closely resembles, then, much of New Age religious or *spiritual* thinking.

But more specifically, as related to messianic expectations, Hasidism believes in what is referred to as the "descent of the Righteous" into matters of this world through supremely spiritual leaders known as *Tzaddikkim* who will, through their authority on earth, elevate the fleshly world back into divine infinity where all is truly "God" in experience. In that role, then, the *Tzaddikkim* usher in a limited messianic role in their lifetime. "The Tzaddiq [Tzaddik] serve as a kind of bridge between the spiritual realm and the people."[7] The most explosive and denoted growth of this persuasion became *incarnated* in the late Chabad-Lubavitch rabbi Menachem Mendel Schneerson, who many devotees passionately contend will be resurrected as the Messiah.

So… what does this mystical Messiah look like through Hasidic eyes? What do they expect that will help all to better comprehend the broader mystery of Messiah now confronting the world—both Jew and Gentile?

The following quotes perhaps best reflect these views and their implications. They are taken from a lengthy interview posted February 5, 2021, on *Arutz Sheva, Israel National News*, by Hasidic Rabbi Reuven Wolf of the Maayon Yisroel Chassidic Center on "The Accidental Talmudist." The Rabbi's mystical views of the Messiah reveal the unresolved mystery of our moment in history, yet the profound expectation of this messianic age.

"The reason the Moshiach isn't here is still a mystery."

"The Moschiach will just show up. He may be any of us."

"The main truth of Moshiach is our awareness…to see the true energy in the physical world."

Judaism's View of Jesus

The belief that Jesus (Yeshua) is God, the Son of God, or a person of the Trinity, is incompatible with traditional Jewish theology. Jews (other than a small minority to date who have embraced Yeshua as Messiah), do not believe that Jesus of Nazareth fulfilled messianic prophecies. Judaism rejects Jesus as God, Divine Being, intermediary between God and humanity, messiah or even holy. Furthermore, Judaism rejects many tenets of Christianity.

More specifically, regardless of all the multiplied Jewish arguments against Jesus as Messiah, these are the two that stand out as foundational to all other contentions.

1. Moses, the revered prophet of the Exodus, foretold to the Israelites before their entrance to the Promised Land:

    "The LORD thy God will raise up unto thee
    a Prophet from the midst of thee, of thy

brethren, like unto me; unto him ye shall hearken" (Deut. 18:15).

While Yeshua was a Jew in the midst of his brethren and was perceived by many to be a prophet, the Jewish leaders maintain that since he claimed to be the Son of God also, he was not a prophet like Moses—but only a mere man.

Therefore the Jews look not for a divine Messiah but for a charismatic leader like Moses.

2. Because Yeshua claimed that God was his Father and that he was not only "son of man" but also "Son of God," he was by Jewish definition a blasphemer worthy of death rather than of divine reverence as Messiah.

Again, quoting Moses' instruction to Israel in Deuteronomy 6:4, the Jewish rabbis argue that, "The LORD our God is one LORD." Therefore, by their understanding, by claiming Yeshua (Jesus) as both human and Divine, it is a violation of the Oneness of God, and therefore idolatry in violation of the commandment: "Thou shalt have no other gods before me" (Ex. 20:3).

A Shocking Confession

The true expectation of believing hope for both Jew and Gentile Christian is in the soon-coming of the Messiah to rectify earth's wrongs, and to redeem the remnant of those who put their trust in Him, and to judge the world in righteousness (Psa. 96:13; Psa. 98:9; John 16:8).

This hope was shockingly catapulted down the prophetic track of time by one of Israel's most prominent rabbis. Shortly before he died, Yitzhak Kaduri wrote the name of the Messiah on a small note which he requested would remain sealed until one year after his death. When the note was opened, it revealed what many have known for centuries, yet many others (particularly Jews) have categorically rejected. This is the name Rabbi Kaduri wrote: "'Yehoshua', or Yeshua [Jesus], is the Messiah."[8] The secret note said, "He will lift the people and prove that his word and law are valid."

Jewish leaders and readers responded with questioning amazement—the ultra-orthodox with denying scorn. "So this means Rabbi Kaduri was a Christian?" they lamented. Yet two of Kaduri's followers in Jerusalem admitted that the note was authentic, but confusing for his followers. A few months before his passing at the age of 108, the Rabbi surprised his followers as he gave a message in his synagogue on Yom Kippur, the Day of Atonement, teaching how to recognize the Messiah. Kaduri's grandson, Rabbi Yosef Kaduri, said the grandfather spoke many times during his last days about the coming Messiah and redemption through Yeshua ben Joseph, Yeshua ben David, the promised anointed one.

Who Is The Messiah?

The question then lingers—How would we recognize the Messiah? Upon what authority will His authenticity be established? Will many be confused, deceived or even destroyed by a false hope in a counterfeit?

Not long ago I was interviewed for almost two hours by a Jewish talk show host concerning my book *King of the Mountain*, discussing the global competitors seeking to ultimately rule the world from the Temple Mount. Near the end of the lengthy conversation, I felt led to ask the host a provocative question, "If the Jewish leaders failed to recognize Yeshua (Jesus) as Messiah, what makes you think they will recognize a purported 'messiah' when he soon shows up on the scene?"

There was a pregnant silence followed by, "That's a very good question." So…what makes YOU think you will have better discernment than the modern Jewish Sanhedrin of revered spiritual leaders when the IMPOSTER makes his debut? Where there is the real and the true, there is inevitably an IMPOSTER.

Notably, however, vision for the Messiah is now being increasingly voiced in Israel. "Zion Needs the Messiah" declared the Arutz Sheva (Israel National News) headline. "There is disillusionment" with various military and political leaders who "have failed to bring us redemption." "This disillusionment should increase our yearning for the spiritual leadership and vision of the Messiah…." "The belief in the coming of the Messiah is deeply embedded within the consciousness of the Jewish people… even the secular…." "We are therefore awaiting the arrival of the true Messiah…." "Even though He may tarry, we are not to lose hope."[9]

Chapter 6

THE "AGE OF AQUARIUS"

*"The promised 'dawning of the Age of Aquarius'
began at the end of December 2020."*

"THIS IS THE DAWNING of the Age of Aquarius" declared the catchy musical prophecy of the musical troupe "5th Dimension" in *Hair*, the Broadway musical of 1967. Few could forget the tune but few also have understood its purported truth.

The Mystery Deepens

If 1967 was the *dawning* of the *Age of Aquarius*, what then is this *Age of Aquarius*, when will it culminate, and does it have implications for the messianic age or the coming of a messiah?

For many, the plot is thickening, depending of course on the significance one attaches to the prophetic implications of astrology. As goes the famous tune:

When the moon is in the Seventh House
And Jupiter aligns with Mars
Then peace will guide the planets
And love will steer the stars.

So…let the sun shine in, the sun shine in.

(But why? What is this *sun* to shine in? And then we get a glimpse into New Age eschatology as the lyrics continue)

> Harmony and understanding
> Sympathy and trust abounding
> No more falsehoods or derisions
> Golden living dreams of visions
> Mystical crystal revelation
> And the mind's true liberation.

This is the dawning,,,,

What is "The Age of Aquarius?"

The concept of *The Age of Aquarius* is rooted in Astrology. And Astrology is the study of the stars in their movements as these movements purport to have significance for the inhabitants of earth, including believed prophetic implications defining the future. Astrology is thus different from Astronomy, which science, while studying the stars and planets, makes no effort to induce a spiritual or mystical application to humankind.

Astrology divides history and time into "great ages" or epochs based upon the precession of the equinoxes through constellations that form the signs of the zodiac." As the equinoxes progress through the zodiac signs, they merge or connect over just over 2000 years. Understanding these esoteric connections thus is deemed to "help us to understand what is meant by the huge shifts in human consciousness and civilizations...."[1]

"During the age of Pisces (the past 2000 years) we saw the rise of Christianity (with the sign of the fish) and Islam, faiths which have, as a central tenet, the notions of heaven and a life beyond this one." "...and it's no accident that some astrologers date the beginning of the Pisces age to around the time of the birth of Jesus and the development of religions where faith, peace and universal love are at their core." "So, it should go without saying that the shift from one astrological 'great age' to another is a monumental event as each marks a distinct place in human history."[2]

Has "The Dawning" Taken Place?

The promised astrological "dawning of the Age of Aquarius" began at the end of December 2020. That is the foretold event where "Jupiter joins Saturn in Aquarius" and "marks the beginning of a new 240-year cycle which will change society and the ruling structures of the elite world."[3] It will bring a revolution, yet has already… "the 'enlightenment' and everything from the American and French revolutions to the cultural revolution of the 1960s and 1970s resonates (literally) with the age of Aquarius."[4] "So are we there yet? The importance of 2020 can't be underestimated because it feels like this year is the dividing line between the past and the future…."[5]

Start of a NEW World Order

"FREEDOM, freedom, freedom…," that is the promise of Aquarius. The astrological conviction is that "2020 [was] The Start of a NEW World Order!" "Knowledge and science will become the new power!" "…finally, a true democracy will come to reign on earth." "The new energy source will become wave technology, quantum technology and the power of the air." "Jesus Christ initiated the age of Pisces with His sacrifice (Pisces) and the start of a 2100 year period for humanity when the 'sins' are washed away." "Having liberated ourselves from the collective karma of humanity…we are gradually starting to have more and more undivided freedom and free will." "The 'age of Aquarius' ultimate goal for humanity is freedom." "Social benefits and care for everyone in society will become the new moral and political norms."[6]

And that is precisely the promise of a soon-to-be revealed counterfeit Christ figure who will incarnate the very hope and promise of this astrological age. Thus, the mystery of the ages, the unveiling of Messiah dramatically deepens. As John Kerry, former U.S. Secretary of State, boldly proclaimed in a World Economic Forum panel, "I personally believe…we're at the dawn of an extremely exciting time."[7] "The notion of a reset is more important than ever before," he said. John Kerry was appointed by then putative president Joe Biden as his Environmental Czar to rejoin the Paris Climate Accord and to "help propel the World Economic Forum's globalist 'Great Reset' plan to use the coronavirus pandemic to transform the world's economy, all as embraced by European Commission President Ursula von der Leyen."[8]

And what is that *Great Reset*? The Great Reset is a plan presented by Klaus Schwab, founder and executive chairman of the World Economic Forum, calling for a "Great Reset of capitalism," declaring, "the world must act jointly and swiftly to swamp all aspect of our societies...."[9] Schwab further pronounced prophetically: "Every country, from the United States to China, must participate, and every industry, from oil and gas to tech, must be transformed."[10] Thus the proposed Great Reset is merely an expression for a declared New World Order. And it is the putative president Joe Biden who has deceptively imposed upon America on behalf of desperate globalists to "open the door to the globalist 'Great Reset'". For this reason, Mr. Biden, throughout his presidential campaign, adopted the New World Order slogan "Build Back Better" from the World Economic Forum.[11]

"Time for Revolution"

Revolutions are born of resistance, but the real import of any "revolution," is not in resistance itself but in the nature of that which is resisted, why the need for resistance is perceived, and more importantly—the heart motivation and direction with which the resistance purports to lead and to what defensible end.

In so-called "modern" times, there have been many revolutions but arguably the leading, most destiny-defining of such revolutions have been:

The American Revolution	1776
The French Revolution	1789
The Bolshevik (Russia) Revolution	1917
The Chinese Communist Revolution	1949

Each of these revolutions were led by quasi-messianic leaders as perceived by the people, and each had a very significant vision for the future. Interestingly, however, only one such leader, George Washington, was a God-fearing man. The others openly and vehemently rejected the God of Creation and were driven by an anti-authority spirit, elevating themselves to veritable god-hood. But when they went to make George Washington king, he declined, causing the colonists to cry out: "We have no king but Jesus." And viewpoint always defines destiny, and to this fulcrum moment in American history, has directed her destiny, which "destiny" is now destined to be cast into the dustbin of history by the Aquarian Revolution and the New World Order.

But now, the spirit of rebellion is growing again—this time world-wide—a revolution defined increasingly by rebellion not so much against all authority but particularly against spiritual authority—against the God of Creation Himself, with Evolution as its "alternative creation" platform. Men and women are thus collectivizing themselves against God and His *Messiah*.

Since it is said that "Nature abhors a vacuum," that God-shaped vacuum is being increasingly replaced by humankind (mankind) and the creation itself. This is the New Age revolution driving the *spiritual* dimension of The New World Order. The restoration of the government of God as Creator as promised in the Hebrew Bible in Isaiah 9:6-7 is being repudiated, both by rabbinic Judaism and New Age religious pursuits, all redefining the essential expectations of a coming Messiah. Ultimately, man must become his own *messiah*—his own *christ*—his own God. Disastrously however, as with all revolutions, the people ultimately repose the heart of their rebellion in a single leader—a dictator—in whom they trust until eventual terror reveals their false trust.

Let us listen to the Aquarian voices of revolution boldly proclaiming a New World Order of utopian freedom—a freedom from God rather than under God—freedom from law in pursuit of Self and self-indulgent *liberty*.

Aquarian revolution is a type of change that makes possible things we previously considered impossible. [The rebuilding of Babel through a "Great Reset" to achieve a New World Order or One World Government.]

> The age of Aquarius, therefore, will be an epoch that begins with a few things being turned on their heads to say the least…that process is already underway.

Post 2020 we'll be leaving an old world behind…we will experience a "new normal"…Though be aware the age of Aquarius will be full of… shocks and surprises.

Essentially, Aquarius is concerned with the new. So, revolution, rebellion and shocks are as likely as originality, progress and innovation.

The past is left behind and we will experience new ways of being and new ways of doing things that affect every area of our lives.

We are already seeing challenges to authority and changes in the nature of authority in many countries. What the Age of Aquarius implies is that our revolutions may have unexpected results.

One of the biggest surprises may be revolutions against so called revolutionaries. In the Age of Aquarius we may be pushed to the extremes in every department—and the outcome will be unlike anything that went before.[12]

The Aquarian Messiah

The heritage of Aquarian messianic voices arguably began with Madame Blavatsky through her *Secret Doctrine* written in 1888, which initiated many prominent figures into a new realm of spirituality eventually embraced under the broad banner of New Age spirituality. In that voluminous writing, she wrote:

"Satan is that Angel who was proud enough to believe himself God."[13]

"…Lucifer or 'Light-Bearer,' is in us: it is our Mind—our Tempter and Redeemer, our intelligent liberator and Saviour from pure animalism."[14]

"Lucifer is divine and terrestrial light, the 'Holy Ghost'…."[15]

"He was transformed by the Church into Lucifer or Satan, because he is higher and older than Jehovah…."[16]

One of the most influential Theosophists was Alice Bailey. By the time she finished her work in 1949, she had become the greatest force in presenting and defining what is now known as the New Age movement. She compiled 24 books, comprising over 10,000 pages, most of which were purported translations of trance revelations from her spirit guide Djwhal Khul, the Tibetan.[17]

Bailey founded Lucis Trust in 1922, under the name Lucifer Publishing Company, which boasted thousands of members—renowned financial and political leaders—people who ran the Council on Foreign Relations (an elite organization responsible for the founding of the United Nations). Some of these notables included: Robert McNamara, Henry Kissinger, David Rockefeller, Paul Volker, and the recently deceased George Schultz. Lucis Trust was headquartered at the United Nations Plaza for many years.[18]

Alice Bailey, like those before her, held "extremely vicious anti-Christian and anti-Jewish views."[19] Today, Lucis Trust continues disseminating the trance voice of Bailey, the supposed esoteric teachings of the Masters, including "their ideas on meditation, energy and how to invoke the appearance of 'the Christ' and his New Order, particularly revealed in her invocatory prayer on 'the Christ' and his Hierarchy. She calls forth…

Come forth, O Mighty One.
The hour of service of the Saving Force has now arrived.
Let it be spread abroad, O Mighty One.
Let Light and Love and Power and Death
Fulfill the purpose of the Coming One.[20]

And just who is the "Coming One" whom she invites? We must explore that in the following chapter.

Chapter 7

THE NEW AGE MYSTICAL "MESSIAH"

"The belief "we are all on a journey soon to culminate in our becoming 'Christs' through globalization of 'Christ consciousness'."

YOU ARE BECOMING GOD! According to New Age Religion in the *Age of Aquarius*, godhood is evolving in you as you progressively, in the spirit of this "NEW AGE," develop increasing global "Christ consciousness." As mankind universally embraces this amorphous global consciousness, Global Unity will be achieved through universal harmony, economic unity and a one-world religion supporting political oneness in a ONE WORLD ORDER or government.

Every human who embraces this universal, non-dogmatic, spiritual consciousness becomes his or her own *Messiah*. Those who reject or refuse to embrace this mystical, esoteric system are not only outliers but must be eliminated as enemies of world harmony and peace. As the catchy tune of yesteryear said, "How can it be wrong when it feels so right?" Such thinking seems especially true when any claims of absolute truth or morality seem so divisive. Has the spirit of Darwin defined our concept of deity?

False CHRISTS or Future "Christs"?

If, as New Age beliefs contend, we are all on a journey soon to culminate in our becoming "Christs" through a globalization of "Christ-consciousness," there remains no room for the Christ or *Anointed One* of the Christian faith, since we are all destined for deification as we unite the world in utopian Oneness, requiring any who *disbelieve* this new doctrine to be "selected out." But if some…or many…are subject to be removed from the glorious manifestation of global oneness, how can it be said we have become *One*? And why is the word *Christ* embraced as the veritable incarnation of Godhood in humankind if the very Christ of the Christian faith is rejected or re-defined? This reveals the increasingly mysterious nature of the mystical New Age spirituality.

The mystical mystery of New Age religion or spirituality might be best summarized as the progressive self-exaltation of SELF, as all claims of absolute truth, morality and defined destiny are abandoned in rejection of a Creator's authority. This renders every evolved human to be a law unto himself. Purportedly, the law proceeding from Godly authority is replaced by a strangely new "law of love" that mysteriously grows the more we each become Self-actualized in loving ourselves exactly as we are, allowing all others the same privilege, so long as you agree with the fundamental *truth* that we are each, in our own way, becoming the God whose authority, as Creator, we have determined to reject.

If this all sounds a bit confusing or mysterious, it is not surprising. But to those who have embraced this mystical mindset, it becomes the glorious hope of salvation of the world, needing no actual Messiah to come, to deliver, to save and to judge. For all such is anathema, except for those who refuse to embrace the New Age dogma of absolute relativism that promises a new "heaven on earth." Those who reject are banished, through force or threat of force, in the soon-coming "selection process."

The Salvation of Syncretism

Syncretism is the operating system of New Age theology. Syncretism, for New Agers, is the patching together of many religious, philosophical and psychological beliefs from around the world that become the context in which facets of all such beliefs and viewpoints are joined to achieve what purports to be a more universally favorable set of *doctrines* to guide the world to global unity. Foundational to this syncretistic *salvation* is what is called *ONENESS*, the belief that all is God, God is One, that all are becoming one in God (including nature), and therefore we are necessarily and inexorably moving toward global salvation in one glorious utopian unity. Under this basic presupposition, the very concept of or need for a Messiah does not compute.

The New Age religious belief system can reasonably be distilled into two *doctrinal* propositions gathered syncretistically from world religions, philosophy and psychology.

1. **EVOLUTIONARY GODHOOD** — Here, the Darwinian concept of man's evolution is extended beyond the physical to the spiritual, constantly pushing mankind in unified enlightenment toward god-consciousness. Any who resist this claimed evolution to "Christ-consciousness" are deemed unfit and a hindrance to evolutionary forces.

2. **GLOBAL UNITY** — Evolutionary Godhood implies that humankind will soon see itself as god. New Age teaches we are basically good, inherently divine, and we can create our own reality. In order to achieve this mysterious and ever-elusive global unity, we must be convinced of three fundamental *truths*.

   a. **Man Unified with Man**—As we all reach our true divine relationship with one another, we will achieve true harmony resulting in economic unity and ultimate political unity through the spiritual unity of a one-world religion, thus, a truly ONE WORLD ORDER.

   b. **Man Unified with Nature**—Since, through Monism – *ONENESS* – god is everything, in everything, and everything is god, we are unified in and through Nature, hence the globally unifying pseudo-religion of environmentalism.

   c. **Man Unified with God**—Since all is One, God is all, all is God, we also are becoming part of the cosmic

ONENESS as we realize our own divinity and divine goodness. Therefore, mankind is neither accountable to any external notions of moral law or absolute truth. We will be tolerant of all views as equally valid and authoritative, since they are expressions of other divinities in the making. Thus, unfettered relativism is the cultural earmark of New Age religion, all purportedly undergirding growing unity in pursuit of the long-sought ONE WORLD ORDER where peace and love abound.[1]

A Revolutionary Messiah

The ancient past is defining NEW AGE destiny. To best understand the present spiritual direction and near-future NEW AGE faith, it is necessary to take a quick journey through modern times to our time, a period or epoch beginning in the eighteenth century and now emerging into a global phenomenon purporting to spiritually unite the world in Oneness. Many seemingly disparate threads must be woven together in order to truly see the emerging tapestry of NEW AGE *truth*.

We begin with the so-called Age of Enlightenment centered broadly in Europe but specifically in France. The French Revolution and the lawless spirit of rebellion that drove it defined for the emerging modern world a new way of pursuing "Liberté, Égalité and Fraternité." Historically, these goals were pursued through pursuit of Creator God, as supreme power over all creation, including mankind.

The French Revolution boldly and even blasphemously not only rejected God's authority but God himself as Creator. Thus, the creature—humankind—became his own "god in the flesh." Even dates, times and calendars were changed to enforce this new anti-faith *faith* upon the citizens, and all who resisted were either culturally marginalized or exterminated in this radical pursuit of a new "peace on earth" born of an enforced unity.

The philosophers of the day paved the way, whether through Rousseau and his godless *Social Compact* theories or through René Descarte's famous declaration "I think, therefore I am." In this way, the western world began to increasingly think of human beings as their own *I AM*...or god...in complete opposition to the biblical under-standing of ages past (3000 years) since the God of Creation, Jehovah, who would deliver the Israelites (Hebrews) from 400 years of bondage declared Himself to be the I AM (Ex. 3:14).

The spirit of the French Revolution thus echoed throughout the western world, as a large pebble dropped in a global pond, and now is manifesting itself in a massive messianic re-definition as the New Age movement declares all to be their own god, their own messiah, their own *I AM*.

It is indeed fascinating, however, that just as these alternative mes-sianic messages emerged through the so-called Enlightenment, George Frideric Handel penned MESSIAH, his musical oratorio, in 1752, the messianic message of which has been rehearsed annually through churches and community cultural groups worldwide. Thus, the com-peting views defining the messianic "Mystery of the Ages" continues.

Evolution of the New Age

Although the term *New Age* was used as early as 1809 by William Blake and the Freemasonry journal of the 1800s was titled *The New Age*,[2] the seeds of the real movement were *hidden* in the appearance of Mormonism, which, while claiming to be "Christian," inserted a shockingly *new* doctrine that man can become God. While Joseph Smith claimed to have received the tenets of Mormon doctrine through revelations of the angel Maroni in the 1820s and Smith died in 1844, the first president of what became The Church of Jesus Christ of Lat-ter-Day Saints made an astounding declaration of doctrine. Lorenzo Snow, who met with and received "sacred communication" from Prophet Joseph Smith, made public the proclamation received from Smith that would define the "dark saying" of Mormonism.

As man now is, God once was:
As God now is, man may be.

This *doctrine* has never been repudiated by the Church of Jesus Christ of Latter-Day Saints, but has actually been reinforced repeat-edly throughout Mormon history.[3] Since the foundational essence of the doctrine is that God himself has *evolved* from manhood, man therefore can *evolve* to Godhood.

The year of Joseph Smith's death in 1844 saw an explosion of new variations of the *Christian* faith that continues to this day. Is it not fascinating that this all should occur within the generation inaugurating Darwin's theory (deemed doctrine) of man's evolution in 1859? And the *evolution* continues as we shall see through the progressive embracing of New Age religious belief that indeed, man is becoming God.

Tracing the Theosophy

From 1844 to 1886, numerous and varied new religious groups or cults emerged, most fashioning themselves as *Christian,* yet blending their core beliefs with evolving spiritualistic concepts that actually re-defined or defied foundational biblical truths, creating an increasing smorgasbord of *spiritual* offerings to those seeking to be *spiritual* yet rejecting the definitive doctrines of the Christian faith. Then came Theosophy birthed by Helena Blavatsky in 1875.

Blavatsky organized the Theosophical Society and the Theosophical Publishing House which published her two extensive works titled *Isis Unveiled* and *The Secret Doctrine*. Through these, "ascended masters" or spirit guides presented a "cosmic gospel" diametrically opposed to orthodox Christianity. The central teachings of Theosophy are summarized in the book *Elementary Theosophy*, by L.W. Rogers:

God and man are but two phases of the one eternal life and consciousness that constitute our universe!... This conception makes a man a part of God, having potentially within him all the attributes and powers of the Supreme Being

…then man, as a literal fragment of the consciousness of the Supreme Being, is an embryo god, destined to ultimately evolve his latent powers into perfect expression…an evolutionary expression of the Supreme Being[4].

The Theosophical Society set the religious trajectory within world events, permeating either blatantly or subtly the religious and philosophical belief systems of the world, much as a virus invasively permeates the programs and operational systems of a computer. Neither time nor space permits us to track and identify the amazing pervasiveness and influence of Theosophical *theology* that has even bound itself to much so-called *Christian* thinking and applicational theology. But there is yet one major Theosophist we must probe in order to fathom the future of purported *faith*.

Unveiling the Plan

"Of the major Theosophists, Alice Bailey was probably the most instrumental in developing the infrastructure and presenting the strategies of today's New Age movement." As noted in an earlier chapter, she founded Lucis Trust in 1922, under the name Lucifer Publishing Company.[5]

A century later, we are now catapulted into the era of culmination in this Age of Aquarius. Let us remind ourselves…we are "Unveiling the Mystery of the Ages" as it relates to Messiah, who He is, how He is to be identified and when He will appear. New Age leaders are convinced—and are intent on convincing you—that they know "the plan" and that it is now taking its final shape for global salvation.

Their solution to terrorism and global tribulation is a "New Age Peace Plan" defined in a ubiquitous global Oneness enforced by a selection process" to eliminate those who oppose it. Therefore, through the pursuit of peace as collective New Age *Christos*, those who follow the Christ of the Bible called "the Prince of Peace" must be selectively removed from society as enemies of the new global peace project. Thus, the inhabitants of earth will *save* themselves and *save* the world. And the hour for this plan's promise to be fulfilled is late.

The "Messianic" Moment is Now

This is the generation of New Age Godhood as the emerging global *Christ* within becomes realized by all who yearn for the Aquarian promise of peace but reject Jesus as **THE** Messiah, seen only as a mere avatar of humanity's ultimate Christhood as individual *I Am's*.

In order to understand this historical and prophetic moment, we must now leap to the mid-twentieth century and follow the trajectory of claimed New Age revelation. That leads us to 1965 and Helen Schucman, a Columbia University professor of Medical Psychology, who heard an *inner voice*, "identifying itself as Jesus," which declared, "This is a course in miracles." The purpose as declared by the voice, was "because of the acute emergency" in that the slow-evolutionary process is being by-passed in what might be described as a "celestial speed-up."

For seven years Schucman took periodic dictation from the voice that became *A Course in Miracles*. This became the *Testament* of a New Age/New Gospel revealing a revised *Jesus*, in the name of Jesus, re-constructing dramatically the doctrines of the Biblical Jesus identified as Messiah. Teaching that *Christ* is in everyone, the clear message became "man's only *sin* is in not remembering his own perfect, sinless, divine nature. The only *devil* is our illusion that we are not divine and part of God. Therefore, global salvation comes when all come to understood that "all is love and all is God," so that "inner peace" and "world peace" will emerge triumphant.[6]

Then came the fulcrum moment for the globalization of New Age *faith*. In 1992, a little-known author named Marianne Williamson presented her book, *A Return to Love: Reflections on the Principle of A Course in Miracles*. Oprah Winfrey told her viewers that she had already purchased a thousand copies, and thereby catapulted the book to the New York Times best-seller list where it stayed for months, thus mainstreaming the New Age/New Gospel to millions. The New Age *Christ* was suddenly "out of the closet."[7] So great was the Oprah-fired influence of Williamson throughout America that she, in 2020, actually ran for president in the Democrat primary.

By 1997, her new book, *Healing the Soul of America*, enabled her to transition the New Age *Christ* as a political savior for world peace. She linked with Neale Donald Walsch, author of the best-selling *Conversations With God*. Oprah Winfrey persistently promoted him to prominence, actually devoting her fame and fortune to launch a *discipleship* course to spread this new *gospel* of self-salvation throughout the world.

Williamson and Walsch then co-founded The Global Renaissance Alliance on the board of which sat Barbara Marx Hubbard, who claimed to have received "new revelation" from an "inner voice" claiming to be "Christ." She claimed she first heard this "inner voice" in

1966. Since then, she fulfilled her "commission" to tell the New Age/ New Gospel story from NASA to the former USSR to the United Nations. She co-founded the World Future Society, became a globally-respected "world citizen" and described herself as part of the "New Order of the Future." At least three of her books were funded by Laurence S. Rockefeller through his Fund for the Enhancement of the Human Spirit. For this Hubbard thanked him for his intuition about the "Christ of the 21ˢᵗ Century."[8]

Neale Donald Walsch declared that humanity is standing on the threshold of a "golden" New Age— "the golden age of the New Human." "The twenty-first century," he wrote, "will be the time of awakening, the meeting of The Creator Within." In his *Conversation With God*, celebrated continuously by Oprah Winfrey, Walsch declared that God told him…

> All of our life you have been told that God created you. I come now to tell you this: You are creating God.

In his purported conversations with God, as declared in his book of that title, Walsch reported that God told him the importance of bringing this new spirituality into politics and government…that "all spirituality is ultimately political." Walsch asked his *God*— "Are you talking about a one-world government?" To which query God ostensibly responded, "I am." Walsch then claims God gave him a new Great Commission to launch this new spiritually-based new world order.

> Go, therefore, and teach all nations, spreading far and wide The New Gospel: WE ARE ALL ONE.[9]

The Universal "Christ"

Enter Maitreya, an "advanced spiritual entity" holding the *Office of the World Teacher*. The messianic Maitreya is linked to both Buddhist and Hindu religious traditions, representing a "hidden Spiritual Hierarchy," the so-called *Masters of the Ancient Wisdom*. In Theosophical texts, Maitreya is said to have manifested in various personages of the ancient world and as Christ during the three years of the Ministry of Jesus.

Alice Bailey referred to Maitreya as the Cosmic Christ, claiming his Second Coming would occur sometime after the year 2025.[10] Most non-Buddhist New Age groups teach that "Maitreya will unify all religions through his teachings and rescue humanity from economic and other crisis by teaching a universal brotherhood. Many names were given to Maitreya, including Christ, the Messiah, Krishna (a Hindu god) and Teacher."[11] Perhaps shockingly, the former Soviet leader Mikhail Gorbachev, openly acknowledged that he was/is working with Maitreya "to bring peace to the world" and had "no problem with the public knowing that he had met the Christ [Maitreya]."[12]

Suddenly, "spiritual politics" became center stage as the New Age "Christ" brought new updated "revelations" into living rooms worldwide. The historic Babylonian dream of a New World Order became an increasing demand.

"We shall have world government, whether or not we like it," roared James Paul Warberg February 17, 1950, before the United States Senate. "The only question is whether World Government will be achieved by conquest or consent."[13]

Forty years later, September 11, 1990, U.S. President George Herbert Walker Bush, a consummate globalist, stood before a joint session of Congress, and *prophesied* these amazing words:

Out of these troubled times…a new world order can emerge:
a new era—freer from the thrust of terror, stronger in the
pursuit of justice, and more secure in the quest for peace.

That "new world," declared America's 41st president, is struggling to be born." The "opportunity" he so eagerly desired to seize was the building of a "new-world order," which he went on to historically declare over 200 times during his administration. Just eleven years later after the September 11, 2001, Islamic attack on the World Trade Center Towers, then Prime Minister of Britain, Tony Blair, could not contain his globalist enthusiasm, declaring:

This is the moment to seize. The kaleidoscope has been
shaken…let us reorder this world around us.[14]

On May 29, 2008, the same Tony Blair, who had just converted to Catholicism after meeting with the Pope, announced the Tony Blair Faith Foundation from the locus of the United Nations in New York. He said…

> I'll dedicate the rest of my life to uniting the world's religions. Faith is…an essential part of making globalization work.

But Mr. Blair did not stop there. He made clear that "Religion is the new politics." "Religious faith will be of the same significance to the 21st century as political ideology was to the 20th century." His goal, he said, was to bring the six leading faiths together in Oneness. *TIME* magazine observed in response: "The Catholic Church has long embodied the attributes of globalization that now engage Blair."[15]

Thus, the trajectory of religious *truth* would forever be redefined to serve what would be accepted as the greater good—a global embrace of a unified *faith* to achieve ONENESS in a divided world. We could save ourselves if only we could redefine the perceived messianic age as not expecting an actual *Messiah* but a virtual version through a unifying spirit of growing ONENESS or unity. Unity had become the ultimate goal rather than the fruit of actual truth that would bind a broken world together. In this amazing spiritual sleight of hand, a One World Government would replace the God who created the world.

Man, who was created in God's image, would now re-create God in his own image and become his Self-Salvation. The world will then enter its ultimate utopian "peace on earth" with "good will toward men" enforced by the seeming wise and benevolent hand of a counterfeit messiah. The world will repose its trust in him…before unprecedented global terror destroys the spiritual charade through the Luciferian imposter who imposes a satanically inspired tyranny, dispelling all doubt as to the false trust invested in a human savior.

Syncretism is the pathway to this New Age salvation, led by politicians, presidents, prime ministers, pastors, priests and even popes… as we shall see.

The Resurrecting Rome

POISED FOR PEACE. That is the growing conviction throughout the globe, but particularly among the so-called West or western nations which are the inheritors of the spirit of ancient Rome prophesied to be the final great empire on earth (Dan. 7:7).

Unity Fever

The "peace of Rome," secured by its ever-present legions, has been called the *Pax Romana*. And now, nearly 2000 years later, what *gospel* will now gather and what glue will now bond the world into a bold new order of the ages, a resurrected *Rome*? Rome was pagan, but at least it promised an elusive peace. *Rome* is now the entire western world in hot pursuit of a new pagan peace — a utopian world of unending compromise to wed humanity into a world government in which unity is the only requirement for heaven on earth.

The pressure for and toward world unity, at every level, is unprecedented. This pressure has reached a fever pitch. The flames of global fever are fanned by fear of global conflagration and by a utopian vision for the global peace and prosperity that has heretofore escaped man's grasp.

The great and growing river of unity gradually becoming a global sea is fed by the confluence of many streams and tributaries, both religious and secular. Neither time nor space here permit detailed delineation of the vast and pervasive scope of this movement. We must therefore limit our latitude of observation to that which enables us to bring into focus the emerging sculpture of a global order being forged as man's ultimate achievement and salvation.

This emerging global-ism is being forged out of the multitude of prevalent isms in our world, the most significant of which we can broadly distill as the "science isms," "social-isms," "political-isms" and "religious-isms," with the ultimate goal of unprecedented material-ism. While seemingly separate in their respective disciplines, upon closer inspection one cannot escape the merging and synergetic interaction of these various broad categories of isms, each reinforcing the other and developing a kind of "magnetic" attraction, chasing each other ever closer into an uncanny bond now universally defined as *global-ism.* While jointly and severally becoming mutually interdependent, it is the religious isms that globalists increasingly, although often reluctantly, acknowledge as the ultimate catalyst to bind the world in the final thrust for global unity.

It is fascinating to watch the threads of the emerging global tapestry being woven into a discernible pattern through the unprecedented pursuit of unity. One can easily be trapped in its seductive web of deception, especially because of the sheer weight of the supposed authorities and their massing majorities embracing global-ism as a veritable new *gospel.*

Social Oneness

From the mid-1800s, just as New Age religious convictions began to emerge, so too did Darwin's theory of evolution. Evolution became the unseen bond, facilitating the emerging world unity in virtually every sphere, whether political, scientific, social or religious…even material and legal.

Into the growing spiritual vacuum of the soul, sweeping like a plague throughout the western world as evolution sucked the god-image from man, came a new unifying alternative to the Creator's gospel of the soul. Freud's war against God meshed well with man having been cut loose from his Creator through evolution.

Humankind needed a new bond to unify socially. A new *acceptable* version of love was needed—SELF love. Through Freudian psychology, feelings replaced biblical faith and human experience replaced biblical truth. Eros and phileo love supplanted the selfless agape love of Scripture. Oneness of *feelings* now progressively replaces oneness in biblical *faith* as experience trumps truth even in our churches. Psychology had become the unifying ethos of an emerging global social order where increasingly godless men could embrace *feelings* as lord and *SELF* as king.

The church divorced the God of mercy from the God of truth, abandoning the fear of the Lord for the fear of man, thus baptizing the new psychologized *gospel* with the aura of a man-centered faith. Few can resist the universal secularization of *feelings.* The spirit of the faith "once delivered to the saints" has been suffocated, replaced by a soulish *sacrifice* of ever-evolving feelings to be offered on the altar of world peace to usher in the enticing era of global oneness. Unity born of feelings has been deemed vastly preferable in the emerging global culture to the *divisive* unity that sets people apart as followers of an exclusive truth in Messiah Yeshua (Jesus) that alone will make and keep men free (Jn. 8:31-32, Jn. 17:17-19).

Political Oneness

Just as Israel, the "apple of God's eye" (Zech. 2:8), was entering the prophetic birth canal to be re-born as a nation, the Deceiver sought to pre-empt the divine drama with an equally dramatic birth.

PURSUIT OF PEACE AND PROSPERITY

World War II had shaken the world. Germany had decimated the Jews. The nations were in despair and Europe was destroyed. And so the United Nations was founded to provide "world peace and security." Interestingly, the Hebrew word *shalom* might be best translated "peace and security" or "security and prosperity." The divine plan was to send forth His Anointed One, the Prince of Peace, to unify the "Israel of God," genuine believing Jews and Gentiles, into "one new man in Christ," "so making peace" (Rom. 2:28-29, 9:4-8, 11:25-26; Eph. 2:12-22).

SATAN'S COUNTERFEIT

But Lucifer (Satan) seduced the nations with his own alternative peace plan. Unite the nations, contrary to God's express command, and let them build a global *tower* system that will reach heaven, or at least create man's best heaven on earth, thus "saving" the earth from the inevitable consequence of sinful rebellion. Unwittingly, history would repeat itself. The God-dispersed tower of Babel of Genesis 11 would now become global. The world would become one, under the Deceiver's direction, until its final destruction.

The United Nations was thus founded in 1945. One of its earliest official acts was to partition the land of Palestine, which God had eternally deeded to Israel, into two nations, one for the Jews and one for Arabs. The partition was to transpire in 1948. The Deceiver was deft in his direction: Divide Israel, which God decreed to be united as one, and unite the nations which God had commanded to separate. The divine penalty would be severe…ultimate divine judgment (Joel 3:1-2; Zech. 12:8-9), Israel was re-born May 14, 1948, and the world has been haunted for its division to this day, and will repeat that debacle.

Just as God would breathe life into the house of Israel (Ezek. 37:1-5), so Satan would breathe life into the unifying of the Gentile nations. Satan's counterfeit is nearing completion. Let us further trace Satan's historical tracks in our time and his deceptive plan for global dominion.

A GLOBAL PHENOMENON

From the ruins of World War II, a global phenomenon began. Just as Israel began its phenomenal resurrection from historical obscurity in fulfillment of biblical prophecy on May 14, 1948, so Europe began a breathtaking rise to world prominence in 1951 with the establishment of the European Coal and Steel Community or "Common Market." Established by the Treaties of Rome in 1957 and 1958, the declared aim was to give Western Europe greater influence in world trade and economic affairs. By 1999, a single European currency, the Euro, was created, and now competes with the dollar for global acceptance.

The Maastricht Treaty of 1993 established the political entity known as the European Union. The renowned Roman Empire of antiquity faded into diverse peoples and countries from the Mediterranean to the Baltic and North Seas for 2000 years. As the curtain is drawn on the "church age," and countries now clamour to be included in the spectacular "resurrection" of "Rome." Twenty-seven nations, historically at enmity, now embrace as political *friends*, all in pursuit of *security* and *prosperity* (shalom), although Britain has now withdrawn.

Never before in history has a nation, obliterated from its roots and dispersed to the four winds for two thousand years, been resurrected in its own land, as has Israel, against all social, political and economic odds. By contrast, never before in history have so many countries and peoples, now nearing 500 million, voluntarily come together in time of peace, as has the European Union. Said Jaques Delos, former head of the resurrecting *Rome*, "We must hurry. History is waiting."

Prophecy is not waiting, but rather surging inexorably toward the Second Coming of Messiah, God's promised "Prince of Shalom" (Isa. 9:6). In less than a generation of seventy years, the world has witnessed the rebirth of Israel, the "apple of God's eye," and the rebirth of *Rome*, the Deceiver's counterfeit, merging the spirit of Egypt, the spirit of Babylon and the spirit of Rome into one global enterprise destined to declare dominion over the souls of men. Babel of Babylon (Gen. 11) is being rebuilt in men's hearts as "Mystery Babylon" (Rev. 17:5), just as the Kingdom of God, through the "Israel of God," is being given life through the hearts of men as the "Mystery of God" (Rev. 10:7).

THE REVIVING ROMAN EMPIRE

The two kingdoms are coming into mortal and eternal conflict. Satan as the "god of this world" (II Cor. 4:4), is drawing the peoples of this planet into godless oneness. In drafting the historic Treaty of Lisbon as the constitution for the reviving Roman Empire, the European Union elite refused even to recognized God, having embraced the godless antipathy of the French Revolution. Rather, this expanding union chose to declare its rebellion against the Creator by adopting symbols to set itself blatantly against Messiah's coming kingdom.

The twelve stars of the European Union flag set themselves against Christ's twelve disciples and the twelve tribes of Israel. The Tower of Babel, through a variety of European posters and other depictions, displays open contempt for oneness in Messiah, boldly declaring man's intent to unify for his own salvation. The European Parliament in Strasburg is even architecturally designed to visually replicate, with a modern flair, the ancient Tower of Babel, now to be more dramatically replicated in America's Capitol as Amazon's headquarters.

A RADICAL NEW DREAM

But the political rebuilding of *Rome* is not yet complete. The nations, observing the seeming phenomenal success of the European Union in such historically short order, are seeking to create similar regional unions throughout the world, all for *security* and *prosperity*. The goal is *global consciousness*. The first transnational political entity in history, the United States of Europe, represents "the rise of a new ideal that could eclipse the United States as focus for the world's yearnings for well-being and prosperity [shalom]," declared Jeremy Rifkin in a profound editorial analysis.[16] Rifkin noted, as an American, "Yet out country is largely unaware of and unprepared for the vast changes that are quickly transforming the Old World and giving birth to the new European Dream." His words should grip the heart and soul of every Jew and Christian believer worldwide.

> The European Dream, with its emphasis on inclusivity, diversity, sustainable development, and interconnections is **the world's first attempt at creating global consciousness.**

Interestingly, it was precisely Barack Obama's open embrace of this vision that connected him so powerfully with America's youth and ingratiated him as a veritable "rock star" throughout the European continent, earning him the moniker of *messiah* by *Der Spiegel*, a German magazine.[17] Oprah Winfrey announced the Obama election as "a change in global consciousness." His presidential campaigning counterpart, John McCain, also embraced the new global vision, calling for creation of a new "League of Democracies" which its boosters argue, "would have not only the moral legitimacy but also the will to right the world's wrongs effectively"…[18] a utopian vision.

Columnist Jeremy Rifkin reveals the cataclysmic "change" that is energizing the vision of global-ism modeled by the New "European Dream," replacing the American Dream whose life support has been nearly severed from its original Godly roots. Europe now represents *peace* and *prosperity* to the world.

"Utopian as it sounds," notes Rifkin, "remember that 200 years ago, America's Founders created a new dream for humanity that transformed the world. Today, a new generation of Europeans is creating a radical new dream." "Romano Prodi, the President of the European Commission, has admitted that the EU's goal is to establish a 'superpower on the European continent that stands equal to the United States'." When Prodi was asked to explain what he meant, Rifkin notes, "he spoke of the European vision as one of a new type of power…a new kind of superpower based on **waging peace**."[19]

Imitation as Flattery

It is said that imitation is the ultimate flattery. If that be so, the European Union, the resurrecting bones of the Roman Empire, stands profoundly flattered, for the entire world is in hot pursuit of "waging peace" to achieve *security* and *prosperity* (Shalom) by forming regional unions.

Most prominent, perhaps, has been the "Security and Prosperity Partnership" or SPP signed in secrecy by U.S. President George W. Bush with Mexican President Vincente Fox and Canadian Prime Minister Paul Martin in Waco, Texas on March 25, 2005. Although long publicly denied, the North American Union to merge the United States, Mexico and Canada was well underway to emulate the European pursuit of *security* and *prosperity*, all without act of Congress. It was continued, under cover, by President Barack Obama, emerging once again from the shadows into the supposed glorious light of globalism.

On April 30, 2008, President George W. Bush signed the "Transatlantic Economic Integration" agreement between the U.S. and the European Union, citing the same ostensible economic purpose to which the rise of the European Union was attributed. Co-signatories included German Chancellor Angela Merkel, president of the European Council, and European Commission President José Manuel Barroso. The United States became committed to a Transatlantic Common Market between the U.S. and the European Union by 2015, a period of seven years, without ratification of a treaty or act of Congress.[20]

This plan, being implemented by the White House with the aid of six U.S. senators and 49 congressmen as advisors, appeared to follow a plan written in 1939 by a world government advocate who sought to create a Transatlantic Union as an international governing body. An economist from the World Bank agreed in print that the foundation of this Transatlantic Common Market "is designed to follow the blueprint of Jean Monnet, a key intellectual architect of the European Union," who admitted the true purposes of the Common Market were intentionally not disclosed to Europeans, intending rather that it lead inevitably from economic integration to political integration and a European superstate.[21]

Where will this process now end, and what are its implications not only for the world but for Israel and for those who profess ultimate allegiance to Jesus?

On February 1, 1992, then President George Herbert Walker Bush, having over 200 times announced the coming New World Order, declared:

> It is the sacred principles enshrined in the UN Charter to which we will henceforth pledge our allegiance.

In 1993, President William Jefferson Clinton pushed congressional approval of NAFTA, the North American Free Trade Agreement and in 1995, CAFTA, the Central American Free Trade Agreement. These laid the foundation for George W. Bush's North American Union and an ultimate merger with the European Union.

The echo of these events continues to circle the earth. The Mediterranean Union has now been declared, established July 13, 2008, to "form a bridge between Europe, North Africa and the Middle East." It was the brainchild of French President Nicolas Sarkozy, composed of 43 member nations. The Union committed to "peace, stability and security" (Shalom), was formed "to ensure the region's people could love each other instead of making war," emulating the European Union. Announcement was timed to coincide with the French presidency of the European Union. As *The Guardian* in Britain noted, "Sarkozy's big idea is to use imperial Rome's centre of the world as a unifying factor, linking 44 countries that are home to 800 million people."[22]

Now established or in process are the following global unions, some with overlapping nations:

European Union	26 nations	Actual
Mediterranean Union	43 nations	Actual
North American Union	3 nations	Formative
Trans Atlantic Union	30 nations	Formative
South American Union	12 nations	Actual
Central American Union	8 nations	Actual
Pacific Union	13 nations	Formative
Russia and Belarus Union	2 nations	Actual
Indian Union	25 states	Actual

African Union	53 nations	Actual
Central Asian Union	5 nations	Formative
South Asian Union	44 nations	Formative

Upon the election of Donald J. Trump as U.S. President, his campaign declaration of MAGA— "Make America Great Again" was seen by globalists in America and worldwide as an existential threat to their nearly realized goal of a New World Order, thus making it necessary (from their viewpoint) that he must be destroyed whatever the cost. Global peace demanded radical domestic revision and destruction.

The Anti-Gospel

Global governance is not a conspiracy theory but a confrontive truth. The *gospel* of global government and the unification of the world is secularly described as global-ism. Its spiritual roots draw life not from trusting God's wisdom, grace and power but rather from man's desire to sever dependence on his Creator and to depend upon mankind's *good nature* to do the right thing for the *common good*, and hence save himself. It is the *anti-gospel* precisely because it denies man's fundamental sinful condition necessitating a savior other than himself, shifting ultimate trust to the "arm of flesh," which brings a curse (Jer. 17:5).

Israel, continuing her search to be like all the other nations (I Sam. 8:5-7), and to be included among them despite God's declaration they "shall not be reckoned among the nations" (Numb. 23:9), now seeks inclusion in the European Union and has been received into the Mediterranean Union. Having rejected her Messiah, she continues to proclaim, "We have no king but Caesar" (Jn. 19:15), trusting the proffered *shalom* (security and prosperity) of man's systems rather than her Savior's sacrifice. And so a European Commissioner wrote in one of Israel's key daily newspapers, "We will also work with Israel to promote and uphold the values we share and which we believe hold the key to prosperity in Europe and everywhere else in the world."[23]

America, as a Gentile "New Canaan," has followed the path of Israel. Having progressively abandoned the God of her fathers and the fear of the Lord, she now fears man. Having lost actual trust in the Creator, she desperately clings to a motto, *In God We Trust*, that has become little more than a faded symbol and an empty mantra. The God who "made and preserved her a nation" had set her apart from all other nations, yet now, in growing fear, she seeks to wed herself to their pagan global enterprise for *shalom* (peace and prosperity).

THE UNBELIEF OF FALSE TRUST

Both Jew and Gentile, "God has concluded them all in unbelief…" (Rom. 11:32). The rabbis of the Supreme Judicial Court of the Jewish People, the Sanhedrin, reconstituted in 2004 after nearly 2000 years of dispersion, have presented their "peace initiative." In a letter drafted in 70 languages to "all governments of the world," the rabbis warn that "the world is nearing a catastrophe" and that the "only way to bring peace among nations, states and religions is by building a house for God." The rabbis, having little seeming trust in God as their I AM, call on "non-Jews to help the people of Israel fulfill their destiny and build the Temple, in order to prevent bloodshed across the globe."[24]

Nature abhors a vacuum. When our genuine trust in God and His Word wanes, Satan is quick to interject an alternative, inevitably shifting our focus from authentic faith to a fleshly counterfeit. Israel, as with the West and the western Gentile church, suffers from acute spiritual anemia. We are wide open for Satan's final spiritual deception. It has been well designed to entrap both Jew and Gentile, and its final manifestation is soon to be revealed for those who have an eye to see.

For the Jew, the Temple may well be the perfect trap, diverting trust from God's *Anointed One* to Satan's appointed one, the "Son of Perdition" who makes ingratiating promises as "the little horn" emerging from the "ten horns" of the resurrecting Roman Empire (Dan. 7:7-8). He will "speak great words against the most High, and shall even wear out the saints…", both Jew and Gentile (Dan. 7:19-25), once he gains power. The mere flattering promise of security and prosperity will be sufficient bait to ensnare and co-opt the trust of most Gentiles, for by pursuit of peace the imposter will destroy many (Dan. 8:23-25).

Yet, for this latter-time trader in trust to gain global dominion so as to invite men to sacrifice their eternal souls for the promise of temporal peace and prosperity, Satan's global governmental "gospel" must become nearly universally embraced. Shockingly, even now, "Anyone who Resists the EU Is A Terrorist" according to former Italian President Giorgio Napolitano at a news conference. The former German President, Horst Köhler, also present at the Siena conference, nodded in agreement.[25] But those broadly labeled *terrorist* today will be deemed *traitor* tomorrow. Just as with ancient Rome, the resurrecting end-time *Rome* will brook no opposition once enthroned. And now, America's new government under putative President Joseph Biden has declared all who refuse the globalist agenda as "domestic terrorists."

How will such universal acceptance be achieved? What will win the mind and heart of the world to passionately embrace global-ism as the ultimate *gospel* for "peace on earth, goodwill toward man" (Luke 2:14)?

Will you recognize Satan's duplicity in the hour of deception? Or will you dance with the Deceiver, seduced by his offer of counterfeit *shalom*, packaged alluringly in religious robes calculated to convince all but those who "keep the commandments of God, and the faith of Jesus" (Rev. 14:12)? Is it not time to "prepare the way of the Lord" in your life and in the lives of those in your sphere of influence so that you "may be able to withstand in the evil day" (Eph 6:13)?

Religious Oneness

Massive spiritual deception is mounting as the final bridge, bidding politicians, pastors, priests, parishioners and parachurch leaders to cross over a worldly "Jordan" into a counterfeit *Promised Land* of global *security* and *prosperity* (Shalom). The rivers and rivulets of the world's religious isms are now combining to propel even professing Christians and Jews in the powerful currents of global *oneness* into the counterfeit Christ's new global order. As Jesus well warned, "if it were possible, they shall deceive the very elect" (Matt. 24:24). Globalism is, in reality, the "Anti-Gospel," choreographing an increasingly faithless, feeling-driven world in a final collective rebellion against God in the battle for *KING of the Mountain*.[26]

PART 3

MOLDING A MODERN MESSIAH

"WHAT IS PAST IS PROLOGUE" wrote Shakespeare in his play *The Tempest*. Those words are inscribed on the monument/statue named *Future* standing at the corner of the National Archive Building in Washington D.C. But what does it mean or imply, and why does it matter?

In contemporary usage it simply means that the past sets the stage for the story that is to come. It strongly implies that history sets the context for the present. Thus, by further natural implication, the present can be seen as setting the trajectory for the future. A yet further implication is that an event, decision or act today will likely lead to another tomorrow or in the near tomorrow.

In the chapters to come we will see how the lack of definitive resolution of the mystery surrounding the word and understanding of *messiah* is putting pressure on the world's peoples, demanding such resolution in the pursuit of shalom—peace, security and prosperity—so as to somehow unify mankind by, in effect, molding a more definitive—or at least universally acceptable—"messiah."

Indeed, if our eyes had been even moderately open, we would have clearly witnessed this pattern for the past century. Or, to put it in the very words of *TIME* Magazine April 5, 1993, "Americans are looking for a custom-made God, One made in their own image." What then is the future?

Chapter 8

SALVATION BY SYNCRETISM

"It is as if it has become the global 'gospel' unifying the planet in full-fledged embrace of the Age of Aquarius."

"WE HAVE TO WAGE PEACE!" declared the New Age spiritual leader, Marianne Williamson, in her post September 11th prime-time interview on *Larry King Live*. Her inclusion on the high-powered CNN panel after the 9-11 debacle reflected her newfound status as both spiritual and political commentator.

She was emphatic. "We have to wage peace…to dismantle hatred. And hatred is our real problem." Few viewers likely understood that the peace she was proposing was completely based on New Age/ New Gospel principles.[1]

The Promise of Peace

Almost everyone on the planet desires peace, that is unless some other lurking desire leaps to the forefront for a time that, we suppose, will ultimately provide a better peace. Yet we well know that real and lasting peace has been perpetually elusive on planet Earth. How can this ever-elusive prize be finally grasped? That is the overarching "salvation" question with which the New Age/ New Gospel "believers" grapple. And they are convinced they have, at this ultimate moment of history, grasped the solution. It is **SALVATION BY SYNCRETISM.**

Peace will be the fruit of the syncretistic roots, bringing the world and its peoples into global oneness.

The pathway to this emerging peace is winding but broadening, as we shall see. Its promise is capturing the political and spiritual imagination of millions and the world's foremost leaders, whether of government, business, education, economics, legal, political or religious orientation. It is as if it has become the global "gospel," the great "good news" unifying the planet on full-fledged embrace of the AGE of Aquarius.

It is the great hope of the ages that the messianic key will be soon in our grasp to open the door, at long last, to the "Promised Land" of peace on earth and global unity where we will all wage peace rather than war. And who could possibly be resistant to such promise?

Yet perhaps, before an uncontrollable euphoric state grips our imagination, we should consider a further question… AT WHAT PRICE, PEACE? What is to be sacrificed in order to achieve this glorious "salvation?" What beliefs, convictions and truths must be denied and what new *truths* must be embraced to produce this universal ONENESS?

Perhaps shockingly, even the most stalwart proponents of this seemingly irresistible promise of NEW AGE peace are not convinced that all will succumb to the promise of global peace because of its underlying demand that we declare ourselves "God." This is especially true in light of the conviction that these ideas about peace come directly from the New Age "Christ" who teaches we are in the final stage of spiritual development—the collective realization that we ourselves are actually a God in the making. This new "Christ" warns that those who are unable to "move to the highest level of their nature" by acknowledging their progressive God-hood as being actually "part of God" will not be a part of his *peaceful* future. And this new "Christ" further states that anyone opposing his peace process will be submitted to his "selection process"—a euphemism for being eradicated from the planet as an enemy of world peace and harmony.[2]

The Mystery of Syncretism

Alice Bailey made clear that "The spirit has gone out of the old faiths and the true spiritual light is transforming itself into a new form which will manifest on earth eventually as the new world religion."[3]

"The New Age is upon us," wrote Bailey, "and we are witnessing the birth pangs of the new culture and new civilization"…language echoed by former President George H. W. Bush a century later, declaring before Congress September 11, 1990. "Out of these troubled times…a new world order can emerge: a new era…in the quest for peace." That new era, he described, as a "new world, struggling to be born."[4]

Perhaps this expectation of a new world, a new era of perfect peace, a utopian heaven on earth, is best summarized again by Alice Bailey.

> Humanity in all lands today awaits the Coming One—no
> matter by what name they may call him. The Christ is sensed
> on His way.[5]

Professed *experience* will progressively replace theology or actual truth about God, since we are God in the making. Again, as Alice Bailey so poignantly stated:

> Therefore, in the new world order, spirituality will supersede
> theology; living experience will take the place of theological
> acceptances.[6]

Thus, the foundation was laid for a global unity movement that, beginning as an embryo, grew rapidly and was progressively perverted, until its syncretistic deadly tentacles metastasized throughout the earth, mysteriously appearing in virtually every religious persuasion, whether or not invited. Engines of diabolical deceit have fostered and fertilized the movement to establish in this final moment of history the Deceiver's greatest goal— "I will be like the most High," and "I will ascend into heaven, I will exalt my throne above the stars of God: I will sit also upon the mount of the congregation [the Temple Mount]," "I will be like the most high" (Isa. 14:13-14).

Syncretism is Seduction

The pursuit of ever-elusive peace and global prosperity is, to mankind, akin to seeking the pot at the end of the rainbow. Without recognizing the inherent sinful condition of our species, and believing that we need only be a little more patient to experience the fulfillment of our individual "divinity" in global unity and ONENESS, there is no ultimate need for a savior or Divine Messiah. Our real need, we reason, is not to be reconciled to God but to be reconciled only to one another because, after all, we are all metamorphosing into God and will thus save ourselves and the planet.

In order to more deeply grasp the globalization of the new spirituality synthetically forming the New World Order's one-world, unifying religion based upon trust in self-salvation, we must follow its seductive pathway through more modern times.

The Evolution of Hope

The "Prophet of Hope" is the unusual title ascribed to Dr. Robert Muller, former Assistance Secretary General of the United Nations. Dr. Muller has made it clear that world unity cannot be achieved simply through political unions and alliances. Such unity, according to Muller, requires a one-world religion.[7]

A Counterfeit Body

In his book, *New Genesis: Shaping a Global Spirituality*, Robert Muller reflects: "I would never have thought that I would discover spirituality in the United Nations…! Perhaps spirituality is such a fundamental human need that it always reappears in one form or another in life and throughout history and we are about to witness now its renaissance in a global, planetary context."[8] In 1993, Dr. Muller delivered the historic Parliament of World Religion's first keynote address, calling for a "permanent institution" dedicated to pursuing religious unity.[9]

Dr. Muller believed we were entering "a new period of spiritual evolution," a period of rising planetary consciousness and global living which is expected to result in the perfect unity of the human family. Central to his theology are views of "a divine United Nations" and a "cosmic Christ." "If Christ came back to earth, his first visit would be to the United Nations to see if his dream of human oneness and brotherhood had come true," wrote Muller. "I often visualize," said Dr. Muller, "of a United Nations which would be the body of Christ."[10]

In every chapter of *New Genesis*, writes Gary H. Kah in his *The New World Religion*, Robert Muller calls for a U.N.-based world government and a new world religion "as the only answers to mankind's problems." "Through it all," notes Kah. "Muller maintains his status as a Catholic Christian," ultimately linking the U.N.'s mission to Roman Catholicism. Note well his passionate pseudo prophecy.

Pope John Paul II said that we were the stone cutters and artisans of a cathedral which we might never see in its finished beauty.

All this is part of one of the most prodigious pages of evolution. It will require the detachment and objectivity of future historians to appraise... the real significance of the United Nations.[11]

The De Chardin Connection

Pierre Teilhard de Chardin was born in France in 1881. Evolution was the passion of his life. As a Jesuit priest of the Catholic Church, Teilhard pursued his first love—blending the physical and spiritual worlds under the banner of evolution.[12] The "Christ" of de Chardin was not the Christ of the gospels. For him, Christ had to fit into the theory of evolution. According to Teilhard's concept of evolution, God had not previously evolved enough to express himself through human consciousness. Chardin's process of evolution concludes with man becoming conscious of who he is— "God".[13]

"Christ is above all the God of Evolution," wrote de Chardin. "He is the supreme summit of the evolutionary movement... evolving into a Super-Christ. Humanity is the highest phase so far of evolution... beginning to change into a Super-Humanity... the Omega Point."[14] He is the most widely-read author of the New Age movement, and his ideas "gained acceptance among many Catholic leaders, including Pope John Paul II."[15]

Father Teilhard de Chardin influenced most of the prominent United Nations leaders of his day. Norman Cousins, former president of the World Federalist Association, made the connection, writing in the Forward to Robert Muller's autobiography...

Whatever the uncertainties of the future may be… oncoming generations will need living examples of the conspiracy of love that Teilhard de Chardin has said will be essential to man's salvation. Rubert Muller is involved in such a conspiracy.[16]

Muller, in *New Era Magazine*, made the final connection, saying, "It is necessary that we have a World Government centered on the United Nations…. we can credit the coming World Government to the 'influence of the writings of Tielhard de Chardin'."[17]

Bringing all the world's religions into cooperation with the United Nations was Robert Muller's top priority. "My great personal dream" he explained, "is to get a tremendous alliance between all the major religions and the U.N.". Muller, in 1997, exulted, "…during the 50th Anniversary of the United Nations… we launched again the idea of United Religions… and a meeting… to draft and give birth to a United Religions…. I will be the father of the United Religions."[18]

The March of Inter-Faith Ecumenism

Even as the vision for uniting the nations through a common religion advances through the United Nations, the systemic spirit of inter-faithism and ecumenism is marching lock step to the spiritual drumbeat of a deceptive *unity* movement worldwide. The cry of "UNITY" in our churches, cities and throughout the various religious expressions globally, as well as through a variety of governmental and (NGO) non-governmental yet quasi-governmental structures, is in itself becoming a common voice and unifying mantra.

It is profoundly seductive, for who, in the current market of politically-correct ideas, desires or even dares to resist the tide. And where is the deceptive danger?

Exchanging trust in the truth of the Bible as God's revealed Word for trust in man's experience and relationships is becoming the new model of "Christian" ecumenism. It is subtle and it is seductive. To break down walls of division, the new approach is to ignore divine proposition in favor of personal testimony. As Cecil "Mel" Robeck of Fuller Seminary, an Assemblies of God minister said, "We will not get embroiled in disputes involving scripture or homosexuality because it "would have the potential to derail our effort."[19]

Cecil Robeck is on a 12-member committee for Global Chrisian Forum. The *Christian Century* reported, "After keeping a low profile for several years, advocates of a fresh approach to ecumenism are going public...." "About 240 leaders from the Vatican, World Evangelical Alliance, Orthodox Churches, historic Anglican and Protestant communions, and Pentecostal and independent churches" gathered November 6-9, 2007, for the Global Christian Forum, to advance the new approach based on "personal testimony." Just one month earlier, Catholic Cardinal Avery Dulles admitted the potential for harmonizing doctrines was exhausted, necessitating "an ecumenism of mutual enrichment by means of personal testimony."[20]

"How then can Christian unity be envisaged?" asked Cardinal Dulles. Testimony must trump truth so as to build trust in man. As Dulles declared, "Our words, they may find, carry the trademark of truth."[21] We would do well to remember the warning of the Psalmist.

It is better to trust in the LORD than to put confidence in man.

It is better to trust in the LORD than to put confidence in princes [pastors, priests, popes and presidents] (Ps. 118:8-9).

Once again, this seductive false unity movement requires that you spiritually dance with the devil, the very Deceiver himself. Remember, there is a great eternal battle between Satan and God for the Souls of men, to become *"KING of the MOUNTAIN"* of your heart. Satan seeks to seduce your soul away from the faithful trust and allegiance in HaShem, the one true God, and His Son, Yeshua (Jesus).

The Bible declares Yeshua, the *Anointed One*, the Mashiach, the Holy One of Israel, is the "express image" of God's person, "upholding all things by the word of his power." Yeshua declared, "I and my Father are one" (Jn. 10:30). He said, "He that hath seen me hath seen the Father" (Jn. 14:9). And Yeshua also said, "I am the way, the truth, and the life: no man cometh to the Father but by me" (Jn. 14:6).

Yeshua made clear that the only true unity pleasing to God was that which is in the fruit of being *sanctified* or set apart through God's **truth** as found in the Scriptures. It was this unity "through the truth" that would cause the rest of the world to "believe that thou hast sent me" and would display God's glory as true followers of Yeshua (Jesus) became "one" even as Yeshua was one with the Father (Jn. 17:16-23). Never forget! It is our trust in the truth of God's Word, the Bible, that binds us in biblical oneness. Anything else is a counterfeit, however attractive it may appear and however broadly it may be embraced. We, whether Jew or Gentile, are *in* the world, but not *of* it, if we truly love the God of Creation, as revealed in Messiah.

Yet interfaith-ism and ecumenism march on to a louder and more incessant drumbeat. The Third Parliament of the World's Religions met in December, 1999, in South Africa, with 6000 delegates from more than 200 different religious groups. Catholic theologian, Hans Küng, said he maintains a "horizon of hope" that the 21st century might witness "unity among churches, peace among religions, and community among nations."[22]

The most ambitious organization in today's interfaith movement has been the United Religions Initiative (URI), founded by William Swing, the Episcopal bishop of California. Although this movement is little known to the public, "it now provides a spiritual face for globalization, the economic and political forces leading from nationalism to a one-world system," says Lee Penn, an investigative reporter. The interfaith movement "is no longer… a coterie of little-heeded religious idealists…" he says. "The URI's proponents range from billionaire George Soros to President George W. Bush, from the far-right the late Rev. Sun Myung Moon to liberal Catholic theologian Hans Küng, and from the Dalai Lama to the leaders of governmental-approved Protestant churches in China."[23] Penn warns in his *False Dawn* that the United Religions Initiative and the interfaith movement are poised to become the spiritual foundation of the New World Order—the "new civilization" now proposed by Mikhail Gorbachev, the last leader of the Soviet Union.[24]

Syncretism is "Sexy"

The very word *seduction* is borrowed biblically and throughout the world's cultures from a universal sexual understanding. To be *seduced* is to respond to the wiles of the *seductress* or *seducer*. And seduction, while sometimes appearing innocent, is always intentional to move the intended "victim" off the legitimate pathway to one of illegitimacy and falsity. For this reason, the word *seduction* is often used interchangeably, in a spiritual sense, with the word *deception*.

By way of illustration, a well-known evangelical pastor was asked by the *Los Angeles Times* whether he believed in Hell. His response was fascinating and reveals the process of seduction from proclaimed theological "truth" to the capitulation to a perceived trajectory of cultural acceptance.[25] While the pastor acknowledged his own belief in Hell, he said he no longer preaches about it because, as he declared, "Hell isn't sexy anymore."

The famous George Orwell declared in his novel *1984* that "In a time of universal deceit, telling the truth is a revolutionary act." "Freedom," he wrote, "is the right to tell people what they do not want to hear." Yet such a message is not born first of freedom but of responsibility. If deceit, deception and seduction, however pleasingly presented, are leading humanity toward unimaginable horror, is there not a duty to lovingly, yet with clarity, warn of the supreme danger ahead?

If syncretism is now *sexy*, it must be supremely alluring to the natural mind, even as it is presented surreptitiously and seductively in religious garb.

Global Allurement

Globalization is not merely economic, environmental or governmental but is bound together through sinews of spirituality supporting a cancerous growth now rapidly metastasizing throughout the varied cultures and countries. Rather than being seen as deadly, it is being driven excitedly as the prescription for global salvation. Hope is seduced by this allurement that promises peace and prosperity while permitting—even promoting—every man to do that which is "right in his own eyes" since he is both inherently "divine" and becoming God.

A quick journey across the world's oceans, mountains and deserts will give a better glimpse of this phenomenon.

"START OF A NEW ERA"

- "The German government will be constructing a house of worship for all faiths in Berlin…." Called The House of One, it is "intended to bring all faiths and no faiths together as a sign of coexistence and solidarity." "The idea is pretty simple," said Christian theologian Roland Stolte, one of the organizers of the $57 million project. Said Stolte, "Religious institutions have to find new language and ways to be relevant…."

  Rabbi Andreas Nachama declared that the project is "more than a symbol. It is the start of a new era…."[26]

TEMPLE OF ALL RELIGIONS

- In Kazan, the capital city of the Republic of Tatarstan in Russia, an amazing place captures the world's major religions. It is called the Temple of All Religions or the Temple of Seven Religions or the Universal Temple. The proclaimed purpose is to "achieve harmony and peaceful coexistence."[27]

CHURCH OF ALL RELIGIONS

- "A Church That Embraces All Religions and Rejects 'Us vs. 'Them'" is the title of a *New York Times* article celebrating "D.I.Y" or "Do it yourself" religion. The congregants of the Living Interfaith Church in the Pacific Northwest come from every conceivable background—atheist, Muslim, Catholic, Lutheran, New Age and evangelical Christians. Services draw from Buddhist, Shinto, Sikh, Hindu, Wiccan and humanist sources as well as Bahai. The pastor, donned in vestments adorned with symbols of a dozen religions, states that people have been "Yearning for decades to find a religion that embraced all religions, and secular ethical teachings as well."[28]

BAHÁ'Í AND RELIGIOUS UNITY

- The concept of a global religious community is clearly at the heart of the Bahá'í faith. Established by Bahá'u'lláh in the 19th century, it teaches "the essential worth of all religions and the unity of all people." According to Bahá'í teachings, "religion is revealed in an orderly and progressive way by *Manifestations of God*, who are the founders of major religions throughout history" such as Buddha, Jesus and Muhammad, all of which are "fundamentally unified in purpose." Again, at the heart of Bahá'í teachings is the unity of all people and "the goal of a unified world order" revealed in "the unity of God, unity of religion, and the unity of humanity."[29] (Note: We must, of necessity, discuss the profound influence of the Bahá'í faith in a later chapter. It may be shocking!)

POPE PROMOTES "GOOD ATHEISTS"

— "Redemption for good atheists" was the unifying promise of Pope Francis at his morning Mass on May 22, 2013. "The Lord has redeemed all of us, all of us, with the blood of Christ… Even atheists. Everyone!" He proclaimed: "We are created children in the likeness of God…. And we all have a duty to do good. And this commandment for everyone to do good, I think, is a beautiful path towards peace."[30] The implication, is what is called "Universalism," meaning that all humanity saves itself through collective good works, a concept embraced in Judaism as *tikkun olam*. Therefore, no coming *divine* messiah is needed or to be anticipated.

The Pope's declaration was intended to facilitate global ONENESS regardless of religious beliefs—or the absence thereof—thereby preparing all for a unified one-world religious belief promising peace on earth without the need for the biblically promised Messiah called "the Prince of Peace" (Isa. 9:6-7) who alone, through faith and trust in Him, would bring long-sought salvation to those who put their hope in Him through repentance of sin rather than through self-salvation by good works (Acts 4:12; Rom. 3:17-24). Such is a classic example of "Christian" syncretism.

TEMPLE OF SPIRITUAL SYNCRETISM

— The phrase "House of Prayer for All People" seems warm and welcoming for all, regardless of beliefs (whether atheist, agnostic, Jewish, Buddhist, Hindu, Sikh, New Age, Bahá'í or Christian). As is often said, "The devil lies in the details," an aphorism more true than most believe. Questions arise— 1. What is prayer? 2. To whom or what is prayer directed? 3. For what is prayer being offered? 4. Do all, regardless of religious belief or the lack thereof, have standing or authority to offer prayer? And upon what believable authority can any promise of response to prayer be expected?

For many, these may seem meaningless questions, yet in reality, they reveal held beliefs, whether true or false, that increasingly define destiny. Hidden within our answers are clues as to the likelihood we would believe in a messiah, would in fact recognize such Messiah, or would be prone rather to embrace a seductive counterfeit.

On November 2, 2014, *VOA NEWS* (Voice of America) carried this headline from Israel's Prime Minister, an orthodox Jew.[31]

> Netanyahu: People of All Faiths Can Worship
> at Temple Mount

In seeking to prevent religious and political clashes, Netanyahu opened wide the door to religious syncretism of ALL faiths, blasphemously betraying his own Orthodox convictions that the Temple Mount was ordained by the God of Abraham, Isaac and Jacob as "My holy mountain," the "mountain of the LORD" (Zech. 8:2-3). This syncretistic usage of the Temple Mount as providing a "House of Prayer for All People" has, perhaps inadvertently, opened the door wide to the end-of-the-age mixture of paganism with Judaism and Christianity, just as it was with Ancient Rome, foretold to be the final great "beast" empire on earth, which will usher in a counterfeit messiah known generally as The Antichrist (Dan. 7:1-28; Dan. 8:19-27).

The Sanhedrin (71 elders of Israel) have seized upon this syncretic interpretation of Isaiah 56:7 to promote and promise world peace by sending letters to the leaders of 70 nations insisting they must help to rebuild the Temple if they have any hope for cessation of religious conflict and establishment of world peace. Since the Jews expect no *divine* messiah, the message is increasingly clear—we must "Tower of Babel" style, unite religiously to save ourselves, ushering in a utopian millennial age of "peace on earth, good will toward men" ... a promise made only of Jesus who would "save his people from their sins," bringing the true tidings of messianic salvation and peace available to *all people* who believe and live accordingly (Matt. 1:21-23; Luke 2:8-14).

Yet confusion reigns concerning this biblical phrase "A house of prayer for all people." The phrase is used as the name for many Christian churches. An entire small denomination founded in 1919 bears the name "United House of Prayer for All People of the Church on the Rock of the Apostolic Faith," with headquarters in Washington D.C.[32] Since the words *for all people* are defined by the very existence of this church as "all people who are born again of the Holy Spirit by confession and repentance of sin, believing in the death and resurrection of Jesus Christ," the true interpretation of the phrase "for all people" is clearly opposite of the prevailing Orthodox Jewish interpretation uniting all people of all faiths... or no faiths.

Thus, the mystery of Messiah remains somewhat *mysterious* or unresolved. Does it make a difference? Might such a difference determine eternal destiny?

THE EMERGING CHURCH

– The most recent generation going back to the last decade of the 20th century has introduced the new religious concept known as *The Emerging Church*. The implication of the word *emerging* might be better understood as *evolving*. This evolution is revealed in setting aside historic Christian doctrine and replacing it with a Christianized version of cultural spirituality for a post-modern world denying absolute truth.

As one observed, "…the emerging church in essence is not so much a group as it is a happening that is seeping into American consciousness in a stealthy cultural paradigm shift. Thus, more than a church movement, it is a social movement." "It engages all cultural streams. It is a sacralizing of the world and a desacralizing of the church." Into the increasing "sacred" world of popular culture, it "encounters its most powerful mediator Oprah Winfrey."[33]

So pervasive is this influence in seeming to bind together the various streams of alternative spirituality that it requires a chapter of its own where a real Messiah might scarcely be found…unless he is YOU.

KABBALAH

– Kabbalah is ancient Jewish mysticism that increasingly infuses its influence in conjunction with 21st century spirituality. Because of its rootedness in Jewish religious history among many revered rabbis and because it synthesizes well with emerging views of global spirituality, it commands a unifying spiritualized acceptance for many drawn to New Age spirituality.

"The startling revelation of Kabbalah is that every person is actually Messiah." "When all people achieve communion with their individual Messiah-consciousness, we will then experience the presence of Messiah." "Once we have received unity with this consciousness, we ourselves become filled with the Light of Messiah."

"We, of this generation are so fortunate to participate in this Age of Aquarius. Unlike previous generations, awareness of Messiah's true meaning is available to us… our own Messiah consciousness."[34]

The Kabbalah viewpoint points to your messiahship. How confident are you in establishing your life and eternal destiny on this increasingly embraced conviction now sweeping the planet?

The *Jerusalem Post* recently affirmed the deeply embedded concept that not only does Kabbalah confirm your messiahship, but that this conviction is also confirmed by the most esoteric realms of science in the merging of philosophy and quantum physics. In what is labelled a "ground-breaking book," author Eduard Shyfrin in *From Infinity to Man* "shows the ideas of Jewish mysticism resonate with the ideas of 21st century science." The effort purports to "show the dynamic between Torah and science."[35]

INTERIM NOTE: If it has not already become apparent, each of these influences, rather than directing man to God, actually emphasizes man **becoming** God. Their message inevitably results in humankind becoming messiah in the flesh. And so we continue exploring this phenomena now merging to form the final global message of messianic expectation— "You, as with Lucifer, will become like God, a self-exalted messiah made in your own image—who will ultimately be lead in a world unity by the supreme counterfeit, gathering all earth's self-exalted "messiahs" to be embodied in a glorified Luciferian-anointed Antichrist."

FREEMASONRY AND KABBALAH

— Freemasonry is a secretive *faith system* synthesizing, in effect, all faiths and cultures into a kind of messianic hope of self-salvation IF one keeps secret and obeys the oaths demanded of the various degrees from 1 to 33rd degree. The 33rd degree is the ultimate manifestation and attainment of spiritual enlightenment necessary for spiritual leadership of a new world global order. The initiates are initially made aware of the marketable and desirable public face of the craft, and only gradually become drawn, through sequential oaths, into the deeper private face and faith of masonic adepts.[36]

The predominance of theological Jewish imagery in Masonic rituals reveals that Jewish mysticism embodied into the Kabbalah philosophy likely influenced the spiritual and esoteric nature of Speculative Freemasonry. "In Freemasonry everything is related to numbers and geometry." Similarly, "Kabbalah can be called the mathematics of human thought, the algebra of faith." Kabbalists call this translation of letters into numbers *gematria*. Therefore, *seven* is the symbolic age of the Master in Freemasonry, yet is the biblically significant number related to God's perfection and therefore to the biblically prophesied Messiah himself. By implication, it is not Christians who are called "brothers in Christ" but rather members of the Craft, as in the eyes of the Kabbalist, who are brothers, since "all men are brothers." This then becomes the foundation for global spiritual unity, and for those not accepting this non or anti-biblical concept of one-world order unity, they become anathema.[37]

Similarly, with New Age "theology," the human is, and is becoming divine or God, but with Freemasonry only if you attain the self-salvation of achieving the 30th to 33rd degrees, qualifying you as an *adept*. And who then are you as a candidate for the Royal Arch Degree? When asked, the Royal Arch Mason replies "I am that I am," the very words Jehovah God decreed as His eternal name (Ex. 3:14). When Moses inquired of God as to His name, Jehovah God responded "I AM that I AM." Thus, the Royal Arch Mason, in monumental and blasphemous chutzpah, claims to be deity in the flesh.[38]

Who then is the true God of Freemasonry? For those lured into the Craft in pursuit of the brotherhood, you may well be faced with a most solemn, soul-searching and eternal destiny-determining decision as you, and everyone, consider the words of General Albert Pike, Grand Commander, Sovereign Pontiff of Universal Freemasonry. In giving instruction to the 23 supreme councils of the world, he declared these soul-gripping, destiny-determining words.

> That which we must say to the crowd is, we
> worship a god, but it is the god one adores
> without superstition…we say this and you may
> repeat it to the brethren of the 32nd, 31st and
> 30th degrees—the Masonic religion should be
> by all of us initiates of the high degrees, main-
> tained in **the purity of the luciferian doctrine**.

Albert Pike continued his address, making Masonic religious belief clear beyond dispute.

> Yes, lucifer is god, and unfortunately Adonay
> is also God…for the absolute can only exist as
> two gods, darkness being necessary for light to
> serve as its foil…. Thus, the doctrine of Satan-
> ism is heresy, and the true and pure philosoph-
> ical religion is the belief in lucifer, the equal
> of Adonay, but lucifer, god of light and god
> of good, is struggling for humanity against
> Adonay, the god of darkness and evil.[39]

Is this not precisely the doctrine of Alice Bailey, laying
the foundation for the entire New Age spiritual movement
undergirding the final stages of the rapidly emerging One
World Order?

A 33rd degree Mason, Christopher Earnshaw, revealed
the true undergirding pursuit of Freemasonry in his recent
book *Freemasonry: Quest for Immortality*. At the very heart
of the Craft, in and through all of its Lodges throughout the
world, is the pursuit of becoming gods—a kind of self-salvation by becoming your own "I AM." The Mason, then,
by building his life through the metaphoric image of Hiram
Abiff—the temple builder—ultimately finds the long-
sought "Tree of Life" found in Kabbalah,[40] thus earning
through progressive self-effort the very promises only to
those who trust Him in faith through Yeshua the Messiah
(Rev. 22:1-2, 14).

The Messianic Masquerade Ball

It is all so alluring! God is whoever we want Him to be, even if he is actually ME or I am actually Him…or becoming Him…along with untold billions progressively united in redefining deity while denying observable reality.

TIME set the stage for the messianic masks to come off. It was the cover story of the April 5, 1993, issue. The cover portrayed a cross made up of mini photos of Americans. In the lower right-hand corner were these words.

"THE GENERATION THAT FORGOT GOD"

It referred not to the generation to come but to the previous generation. When you "forget God," you eventually redefine Him or re-invent Him according to personal and cultural predilections. And so the secular news magazine declared it so to be.

The feature article was titled "The Church Search" emblazoned across a double-page spread. Noting that millions of Americans were "flooding back to church" in the fearful wake of Gulf War I, *TIME* made an astute observation, declaring "church will never again be the same." But why? Apparently it took a liberal, secular news magazine to tell a truth that escaped the pastors and priests of a nation professing to be "Under God." The conclusion stripping the masks off of spiritually syncretized Americans—especially professing Christians—was embarrassingly announced:

Americans are seeking a custom-made God, one made in their own image.

And so it is throughout the world in this messianic age. The masquerade will soon be over as the denizens of planet Earth are confronted with one who truly is MESSIAH. When the masks finally come off, the sheer horror of billions of mini messiahs doing obeisance to the world's consummate counterfeit only to discover that he, like them, was masquerading, will be eternally catastrophic.

Chapter 9

SINCERE SEDUCTION

"...the reality of our readiness to be seduced, notwithstanding our professed beliefs to the contrary, is absolute proof...that whenever the right combination of circumstances arrives, we are prone to succumb."

SINCERETY IS NO SUBSTITUTE for truth. As human beings we inherently know that to be true...that one can be sincerely wrong even to the point of disaster and destruction; yet we are cleverly adept at rationalizing why our sincerity alone is sufficient. In no arena of human life and experience is this troubling truth more evident than in our religious beliefs, but why?

The Nature of Seduction

Seduction reveals the fallen state of human nature. We may be reluctant to admit it, yet the reality of our readiness to be seduced, notwithstanding our professed beliefs to the contrary, is absolute proof of our weakness that, whenever the right combination of circumstances arrives, we are prone to succumb.

Whether or not you believe the Bible, as true or as a genuine message of God to humankind, it is replete with the issue of sexual metaphors to describe our propensity to embrace untruth, even in the face of glaring truth. This may seem, at first, to be merely an academic discussion, but it takes on destiny-determining significance if, in truth, there is a TRUE Messiah who, as the Bible declares, is coming "to judge the world with righteousness, and the people with his truth" (Psa. 96:13).

If this is, as vast numbers believe, the messianic age, perhaps it behooves us to explore more sincerely and seriously this "Mystery of the Ages" which, through the prophesy, in both Jewish (Hebrew) and Christian Scriptures, i.e., the Bible foretells of a real, true and long-expected Messiah. And so we explore a variety of prominent "faiths" or religions as well as global religious influences or organizations that many have *sincerely* embraced.

The Mystery of Messianism

Messianism, by itself, is a seductive mystery. Like all other ISMs, it is also an *ism*, a basic truth around which many man-devised beliefs have been conceived and promoted throughout human history until this unique messianic moment.

The heart truth of messianism is the conviction or belief in the coming of a "messiah" who serves as a savior or liberator of a people or of all humanity. While rooted deeply in Abrahamic faiths, it also manifests in other religions with messianism-related concepts, including Zoroastrianism (Saoshyant), Judaism (the Mashiach), Buddhism (Budha), Hinduism (Kalki), Taoism (Li Hong) and Bahá'ísm (He whom God shall manifest).

In Judaism, the traditional expectation referred to a future Jewish king from the line of King David, who would be "anointed" and rule the Jewish people as "Melech HaMashiach" or "the Anointed King." Rabbinic Judaism and current Orthodox Judaism see a messiah, a non-divine charismatic human, who will gather the Jews back to Eretz Israel (the homeland) and usher in an era of world peace. Reformed or "liberal" Judaism, while believing in a Messianic Age of world peace, do not anticipate an actual messianic leader.

Mohammedanism (Islam), while believing in Isa (Jesus son of Mary, as the Messiah) actually believe that Jesus' reign upon his return will embrace and promote the Islamic Mahdi (the 12th Imam) as the true messianic redeemer, restoring global peace by eliminating all religions except Islam.

Perhaps you may have noticed…all of these religious beliefs are called "ISMs." Only one expressing a clearly defined Messiah is not distinguished as an "ISM" and that is Christianity. That should engender heart-probing consideration.

We now briefly explore many of these various "ISMs" as well as a variety of historic or present movements that compound the messianic mystery of the ages.

Rise of Messianic Buddhism

Siddharta Gautana lived in the foothills of northern India; reportedly born around 560BC. Having left his home and family as a young man, he wandered as a beggar for six years, self-sacrificing in order to attain spiritual illumination which eluded him. Realizing he had to look within himself, he sat under a tree for three days seeking spiritual ecstasy. Apparently having accomplished his search, the bodhisattva (holy man) had become the Buddha.

For forty years he wandered northern India, spreading his message: "Cease to do evil, learn to do good, and purify your heart." Only when the sacred state of self-salvation revealed in *bodhi* (enlightenment) was attained could one find the final peace he himself thought to have attained as Buddha. Rather than resurrection of the dead, Buddha believed in multiple reincarnations, whether as humans or animals, depending upon how they had lived their lives.[1]

Messianic Buddhism is the liberation and "salvation" theology of a Buddhist "messiah," who discovered the Four Noble Truths that he preached would relieve or free the mind from suffering, leading to Nirvana.

The two best known Buddhist "messiahs" are the 14th century Dalai Lama, exiled from Tibet as god-king when the Chinese invaded, and ultimately became the dominant religion of China, therefore is arguably the most widely embraced religion worldwide, received predominantly in the West as Zen Buddhism. The other Buddhist "messiah" is Wirathu, known as the terrorist monk of Myanmar.[2] [3]

Under messianic directives, personal "salvation," while ultimately attained by the SELF in pursuit of Nirvana, has been linked to national salvation; with personal religion as state religion.[4]

Confucianism's Self-Salvation

Confucious was China's most important teacher and religious philosopher. His religious, social and political philosophy is known as Confucianism and became the foundation of Chinese life, education and government for 2000 years. Confucianism, however, was not a religion with its own gods. Rather, Confucious, like vast and growing numbers of Americans and Western Europeans, believed that all people are basically good and capable of self-salvation by leading a good and noble life, yet to no defined eternal end.[5]

Awaiting the Hindu Messiah

In the mystical religion of Hinduism there is, perhaps surprisingly, a strong messianic expectation in spite of its polytheistic nature absent a supreme being.

Hinduism believes in the unity of everything. This totality is called *Brahman*, and "we are all part of God." It should then be obvious that Hindu beliefs underly much of New Age spirituality and the emerging religious foundation of the New World Order.

Many deities are worshipped in Hinduism, perhaps hundreds of thousands, yet there is a hierarchy, the top three being Brahma, Vishnu and Shiva. "Vishnu is worshipped as savior, and is second in rank after Brahma." Krishna is the eighth incarnation of the god Vishnu and is one of the special avatars in Hinduism. It is alleged that Jesus was an incarnation of Krishna.... And it is expected that there will be a new incarnation of the avatar...who will be known as the Kalki Avatar as he will be riding on a white horse.[6]

The Kalki Avatar "will fight the apocalyptic snake and achieve final victory over evil on earth, renewing humanity to lead pure and honorable lives." The messianic expectations of all religions will be thus fulfilled in the Kalki Avatar, the "world messiah."[7]

What, then, do Hindus believe about Jesus? To Hindus, Jesus' proclamation "The Father and I are one" confirms the Hindu belief that everyone, through rigorous spiritual practice, can realize his own universal "god consciousness." Deepak Chopra declared, "Christ-consciousness, God- consciousness, Krishna-consciousness, Buddha-consciousness—its all the same thing. This consciousness says, 'You and I are the same beings'."[8] Which means, we are all gods, needing no personal saviour. Our only need is for a world-wide Kalki Avatar or New Age "messiah," bringing universal peace.

The casual reader may be prone to reason that since all of these religions seem to believe the world is nearing "the end of the age" or a fulcrum moment of cataclysmic change and that a messiah-like figure will bring universal peace, that they must be referring to the same thing, coinciding with a Christian Biblical expectation of the Second Coming of Messiah Yeshua, thus unifying humanity in a universal hope, bringing one-world unity. Unfortunately, such a conclusion may well be a deceptive sleight-of-hand seducing billions of unsuspecting denizens of earth to, in the name of global spirituality, embrace a pernicious counterfeit messiah.

Bahá'í And The Promised One

Will the relatively new religion of Bahá'í bring final resolution or solidify confusion as to the messianic mystery of the ages? We shall see.

The Bahá'í Faith teaches the essential worth of all religions and the unity of all people. It was established in the 19th century by Bahá ú lláh, and embraces three principles…

1. The unity of God;
2. The unity of religion; and
3. The unity of humanity.

Bahá ú lláh taught that religion is revealed in an orderly and progressive way by "Manifestations of God" who are the founders of the world's major religions, the most recent of which is Báb followed by the prophet Bahá ú lláh . At the heart of Bahá'í teachings is a "unified world order" ensuring universal prosperity, without nationalism or racism.[9] Sounds growingly familiar, doesn't it?

Bahá'í believes the world, as we know it, is at the "end of the age" revealed in maximum moral and spiritual decline and therefore awaits the coming of the Hindu Kalki Avatar, thus fulfilling prophecies of Lord Krishna. Bahá'í therefore envisions the synthesis of all religions, merging the desirable aspects of each to the fleshly human mind in a religious stew of spiritualized promises of global peace, prosperity or shalom. This reveals the utopian fulfillment of an amorphously defined "messianic age" seductive to the ever-growing masses desiring maximum inclusivity with minimal behavioral and spiritual demands as every man does that which is right in his own eyes, It should then be obvious that both genuine followers of Jesus with absolute commitment to the Bible as "the Word of God" as well as serious and sober-minded Orthodox Jews will, of necessity, be *excluded* from the "inclusivity" of the emerging New World Religion. They will be subject to the "selection process" of globalized persecution to either compel conformity by threat or force or have their lives selectively removed from the planet so as not to negatively impact the rising utopian fervor and fever.

The Convergence

It should be increasingly obvious to a sincere and sober-minded observer that this perceived "messianic moment" is defined by the rapidly progressing merger of all the rivers and tributaries of history and prophecy surging with unprecedented pressure toward a culminating event promising either worldwide shalom or the cataclysmic fruit of devastating seduction. Sincerity alone will provide no bridge nor will good intentions be an eternal life saver as the roiling waters surge inexorably toward the expected "end of the age."

New Agers refer to this phenomena as "The Convergence." Yet there remain other growing global and governmental components joining the religious convergence, driving the choices inevitably to be demanded of all earth's denizens…including you and those you hold dear. These further forces must be disclosed in order to truly "unveil the mystery of the ages."

Chapter 10

THE MYSTERY OF MORAL MESSIANISM

"Moralistic therapeutic deism enables all religions to be universally embraced and unified."

MORALS HAVE BECOME A MYSTERY. The Pursuit of a global morality has taken on a powerfully persuasive messianic tone over the century last passed that is now reaching a crescendo. Yet the very concept of morals and what is "moral" or immoral has changed dramatically over the past fifty years, reaching the level of *dogma* driven by the unholy trinity of political correctness, multiculturalism and religious pluralism. This emergent dogma is now enforced by the high priests of cancel culture and globalism.

The A-Morality of "Morals"

The very word *moral* or *morality* is now wrapped in a mystical cloud of ever vacillating feelings and perceived cultural standards of acceptable or desirable human behavior and attitudes. There is no longer any well-definable fixed point of moral absolutes that has historically guided humanity, leaving us increasingly adrift on a tumultuous sea of relativity where every man or woman does that which, for a fleeting moment, is right in his or her own eyes (Judg. 17:6).

This was the lamentable condition of ancient Israel in the days of the judges, to which the people "would not hearken," so the people "went a whoring after other gods" and "turned quickly out of the way which their fathers walked in, obeying the commandment of the LORD, but they did not do so." They abandoned the moral law and the Ten Commandments, and "corrupted themselves more than their fathers...." "...they ceased not from their own doings, nor from their stubborn way. And the anger of the LORD was hot against Israel..." (Judg. 2:17-20).

This is a vivid picture of "moral" replacement by shifting moral authority. The shift was somewhat gradual, yet within a single generation, moving from the sovereignty of God to the absolute sovereignty of man in the lordship of SELF and purported self-government. Thus man, humankind, became the ultimate arbiter of truth and morality.

This same pattern now prevails throughout the supposedly Judeo-Christian western world. Shockingly, man, in effect, becomes his own mystical "messiah," which is precisely the promise of the rapid convergence of world religions culminating in a New World Order where we are told we will save ourselves, thus ushering in the long-awaited utopia.

This phenomenon was poignantly captured by the secular, prophet-like authors of *The Day America Told the Truth* in 1991. In their piercing analysis of western life revealed in and through American thinking, they asked the probing question: "Who is the new moral authority in America?" Their prophetically-troubling answer was, "You are, pardner. You are the new moral authority in America."[1]

In its 1993, April 3, edition *TIME*, while featuring a cross on its front cover, declared America's shifted moral base and authority with the provocative declaration:

"The generation that forgot God."

But the reasoning behind the conclusion that the previous generation had, like Israel, already "forgotten God," was perhaps even more troubling for the future (which is now the present). In the feature article, "The Church Search," it was noted that after Gulf War I people were flooding back to church – but – "church would never again be the same." We should all take note of the heart-piercing conclusion preached from a secular pulpit. Church will never again be the same because…

> "Americans are looking for a custom-made God, one made in their own image."

TIME's inescapable analysis revealed that America and Americans, even or especially "Christian" Americans, have been busily redefining moral authority, based on their own ever-fleeting feelings and collective viewpoints rather than on a God-breathed immutable moral authority.

This conversion of what formerly and historically was deemed *immoral* was now mysteriously becoming embraced as *moral*, a transition traversing a single generation. This transition from immorality to "morality" was dramatically confirmed by America's 43rd president, Bill Clinton, known to carry a big black Bible (at least for photo ops). In November 1997, he became the first sitting American president to knowingly appear before an exclusive homosexual audience, before which he made what may well be one of the most arrogant statements to have ever been made by an American president purportedly guiding a nation claiming to be "Under God." Here are his shocking words:

We are, in practical ways, changing the immutable ideals that have guided us from the beginning.

Here was a veritable declaration of God-hood for both the president and We the People. "We are," he said, "changing the *immutable* [unchangeable] ideals [morals and laws] that have guided us [been at the very foundation of the country] since the beginning. From that moment forward, Black became White, Evil became Good and acceptable, Truth was abandoned for cultural predilection, and Morality became progressively "im-moral," thus dismissing morality as a virtue and confirming a-morality as a unifying force for ONENESS. It should therefore come as no surprise that *Forbes*, America's foremost business magazine, should devote its entire 75th anniversary edition in 1992 to asking the question, "Whatever happened to virtue in America?"[2]

For an entire generation, the supposed "Land of the Free" has exported a god-defying a-morality as virtue throughout the world, setting the stage globally for a counterfeit virtue of immorality in the belief this will finally destroy divisions and thus enable global citizens to unite in peace under a New World Order. We will have become our own "messiah," gods made in our own image.

Moralistic Therapeutic Deism

The 2021 research report of George Barna and Arizona Christian University was very revealing as to the current worldview of We the People increasingly living amid moral chaos in the United States. For careful observers it should have provided no surprise.

Of seven distinct worldviews characterizing the country, by a significant margin Moralistic Therapeutic Deism took the ascendency at 39%, followed by a Judeo-Christian biblical outlook at 31%.[3] Yet those figures do not tell the total tale. The study found that only 2% of Millennials (born between 1985 and 2002) have a biblical worldview. And not much better were their parents, Gen X'ers, at only 5%. The pattern is disturbingly pervasive. As Barna's Cultural Research Center reported in 2020, "The Christian Church is Seriously Messed Up," stating that "…professing Christians are developing more and more decidedly unchristian beliefs. "Syncretism," he warned, "rules the day." Although Jesus, as declared "Messiah" had declared "I am the way, the truth and the life. No man comes to the Father but by me" (Jn. 14:6), 56% who identify as evangelical Christians profess that what really matters is that one sincerely professes "some type" of religious faith. Unsurprisingly, Mainline Protestants were at 67% and Roman Catholics at 77%. Being "generally good" was the universal criteria for claiming to be a Christian in today's culture.[4]

So…what then is *Moralistic Therapeutic Deism*? It is a term coined by sociologist Christian Smith, in his 2005 book titled *Soul Searching: The Religious and Spiritual Lives of American Teenagers*. While not a new religion as such, it is a combination of beliefs he labels "moralistic therapeutic deism." It consists of five defining points setting the trajectory for a desired spiritual destiny.

1. A creator God does exist who ordered the world and watches over human life.
2. God wants people to be good, nice and fair.
3. The central goal and defining purpose for life is to be happy and to feel good about oneself.
4. God does not need to be particularly involved in one's life, except when you think you really need Him.
5. Good people go to heaven when they die.[5]

These were the views of 3000 teens interviewed by the sociological study conducted by a Roman Catholic University. As Smith and his co-author Melinda Denton conclude, this system of thought and belief is "moralistic" because it teaches that being a good or moral person (however defined) is central to a good and happy life. It is about providing "therapeutic benefits to the adherent" rather than "repentance from sin" or obeying a Creator God who has authority over His creation.

The authors maintain that "a significant part of Christianity in the United States is actually only tenuously Christian in any sense…but rather has morphed into Christianity's misbegotten step-cousin, Christian Moralistic Therapeutic Deism." Morals are thus seen (however one wants to define them at any given time) as the defining characteristic of Christianity, but because all religions ostensibly claim those same standards (however vaguely or varied they may be as we universally evolve into god-hood), moralistic therapeutic deism enables all religions to be universally embraced and unified. As one blogger suggested in 2009, Moralistic Therapeutic Deism is "perfectly suited to serve as the civil religion of the highly differentiated 21st century United States."[6]

As we now swim in the swirling waters of an increasingly globalized and interconnected world, "practicing Christians find the claims of New Spirituality among the most enticing, perhaps because it holds a positive view of religion and emphasizes the supernatural…." The belief that all people pray to the same god or spirit (by whatever name known) and that "meaning and purpose come from becoming one with all that is" has now captured the minds of 27% of professing Christians as of 2020.[7]

Perhaps Catholic priests, Richard Heilman and Bill Peckman best capture the merger of moralistic therapeutic deism with its milieu in popular western culture and culturally re-defined spirituality by declaring…

IT IS THE THEOLOGICAL UNDERPINNING OF UNIVERSALISM.

"Nowhere in the Christian Scriptures are we told to be good or nice," they noted. Rather, "We are told to be humble, merciful, compassionate, bold, courageous, holy, strong, and a whole host of other things…but never to be merely good or nice." The "plea of moralistic deism is to be inoffensive. It is why all religions can be the same…the goal isn't holiness…it's being nice." "Believe in nothing so strongly that one triggers no one." "Conveniently enough, I get to be the arbiter of what constitutes good," and therefore I, on my own sinless merit, declare my certain eligibility for Heaven as "the ultimate participation trophy."[8]

Thus, I become my own "I AM," becoming both judge and jury of my own destiny, defined not by the testimony of faith but by the unassailable testimony of my ever-vacillating feelings. I have become *messiah*.

Chapter 11

THE "CAFETERIA" CHRIST

*"The choice of messiah becomes the
hinge of history, both for Jew and Gentile."*

SPIRITUAL DEMOCRACY is a concept well-suited for our post-modern culture demanding universal choice to fit every individual's predilection, however vacillating it may be. Indeed, if every woman should have the power to choose whether or not to preserve the life of a child who would be born as one made in God's image, surely we all should be empowered to create a god or messiah in our own image—a messiah made like unto us in this gratuitous ME, ME, ME generation.

The Power to Choose

Democracy is a government and attitude of the heart giving man supreme power and authority over himself. Thus, however absurd it may seem, if a woman has the "right" to kill her child for reasons uniquely justified by her, a man therefore might similarly (for reasons uniquely justified by him) claim the "right" to rape. This is the dangerous folly of pure democracy well understood by America's founders and rejected as an unavoidable and unsustainable form of government, where every person does that which is right in his/her own eyes as a perverse and pernicious expression of *liberty*.

America's founders cringed at the concept of pure democracy where man becomes an absolute sovereign—a virtual "god" or self-ordained messiah. Both the historical record of unfettered human passions and the testimony of the Bible convinced America's forebearers of the potential dictatorial tyranny of a collective mass of humankind to carry out, without fear of God, their despotic will, unrestrainable by human government. And so, well-knowing the true nature of mankind, they gave us a uniquely-designed government of human checks and balances subsumed under a divine sovereignty ultimately expressed in the motto "One Nation Under God" and "In God We Trust." And what government were we given… "A republic, ma'am, if you can keep it," declared Benjamin Franklin.

"We have no government armed with power capable of contending with human passions unbridled by morality and religion," warned John Adams (Harvard graduate, 2nd president of the United States of America, and first to inhabit the White House). "Our Constitution was made for a moral and religious (meaning "Christian" to the founders) people," declared Adams. "It is wholly inadequate to the government of any other."[1]

Robert Winthrop, descendant of John Winthrop who served as the first governor of the Massachusetts Bay Colony from 1630 and for forty years, echoed the same conviction as John Adams, but over fifty years later, declaring of American society and government that "…the Word of God is the only authoritative rule." "No evolution produced that Volume, and no revolution of thought, or action, or human will can ever prevail against it." "Men," he warned, "must necessarily be controlled either by a power within them, or a power without them; either by the Bible or by the bayonet."[2]

Thus, pure democracy, unrestrained by both the Word and Spirit of the un-evolved Creator, dooms mankind and nations to ultimate self-destruction. Our human, yet divinely ordained power to choose, therefore entails both temporal and eternal consequences. The power to choose is soberingly consequential. It can proffer either "the best of times," or "the worst of times." It promises either a blessing or a curse. As Adam and Eve learned the hard way in an otherwise God-blessed paradise, questioning what God hath said, however justified by human or satanically-inspired reason, can breed unfathomable sorrow and separation when haunting fear displaces holy fellowship.

Both America and Israel therefore become the ultimate testing ground in this messianic age of the very test failed by our forebearers in the garden. The words of that eternal test echo now in the hearts and minds of these two countries and their citizens… "Hath God said…?" (Gen. 3:1). The destiny of humankind now teeters on the perilous choice of those nations where their very existence was established by covenant with a Creator whose will and way were deemed supreme and sovereign over the fickle and wayward wills of man.

These two nations who alone, both Jew and Gentile, have represented to the world that foundation of the Divine will for mankind, are now facing the supreme choice of either embracing or rejecting that God's sovereign authority, thus leading the world, as did Adam and Eve, to elevate human reason over the Divine, and thereby elevating the creature to godhood in opposition to the Creator. Satan, the cast-out Lucifer, will have seductively and surreptitiously fulfilled his historic goal to become as "the most High God" ruling and reigning over not only the land but over the hearts of men, eternally alienating them from the God who would be their Father.

The choice of messiah, therefore, becomes the hinge of spiritual history, both for Jew and Gentile.

The Cafeteria Plan

People are often drawn to a cafeteria as opposed to a regular restaurant. There are three primary reasons:

1. More choices are made available.
2. The very spirit of choice is amplified.
3. And the cost is usually less.

We therefore can pick and choose whatever foods we so desire at the moment from a vast array of offerings calculated to persuade and provide whatever pleases our fickle pallets. Unfortunately, as it is with the cafeteria plan of infinite choice for food, so it has increasingly become the alluring offerings of a cafeteria system of faith.

This ever-expanding buffet table of supposed faith choices was well prophesied by a famous Jewish zealot 2000 years ago. Known then as Rabbi Shaul, he terrorized Jews who had become followers of Yeshua as Messiah. Amid his zealotry of passionate persecution of these "Christians," he was knocked off his high horse by a dramatic appearance of the One called Jesus of Nazareth who had been crucified and had risen again as witnessed by more than five hundred persons. The historically confirmed consequences of this holy confrontation resulted in Rabbi Shaul becoming the Apostle Paul, all recorded in the Acts of the Apostles (Acts 9:1-30, 13-28).

Rabbi Shaul's conversion changed the world and clarified the choice that both Jews and Gentiles face in this consummate moment of history. A Jewish zealot who once conspired to bring about the death of Stephen, the first man to be martyred (by stoning) for his faith in Yeshua as Messiah, now, in his moment of confrontational truth with that Messiah on the road to Damascus, becomes a global minister of Jesus as Messiah, suffering stoning, shipwreck and death to proclaim the Good News of salvation through Jesus known as "The Gospel." It was that same Apostle Paul who warned of future perilous times immediately preceding the Second Coming of Jesus as Messiah (II Tim. 3:1-8). He particularly noted that "evil men and seducers shall wax worse and worse, deceiving and being deceived" (II Tim. 3:13). He exhorted that we must "hold the mystery of the faith in a pure conscience" (I Tim. 3:9).

This rabbi turned apostle, having been profoundly confronted in glaring light by the manifest presence of the Messiah, now was eternally convinced of the necessity to choose. He warned that many who once chose to follow Jesus as Messiah would "fall away" from the faith, choosing not to press on in the truth (II Thess. 2:3). He warned that the majority of people would be captured by "the deceivableness of unrighteousness" because "they receive not the love of truth," "believed not the truth," but "had pleasure in unrighteousness" (II Thess. 2:9-12).

Paul well understood the assault we would face in these end times with the barrage of competing choices. The cafeteria plan of many "truths" and many choices to please our spiritual pallets would be very enticing. He spoke not of "truths" or of many alternate ways but of **the** truth…

> For the time will come when they will not endure sound doctrine [teaching]; but after their own lusts shall they heap to themselves teachers, having itching ears; and they shall turn away their ears from the truth, and shall be turned unto fables (II Tim. 4:3-4).

Apparently, we are easily seduced by the savor of offerings at the spiritual buffet table that provide temporary satisfaction yet leave us without the enduring sustenance either for life or eternity. The purported democracy of faith is profoundly deceiving and may well lead to perdition. We must choose, but how… and when? Do you have the discernment to choose that which is true amid the "democratic" offerings of feelings-based faith?

We look now at one of the plethora of religious presentations that purports to provide the ultimate spiritual solution to save the world. Enter *Bahá'í Teachings for the New World Order*.[3]

The "Spiritual Democracy"

Welcome to "The Bahá'í World Order." "The concept of a world order—a federation of the globe's nations, a universal tribunal, a Parliament of Man—represents the inevitable next step in our collective maturation; humanity's best hope for peace…" declares baha-iteachings.org. '…the Bahá'í Faith incorporates, at its very core, the democratic ideal. Every Bahá'í decision-making body is democratically-elected, and no clergy exists in the Bahá'í Faith. That fact rules out the possibility of a Bahá'í theocracy. The foundation of this Cause is pure spiritual democracy, and not theocracy—Abdu'l-Bahá, Bahá'í Scriptures, p. 449.[4]

"The Bahá'í Faith encourages the independent investigation of truth, supports the thought and upholds the right of unrestricted individual belief." "…in democracy, because thought and speech are not restricted, the greatest progress is witnessed. It is likewise true in the world of religion," according to Bahá'í. "The new way of looking at faith—as the free exercise of each person's conscience and conscious-ness—differs drastically from many of the old and ossified religious traditions," declares Bahá'í. "To Bahá'í, there are no insiders or outsid-ers, no saved or damned, no clean or unclean, no believer or apostate, no righteous and infidel, no Other."[5]

The seemingly obvious conclusion is that all "truth" is defined exclusively by an individual's personal belief at any particular moment, regardless of how widely or exclusively it may differ from a million other self-ordained beliefs. Each person, therefore, becomes his or her own democratically-ordained and self-anointed messiah. Yet such application of democracy is essential to obtain the otherwise illu-sory goal of one-world unity to undergird the rapidly emerging and divine-defying One World Order. But the democratically-desired and demanded ends must justify whatever means to achieve it, however abused the foundational "truths" upon which they are based may be.

A New World Coming

"Mankind's desire for peace can be realized only by the creation of a world government," declared Albert Einstein.[6] "We stand on the threshold of an age whose convulsions proclaim alike the death-pangs of the old order and the birth-pangs of the new."—Shoghi Effendi, *The New World Order of Bahá ú lláh*, p. 169.[7]

Nelson Mandela made clear his own conviction, declaring, "The new world order that is in the making must focus on the creation of a world democracy, peace and prosperity for all."[8]

From a Bahá'í perspective, the phrase 'new world order'…refers to the progressive, inevitable next stage in global governance—a world-wide spiritual democracy."

Welcome to the dispensation of the Cafeteria "Christ" gloriously presented for your personal selection at the democratic buffet table of Bahá'í.

PART 4

THE GLOBALIST MESSIAH

A GLOBAL "MESSIAH" WILL ONE DAY RULE THE WORLD. That is the very nature of every messianic movement—religious, quasi-religious or otherwise. The contestants are many and varied, but each seeks to be victorious.

Since the underlying, yet often somewhat secret or unspoken goal is global, spiritual and governmental leaders have realized that to achieve the ultimate objective thy must sacrifice some of their unique distinctives so as to join forces (so to speak) to maximize their messianic claim, thus collectively claiming the consummate prize of global dominion and power.

It is therefore now the perceived moment in history to, in effect, rebuild the ancient Tower of Babel in a global "Babylon." The Messiah awaits man's best effort to replace him, since nature abhors a vacuum. Welcome to the birth of a New World Order as the kings and priests of the planet prepare to bow to a false-real messiah.

Chapter 12

THE UNITED NATIONS' SAVIOR

*"A One World Government is the
only way to 'Save Humanity'." ~ Pope Francis*

HE DECLARES HIMSELF THE PROMISED ONE of all nations
and religions. He claims to be the King of kings and Lord of lords, the
world's Savior and Redeemer promised in all sacred Scriptures. His
name is Bahá ú lláh.[1]

Bahá ú lláh was the founder of the Bahá'í Faith in the latter half
of the nineteenth century (late 1800s). His son, 'Abdu'l- Bahá, was his
appointed successor. He gave many public dissertations in America in
1912 which were published in *The Promulgation of Universal Peace*,
declaring Bahá'í to be "The foundation of all the divine religions" …
being "one" (or ultimately consolidated and expressed) in Bahá'í.

The Bábí Dispensation

For anyone not familiar with Bahá'í, what is revealed in this chapter
may seem weird, absurd, arrogant and blasphemous, but we must
realize it is seriously believed by millions and received as a premier
coalescing force by the United Nations for giving ultimate birth to
The New World Order. Bahá'í is believed to be the "gospel" glue to
bind the peoples of our planet into a glorious unity by accepting all

religious, or non-religious, beliefs as equally authoritative to be not only respected but accepted.

Since it should be apparent that the golden threads of New Age spirituality are woven through the claims of Bahá'í, it should also be apparent that any individual, group, or religious/spiritual persuasion that refuses to embrace the fundamental religious "oneness" of Bahá'í, cannot be allowed to enjoy or participate in its purported global peace and prosperity. Such aberrant persons or beliefs must therefore be cancelled out (removed) as enemies of the new glorious global salvation of the planet.

As previously discussed, enforcers or true believers of New Age Spirituality call for such contrarian beliefs to be "selected out" by the "selection process." Alleged "democratic choice," therefore, based upon true and uncompromisable beliefs, cannot and will not be tolerated. They will be deemed dangerous to the grand, unifying redemption of earth. Life on earth will be short for those Jews believing such beliefs to be blasphemous, or, for true followers of Jesus, absolutely committed to the conviction that Jesus is "the only way, the only truth and the only life" ...the "only way" to God the Father.

The Bahá'í library, in proclaiming "The World Order of Bahá ú lláh," declares "That the Bab [is] the inaugurator of the Bábí Dispensation." The most distinctive feature of the Bahá'í Dispensation is the purpose "ordained for the Bab by the Almighty" entitling him "to rank as one of the self-sufficient Manifestations of God." The "most distinctive feature of the Bahá'í Dispensation" is "its uniqueness, a tremendous accession to the strength, to the mysterious power and authority with which this holy cycle has been invested... to a degree unrivaled by the Messengers gone before Him...." "That so brief a span... should have separated the most mighty and wondrous Revelation... is a secret that no man can unravel and a mystery such as no mind can fathom."[2]

"I am the Primal Point... from which have been generated all created things," wrote the Bab. "I am the Countenance of God... the light of God... and "all the keys of heaven God hath chosen to place on My right hand... the keys of hell on My left." "I am one of the sustaining pillars of the Primal Word of God."[3]

(Please take a breath before we continue!)

"The Bab is likewise the Sun of Truth, and His light the light of Truth." "I am the Interpreter of the Word of God." "His Holiness the Exalted One (the Bab) is the Manifestation of the unity and oneness of God and the Forerunner of the Ancient Beauty... the supreme Manifestation of God and the Day-Spring of His most divine Essence." The Bab is "the perfect Exemplar of His teachings, the unerring Interpreter of His Word, the embodiment of every Bahá'í ideal, the incarnation of every Bahá'í virtue." "He is, above and beyond these appellations, the 'Mystery of God'." "I am."[4]

If this accurately describes the heart and foundation of Bahá'í belief, as taken directly from their website, it should not be difficult to see that, while purporting to embrace all religions as culminating in the Dispensation of Bahá'í, there is absolutely no space in such a world religion for a genuine Orthodox Jew or for a follower of Jesus if He truly is the long-awaited Messiah. And so the plot of this "Mystery of the Ages" thickens. Why does the vision of the United Nations and that of Bahá'í seem absolutely congruent? We must explore that fascinating connection.

Uniting the Nations

The Bahá'í "incarnation of God religion is the greatest of all means for establishment of order in the world," declared 'Abdu'l-Bahá.[5]

"The Bahá'í faith sees the United Nations as the vessel by which the unifying of the world's religions into one faith will come to fruition. Their plan for the future of our world and the role of the United Nations and a regionalized world, are an eerily complete and detailed picture of Biblical prophecy." "The Bahá'í Faith is a popular religion of ecumenism and political correctness embraced by the United Nations and other interfaith organizations. The popularity of Bahá'í can largely be attributed to its attempts to unifying all faiths, prophets and the entire human race."[6]

"The Bahá'í temple in Illinois is a nine-sided building representing the world's nine living religions, symbolizing the unity of all religions. It therefore becomes understandable why Bahá'í is promoted vigorously by the U.N. and plays a major part in all United Nations spiritual events." Its International Headquarters is dramatically displayed in Haifa, Israel, a further demonstration of its decisive presence in the United Nations. Bahá'í "eagerly awaits the man [be he Messiah or Antichrist] who will usher in global peace, and holds as one of their central missions the establishment of a united global commonwealth that will control all things political, financial, and spiritual." And Bahá'í's involvement with the United Nations dates back to the U.N.'s founding in 1945. Nearly 130 agencies and organizations operating within the UN system, overseeing vast resources, are all strategic parts of the plan to achieve global governance and eliminate national sovereignty, all undergirded by a growing Ecumenical Interfaith Religion.[7]

"Teachings for the New World Order"

Welcome to the rebuilding of the ancient Tower of Babel, the spirit of which never departed from God-defying humanity determined to democratically define our own destiny without divine submission. The world's elite have determined that the time is short, and that what we do we must do quickly.

Due to brevity of time and space, the "quick" transition must be distilled both in time and trajectory so as to comprehend the calculations of globalists to reconfigure our world, thus placing the spiritual/religious component in context. For that, we turn to the *World Tribune*, May 17, 2021. The headline reads,

"The 'great reset' timeline, from 2014 to 2021."

For those informed by biblical prophecy, it may be more than a curiosity to note the initial timeline for introducing the *Great Reset*, a euphemism for "One World Government," was seven years. Since planting the first official seed for the so-called "great reset" at the World Economic Forum (WEF) in Davos, Switzerland in 2014, leftist elites such as former U.S. Secretary of State, John Kerry, were clamoring for this new global order, and for a global crisis to latch onto. That came conclusively to the world in 2020.

As the World Economic Forum founder, Klaus Schwab, one of the architects of the Great Reset, proclaimed: "The pandemic represents a rare but narrow window of opportunity to reflect, re-imagine, and reset our world…." The great reset calls for "a complete makeover of society under a technocratic regime of un-elected bureaucrats who want to dictate how the world is run from the top down," determined through invasive technologies to "track and trace your every move while censoring and silencing anyone who dares not comply."[8]

The world's wealthiest were quick to jump on board, particularly Bill Gates, founder of Microsoft, who crusaded the world's pundits and politicians through his foundation's association with Dr. Anthony Fauci to demand world-wide vaccination. But the plan seems to have already been decided and prepared by pandemic simulations beginning in 2018.

"In May 2018, the WEF actually partnered with Johns Hopkins to simulate a fictitious pandemic. It was called "Clade X" and was set up to see how prepared the world [would be] if it were ever faced with such a crisis." "In October of 2019," just a few months before the revelation of the COVID-19 virus in January 2020, "the WEF [again] teamed-up with Johns Hopkins and the Bill and Melinda Gates Foundation to stage Event 201, another pandemic exercise." "Less than six months after the conclusion of Event 201, which specifically simulated a coronavirus outbreak, the World Health Organization (WHO) officially declared that the coronavirus had reached pandemic status on March 11, 2020." "After the nightmare scenarios had fully materialized by mid-2020, the WEF founder [miraculously] declared 'now is the time for a *Great Reset*'." Hinchcliffe, in the *Global Research* report, concluded: "And now they're saying that the great reset ideology is the solution to the pandemic, and it **must be enacted quickly**." (Emphasis added)[9] That Great Reset is now set to come to final fruition on or before 2030.[10]

Teachings For the New World Order

By now it should be apparent to any thoughtful reader that the world and its leaders are moving inexorably toward the consummation of a global government merging economics, law, a re-defined morality and spirituality into a New Order of the Ages commonly known as The New World Order. The vision is that history as we have known it will be vacated in favor of the fulfillment of a vast and all-encompassing unity or oneness of humanity that will supersede all previous historical efforts for one-world dominion. Mankind will have finally reached the divine pinnacle where all are honored as becoming gods in their own right, thereby removing all cause for ever and dissention, bringing a heaven on earth in absolute harmony, historically referred to as Utopia. But what universal dogma, or teachings will undergird such a vision? Enter... *Bahá'í Teachings for the New World Order.*[11]

In presenting these foundational principles, it is not the intent here to promote them but solely to inform of the Bahá'í-described resolution of the "Mystery of the Ages," the revelation of which is being progressively revealed through the pages of this book, bearing in mind that there is much more to come.

The Principles of Bahá'í

The following Bahá'í "principles" are excerpts from the public presentations of 'Abdu'l-Bahá in America in 1912 that were published in *The Promulgation of Universal Peace.* It is these "principles" that form the foundation not only of the Bahá'í Faith but also of its embrace by the United Nations, which interestingly Pope Francis and Pope Benedict XVI have declared to be the unifying hope of humanity, and even called for a greater "supranatural" body for the "universal common good" and for a "new evangelization of society."[12]

These Bahá'í principles thus become, in effect, the new "gospel" for global oneness, unity and shalom to which the world's peoples must be "evangelized."

- The oneness of mankind.
- Universal peace upheld by a world government.
- Independent investigation of truth.
- The common foundation of all religions.
- The essential harmony of science and religion.
- Equality of men and women.
- Elimination of prejudice of all kinds.
- Universal compulsory education.
- A spiritual solution to economic problems.
- A universal auxiliary language.[13]

The New World Dogma

Every religious persuasion has its own dogma or doctrine. The dogma of the emerging one-world religion reflects a fusion of man's best human-inspired efforts to replace the need for a God-designed and defined salvation with a glorious stew of utopian geopolitics, environmentalism, socialism, universalism and the best acceptable blend of all religious beliefs, thus envisioning a man-created heaven on earth. The United Nations, formed in 1945, is thus embraced as the institution of world salvation requiring merely a few corrective tweaks for the soon-coming redemptive One World Order, defining the final structure and spiritual unity necessary for the effective "rebuilding of the Tower of Babel" anticipated to endure in perpetuity.

To place this historical moment in spiritual perspective, Pope Francis addressed the United Nations General Assembly in celebration of its 70th anniversary in 2015. There he declared, quoting Pope Paul VI, "the edifice of modern civilization has to be built on spiritual principles."[14] Francis made clear his, and previous popes' position, as to the Vatican's effusive embrace of the U.N. as the geopolitical entity to merge with the Vatican's perceived moral / spiritual aura to bring about the New World Order, referencing even the U.N.'s "2030 Agenda."

This is the fifth time that a Pope has visited the United Nations. I follow in the footsteps of my predecessors Paul VI, in 1965, John Paul II, in 1979 and 1995, and my most recent predecessor, now Pope Emeritus Benedict XVI, in 2008. All of them expressed their great esteem for the Organization which they considered the appropriate juridical and political response to this present moment of history.

I can only reiterate the appreciation expressed by my predecessors, in reaffirming the importance which the Catholic Church attaches to this Institution and the hope which she places in its activities.

The history of this organized community of states is one of the important common achievements over a period of unusually fast-paced changes.[15]

A commentary following Pope Francis' speech to the U.N. on its 70th anniversary and in response to his encyclical *Laudato Si*, also issued in 2015, pierced through all the multiplied nice-sounding words to the heart of the matter.

Francis revealed the dogma that he intends to replace belief in Christ as savior.... He is advocating for Catholics to unite behind a one world government, and surrender their freedom and sovereignty to international interests.[16]

This same submission to globalist dogma was further defined and declared by Pope Benedict XVI in his 2009 encyclical *Carits in Veritate* in which he stated: "...there is urgent need of a true world political authority, as my predecessor Blessed John XXIII indicated some years ago." In his latest encyclical, Pope Benedict XVI called for creating a "true world political authority" with "real teeth," believing that the United Nations can be reformed to be the basis for this new global entity.

This encyclical is binding as Catholic Church teaching or dogma. As one observer noted: "Caritas in Veritate should be seen as what it is: a theological and political earthquake." The Roman Catholic Church, which as once seen as the guardian of tradition worldwide, "now wishes to use radical means (a 'true world political authority') for its own socio-political ends."[17]

Bahá'í Proclaims U.N. Beliefs

Bahá'í beliefs are increasingly becoming the foundation and unifying force of United Nations beliefs and are therefore, through decades of papal proclamations, being merged with Vatican geopolitical and spiritual views, thus becoming congruent. We turn again to those expressed beliefs of Bahá'í as set forth in *Bahá'í, Teachings For The New World Order*, the 2003 Edition.

> The world's equilibrium hath been upset through the vibrating influence of this most great, this new World Order. Mankind's ordered life hath been revolutionized through the agency of this unique, this wondrous System—the like of which mortal eyes have never witnessed.[18]

> Unification of the whole of mankind is the hallmark of the stage which human society is now approaching… World unity is the goal towards which a harassed humanity is striving. Nation-building has come to an end. The anarchy inherent in state sovereignty is moving towards a climax… A world… must abandon this fetish, recognize the oneness and wholeness of human relationships, and establish once for all the machinery that can best incarnate this fundamental principle of its life.[19]

It should be obvious that this language is virtually indistinguishable from that emanating from the papal pens of the last three popes, emphasized dramatically by the proclamations of Pope Francis. But where does it lead? Beliefs are borne out in actions. What actions will this "miraculous" merger of geopolitics and man-centered religion reveal in this historic moment? Bahá'í makes clear the endgame of Vatican vision and globalist Protestant promoters.

The unity of the human race, as envisaged…implies the establishment of a world commonwealth in which all nations, races, creeds and classes are closely and permanently united…

This commonwealth must… consist of a world legislature, whose members will, as the trustees of the whole of mankind, ultimately control the entire resources of all component nations, and will enact such laws as shall be required to regulate the life, satisfy the needs and adjust the relationships of all races and peoples.[20]

Please note! This is the all-encompassing vision of not only Bahá'í but also of the Great Reset planned by the World Economic Forum, supported by the Vatican vision for the "new evangelization" of the world under papal power. Yet we must more deeply explore the full intent of this quasi-religious enterprise. The Bahá'í New World Order Teachings leave few stones unturned, leaving only to the imagination the terrifying consequences of such initially "soft tyranny."

A world executive, backed by an international Force, will carry out the decisions arrived at and apply the laws enacted by, this world legislature…. A world tribunal will adjudicate and deliver to compulsory and final verdict in all and any disputes…. A mechanism of world intercommunication will be devised, embracing the whole planet, freed from national hindrances and restrictions, and functioning with marvelous swiftness and perfect regularity.

A world language will either be invented or chosen…. A world script, a world literature, a uniform and universal system of currency of weights and measures, will simplify and facilitate intercourse….

In such a world society, science and religion… will be reconciled, will cooperate, and harmoniously develop. The causes of religious strife will be permanently removed, economic barriers and restrictions will be completely abolished….[21]

All of these utopian quasi-religious goals as embraced fully by global politicians, priests, pastors and popes, are intended to "stimulate the intellectual, moral, and spiritual life of the entire human race."[22] And finally, the glorious new globalist "gospel," as papally "evangelized" among the world's citizens through United Nations geopolitics, will reach its zenith lead by the "world executive"—a counterfeit "christ" or messiah bringing promised "peace on earth, good will toward men." Bahá'í reveals the consummation.

> A world federal system, ruling the whole earth and exercising unchallengeable authority [will have been achieved].

> [It will be] a system in which Force is made the servant of Justice, whose life is sustained by its universal recognition of one God [the merger of all religions] and by its allegiance to one common Revelation [the Bahá'í Faith]—such is the goal towards which humanity, impelled by the unifying forces of life, is moving.[23]

Prepare, therefore, for the soon manifestation of the United Nations Savior. Your allegiance will be compelled by Force. As Pope Francis decreed, a "One World Government is the only way to "Save Humanity."[24]

Chapter 13

THE SCIENTIFIC SALVATION

"The greater scientific god now is the creation of immortality."
"...the agent of eternal life has been found."
"Transhumanism is man's new quest for immortality."

"TURNING INTO GODS." That was the title of Jason Silva's documentary in 2012. The year before, he noted in an interview with Forbes, America's foremost business magazine, that: "We are the species that transcends our limitations...and so with Turning Into Gods I want to ignite a new conversation about who and what we are as we face exponential change." He made clear the mind-heart-motivational connection, revealing what may otherwise to most be a mystery — "We want to transcend our biological limitations."[1]

Transcending Biological Limitations

What, then, is meant by the words "Transcending Biological Limitations?" The answer to that question defines the heart and soul of the meaning of "Scientific Salvation." It has been said that "As a man thinketh in his heart, so is he."[2] Our thoughts are the innermost substance and revealer of who we really are as human beings. They are or comprise the moral and spiritual essence that defines the intangible reality of our biological presence on the planet.

Yet how might we most effectively—even definitively—know those innermost thoughts, beliefs, ideas, propensities and aspirations of someone? It is first by their words and then by their actions. Sometimes we say that "Actions speak louder than words" because words can easily be manipulated to deceive. Even so, our words are the primary carriers (i.e., like atoms and molecules) of our innermost spiritual nature and being—even our faith.

It is indeed fascinating that the New Testament Scriptures declare of Jesus as Messiah that "In the beginning was the Word, and the Word was with God, and the Word was God." And continuing in the Gospel According to John, "And the Word [referencing Yeshua] was made flesh, and dwelt among us, and we beheld his glory, the glory as of the only begotten of the Father, full of grace and truth."[3] In other words, Jesus known to Israel as Yeshua, was actually sent by God the Father to be the "living Torah"—God's Word on full display so that the truth of the Words would be validated and discerned by corresponding actions, as understood by Christians.

That same "living Word" known to his professing followers, whether Jew or Gentile, as Messiah, made this piercing declaration that has, whether we realize it or not, vast implications for the discussion here at hand. Here are His words:

> I say unto you, That every idle word that men shall speak, they shall give account thereof in the day of judgment.
>
> For by thy words thou shalt be justified, and by thy words thou shalt be condemned (Matt. 12:36-37).

What, then, should be understood from the stated goal—the words "Transcending Biological Limitations?" The meaning and implications are not a mystery. What is simply distilled in those words is a revelation both of the thoughts and intents of the heart and a profound, blasphemous chutzpah, declaring:

1. I am a biological being, yet made in the image of God.
2. I am not satisfied with being merely a being of flesh and blood with heart and soul.

3. I will transcend this mortal being and become immortal through Scientific Salvation, i.e., technology.
4. I will not die, but live forever... eventually through technological salvation.
5. I will become transcendent and together we will finally rule the world.
6. I...and we...will become God.

Is this somewhat shocking? Do you believe this is the motivational trajectory of technology driven by God-denying, God-despising scientists and philosophers? And why do they want to become as God or gods when and while adamantly maintaining their disbelief in both a God and Creator. The dissonance reveals a level of mental and spiritual fragmentation that such scientific techie minds cannot seem to grasp. And yet, if you yet be disbelieving of their heart intent, philosopher May Midgley made it clear. In her 1992 book *Science as Salvation*, she "traces the notion of achieving immortality by transcendence of the material human body...."[4]

"Transcending Biological Limitations" has one ultimate goal... becoming immortal... becoming as God. When might such an achievement reach the pinnacle of human pride? The cover story of *TIME*, February 21, 2011, announced:

"2045—The Year Man Becomes Immortal."[5]

Just in case you breathe a sigh of relief that such a momentous event lies afar off, consider first the claim of Vernor Vinge concerning the consummate event known as "The Singularity," which he exults will "revolutionize the world, ushering in a posthuman epoch." When asked in 1993 when he expected this ultimate progression of human history to virtual godhood, he announced, regarding "The Coming Technological Singularity," "I said I'd be surprised if the singularity had not happened by 2030."

For those interested in the significance of the year 2030, consider that is the year the World Economic Forum has decreed the consummation of "The Great Reset," which former U.S. Secretary of State

John Kerry declared and was ushered in by the Inauguration of Joseph Biden as U.S. President. It is also noteworthy that the United Nations has established for fulfillment of its One World Order globalist intentions "AGENDA 2030."

Discerning the Honorable vs. the Hubris

At this juncture it must be made clear. Science alone is not evil. Science becomes "evil" in the hands of and as the expression of the heart of evil men. A man or woman who strives through science to escape humanity and become virtual deity has, by definition, become evil by lustfully desiring and determining to "go beyond the scope of his / her privilege" as a human, thus superseding the intent of the Creator to configure his / her own design to be "as God."

Whether you are Jew or Gentile, a proclaimed atheist, agnostic and regardless of religious persuasion, you…we… must take this seriously because beliefs have consequences, leading to actions that may affect destiny, whether temporal or eternal. A proponent of this mysterious desire to become as virtual gods…or God…stated it is the "movement that epitomizes the most daring, courageous, imaginative, and idealistic aspirations of humanity." On the contrary, however, the famous futurist philosopher, Francis Fukuyama, described the movement as "the world's most dangerous idea."[6] Are we talking about mere betterment of humanity as "humans," or are we seeking "human enhancement" beyond humanity?

We will now begin a brief exploration of some of those technological developments that may provide great benefit or terrifying burden to our human species. These discussions must necessarily be presented so as to be somewhat understandable to the lay reader rather than to be couched in undue scientific complexity. Yet, as will be seen, "The Mystery of the Ages" has truly taken root in the heart of scientists. Are we awaiting a Messiah… or creating one?

The Genome of God

The decoding of the human genome at the outset of the sixth millennium was the most ambitious biology mission in the life of humanity. The unraveling of the human DNA has become a scientific sign of the "unveiling of history's greatest mystery," opening the door to the purported fulfillment or revelation of this ultimate messianic moment. It might rightly be described as *apocalyptic*, actually meaning "the unveiling."

Consider that the human DNA is being described as "the book of life." Then reflect on the Bible's reference to those embracing Jesus as Messiah as said to be "written in the book of life" (Rev. 21:27). Is this language merely metaphorical, or is it loaded with spiritual vision and aspirations to Godhood, all under cover of science. After all it might be reasoned that if God made man (humankind) in His image, then the human DNA (further unraveled) might reveal how we humans could be like God… or even become God… if scientific minds could just be fully unleashed to fulfill the faith of the future… to be like… or equal to… the God of Creation. No sin, no need for salvation, just science as the savior.

Wow! Is this historical chutzpah, or cause for human hallelujah? Francis Collins, who headed the publicly-financed Genome Project since 1993, and who has professed to be a follower of Jesus as Messiah, has noted that "decoding the book of life poses daunting moral dilemmas… the power to re-engineer the human species." *TIME* translated his concern in its cover story April 10, 2000, titled "Genome—Decoding the Human Body." "Perhaps the greatest unknown is how the completion of the Human Genome Project—learning the function of every gene—will shape our views of who we are. There is great risk, he noted, of succumbing to a manic biological determinism, ascribing to our genes such qualities as personality, intelligence, **even faith**" [emphasis added]. He then made clear, "We do ascribe some sort of quasi-religious significance to our DNA."[7]

Have we achieved scientific salvation, or is it just lurking around under a secretive mantel for the momentous unveiling of our messianic moment? At the White House gala in celebration of the 10-year, 2 billion dollar Genome Project identifying and ordering the 3.1 billion molecules "letters" of the DNA residing in almost every human cell, then president Bill Clinton compared the feat to such paradigm-shifting accomplishments as Sir Isaac Newton's discoveries in physics and the 1969 moon landing. "Without a doubt," he said, "this is the most important, most wondrous map ever produced by mankind," described by the *Los Angeles Times / Washington Post News Service* as deciphering "the book of life."[8] Said Dr. Francis Collins, director of the National Human Genome Project, "We have caught a glimpse of an instruction book previously known only to God."[9]

"Playing God"

Shortly before unveiling the genome "instruction book previously known only to God," thus deciphering the "book of life," *The Cincinnati Post* presented the shocking front-page headline "Playing God," responding to the news of a cloned sheep named Dolly and warning about "humans playing God." A leading figure in biomedical ethics said, "We associate this [cloning capability] with divine power: changing the very structure of nature. It ties into our deep anxieties about the malevolent side to modern science."[10]

If, then, as the book of Genesis informs that God made man in His image, might man now re-create a new hybrid humankind by splicing and dicing the DNA? This was the "messianic" message echoed worldwide in response to the cloning of Dolly with *Newsweek* asking in its cover story "Little Lamb, Who Made Thee?" The cover made clear the looming question hovering over scientific hubris: "Can We Clone Humans?"[11] Plainly speaking: Are we not only playing God but becoming God? Can we "save" ourselves and become immortal without the divine intervention of a "savior" or messiah-redeemer?

Creating Immortality?

Is this now science's "messianic moment?" As the famed reporter Kenneth L. Woodward piercingly and publicly asked "Today the sheep—tomorrow the shepherd?"[12] Richard McCormick, a veteran Jesuit ethicist at the University of Notre Dame, stated that "any cloning of humans is morally repugnant," but since when has morality impeded godless scientists from pursuing scientific salvation as an alternative to confessing sin and embracing a savior by faith. As Rabbi Moshe Tendler, professor of medical ethics at New York's Yeshiva University warned: "In science, the one rule is that what can be done will be done."[13]

The possibilities… and problems… are endless now, prompting the United Nations, in 2005, to adopt a "Declaration of Human Cloning" prohibiting all forms of human cloning. Yet in 2008, researchers successfully created the first five mature human embryo which, after having been studied, were destroyed.[14]

The greater scientific goal now is the creation of immortality. While cloning clones may produce a kind of genetic immortality, means other than cloning are driving scientific "divinity" toward human immortality. One such approach in pursuit of health remedies is called "therapeutic cloning" using stem cells.[15] *TIME* prophetically asked a probing question hovering over the world of bioethics and genetic engineering: "Can Souls be Xeroxed?"[16]

In 2001, Kenneth L. Woodward set the stage for *NEWSWEEK* with his eye-catching title: "A Question of Life or Death," concluding that we "stand at the edge of a new world where human beings can virtually reinvent themselves."[17] Where is this leading, and more importantly, what is the driving motivation revealing the human heart?

For starters we might consider *WORLD* Magazine's article in 1999: "Human farms," with the opening statement, "Someday…scientists will clone a human. As it turns out 'someday' was last November [1988]…when the first human embryo was cloned," euphemistically called "therapeutic" cloning.[18] As noted by Richard Seed, a Harvard-educated physicist, "I've said many times that you can't stop science: [further declaring]…

Cloning and the reprogramming of DNA is the first serious step in becoming one with God."[19]

Six years later (1994) *NEWSWEEK* tantalized with the title: "How Far Should We Push Mother Nature?" Concerning "Making Babies," the author warned: "Technology is evolving faster than our ability to weigh the cost and ethics."[20] But why stop with human cloning? Why not create human-animal hybrids? By 2011 the nightmare announcement came: "150 human animal hybrids grown in UK labs: Embryos have been produced secretively for the past three years." The revelation came just a day after a committee of scientists warned of a nightmare

'Planet of the Apes' scenario, with one disgusted scientist lamenting we are "dabbling in the grotesque."[21] Human-animal "chimeras" are now being created just 10 years later.

Grotesque or not, scientists press on in hot pursuit of god-hood and immortality. "Imagine a man fathering a child—or 100 children—a century after his death. Sound preposterous? Think again." A team of scientists at the University of Pennsylvania and University of Texas Southwestern Medical Center took the first steps in 1996 to create something even more bizarre. As a co-author of the study proudly declared: "We can make any individual male biologically immortal."[22] Hence, they dub it "biological immortality."

The trajectory of technological creationism is to achieve immortality. While admitting the potential temporal benefits in combatting disease Dr. W. French Anderson, professor of biochemistry and pediatrics at the USC School of Medicine, described it as "A Cure That May Cost Us Ourselves." As one of the pioneers of human genetic engineering predicted: "Within 30 years, there will be a gene-based therapy for most diseases." But he fears "the profound dangers of his own work."[23] Consider then, in context, the warnings and fears of many independent scientists, biologists, virologists and epidemiologists regarding the long-range dangers of the COVID-19 "vaccine" that do not actually cure or prevent the virus. What then do—or will—they do?

Cryonics is also now offering immortality — "the possibility of protecting one's body from decay after death, and transporting it into a future with completely new medical possibilities." In an article published in Switzerland, molecular biologist Patrick Burgermeister says, "That we have to die is one of the most brutal thoughts ever."[24] And why is the thought of death so brutal? Is it not just the typical human desire to escape potential responsibility for our actions in life after death…without having to give an account for our lives? As the thinking goes…if I can become immortal in the flesh and/or become "God" myself, the problem of accountability is solved…at least for the moment in my mind. As the Alcor Life Extension Foundation declared on its website, "We are taking action to fight death and achieve indefinite extension of our lives." The underlying motivational message is clear: Cryonics wants to fight death and achieve eternal life medically and biologically, dispensing with any spiritual accountability. While seemingly clever, it does nothing to clear the conscience.

Interestingly, the entire dramatically-advancing technological pursuit of "salvation" through the biological "messiahship" of life extension and physical immortality comes in the context of rapidly shifting global thinking concerning the spiritual dimensions of life, death and purpose. As the *Jerusalem Post* asked: "Is it possible that death may not be a foregone conclusion to life?"[25] It noted that a surprising 33% of Americans now believe in reincarnation and 41% believe in psychic energy.

The powerfully emerging sense of some spiritual dimension is creating a virtual industry to exploit the sensationalism of Near-Death Experiences, past-life encounters and communication with the dead through seances, leading universities to offer courses on the spirit world, all in a seemingly subconscious effort to avert the prospect of a messiah who might either redeem or judge. And Israel is no exception. Professor Ofra Mayseless of the University of Haifa is the founder of the Center for the Study of the Human Spirit. Its goal "is to combine the world of academia and research with the endless, eternal landscapes of the spirit and mind." She noted: "I look in all directions, researching spiritual traditions in Judaism, Buddhism, Hinduism, Christianity." She noted that her course is all about feelings and experiences, palatable and non-threatening.

The *Jerusalem Post* life-after-death article is very lengthy, revealing several salient points for our consideration in the "University of the Mystery of the Ages."

First: "Somewhere around 75% of people in the world believe in something beyond...."

Second: "There is a notable change in society's reaction to the possibility of an afterlife."

Third: "The whole subject is definitely more acceptable now."

In wrapping up this inexorable pursuit of immortality, we might aptly call it: TELOMERE THEOLOGY. In exploring why cells die, biologists looked for a gene that enforced cellular mortality, but found nothing. But what they found, instead, was a small tip of chromosomes that seemed to have no purpose, until they discovered that almost every cell in the human body showed "telomere loss." Molecular biologists, in 1984, discovered a telomere-preserving enzyme they dubbed "telomerase." In 1989, the results of the study of 1984 were confirmed.

Consequently, *TIME* declared in its cover story "Can We Stay Young?" (1996) stating that "the agent of eternal life had been found."[26] Thus, "the mystery of aging" was deemed solved, embracing the human hope that we can now live forever without divine intervention or demand. Yet the finality of "scientific salvation" had not been deemed to reach its pinnacle of universal dominion and glory, as we shall soon see.

"Ascending The Human Race"

Will humans be satisfied to be "like" God or will we persist to "become" God? According to the biblical record, we were made (created) "in the image of God," however that might be construed. But science, rejecting being created in the image of God by embracing the theory of evolution, now is in a full-court-press to self-create God in our own image. The goal is to "ascend the human race." As Big Tech continues to expand its control over all things, "a new alarm is being sounded over...its next targets: the human body and soul." This warning has come from Andrew Torba, the CEO of Gab.com, who asserts that the tech giants are looking at creating a "post-human race"... destroying our humanity by appending technology to our bodies and, they believe, to our souls."[27]

"When you talk about this transhumanism, warned Forbes, "this mindset that they have, they truly believe that they are God." They want to take the current digital addiction of the masses to the next step — "to enslave our biology..." "by planting chips or altering DNA" ..."to control us," "while using that same technology to lift them up as gods to live forever and control the rest of us as digital serfs." Torba stressed that the leaders of Big Tech "consider themselves as powerful as divine beings." "They want to live forever. They want to be gods...."[28]

"In fact, it can be fairly argued that technology is a modern qua-si-religion whose daily miracles are commonplace." "…we witness the birth of transhumanism before our very eyes." "Humanity now stands at a crossroads."[29] Transhumanism is "Man's new quest for immor-tality."[30] Since the human body is finite in and of itself, science seeks to meld man and machine so as to keep one's consciousness alive in perpetuity. This pursuit is called *transhumanism*. Most Christians and many Jews, therefore, decry the very concept and pursuit of transhu-manism as dangerous and perverse, seeking to de-humanize mankind while trying to make him immortal.

"Technocracy and Transhumanism are in control of the very course of human history at this very moment," observed Patrick Wood in *Technocracy News and Trends*. Transhumanism's "ultimate goal is for humans to escape death and live forever in a state of immortality,"[31] thus forever delaying any ultimate divine accountability for one's life on earth.

Although some transhumanists report having religious or spiritual views, they are for the most part atheists, agnostics and secular human-ists. Secular transhumanists are strong materialists and naturalists who do not believe in a human soul. Pierre Teilhard de Chardin, a pale-ontologist and Jesuit theologian, foresaw such a movement with his forceful quasi-religious embrace of evolution; anticipating the devel-opment of an encompassing "global consciousness," thus making him an early New Age "guru." Religious and secular critics maintain that transhumanism is itself a religion or, at the very least, a "pseudo-re-ligion," faulting "the philosophy of transhumanism as offering no eternal truths nor a relationship with the divine."[32]

"What ideas, if embraced, would pose the greatest threat to the welfare of humanity?" This was the question posed by the editors of *Foreign Policy* to eight prominent policy experts. One of the eight, Francis Fukuyama, professor at Johns Hopkins School of Advanced International Studies and member of the President's Council on Bio-ethics, made clear his choice, declaring that the "most dangerous idea" is TRANSHUMANISM![33]

Another, however, called it a "movement that epitomizes the most daring, courageous, imaginative, and idealistic aspirations of humanity."[34]

Indeed it is both human chutzpah beyond anything heretofore so overtly manifested in human history since the Tower of Babel. The "created" now boldly challenges the Creator, grasping for the glorious personification of godhood in posthuman emulation of Lucifer's defiant declaration, "I will be like the most High God" (Isa. 14:14).

The Covid Transition To Transforming Humanity

The geo-politically proclaimed Covid pandemic became the triggering catalyst to catapult the world into the ultimate merger of biotechnology and digital technology to transform humanity. "The anticipated Great Reset would bring a world in which giant corporations and government would seamlessly merge." Klaus Schwab, founder of the World Economic Forum, has predicted a "fusion of our physical, digital and biological identities." He wrote that microchips and other technology will "lift humanity into a new collective and moral consciousness."[35]

"Such technology, which can turn humans into digital assets in the new [world] order, enables a cashless society. One's ability to buy or sell could be instantly cancelled."[36]

The mRNA vaccines, we are assured, do not affect the human genome. What should we conclude, then, from a TED talk by Tal Zaks, Moderna's chief medical officer, who boldly and proudly declared: "… we are actually hacking the software of life."[37] "Genetic engineering, along with robotics, molecular nanotechnology, and artificial intelligence, is seen as a tool for transforming humanity into a post-human species."

"The Pfizer/BioNTech and Moderna COVID vaccines insert genetic material into your cells," declared the Association of American Physicians and surgeons, and as Bill Gates described it, "you essentially turn your body into its own manufacturing unity": you become a spike protein factory. "You literally become a GMO."[38]

The goal is not defined by the superficial pretense of health and healing but rather is the inner intention that the human creative advance to godhood by re-creating himself, thus shaking humanity's collective fist in the face of the Creator, declaring equality with his Maker. As Dr. Stephen Hoge, president of Moderna explained:

"mRNA is really like a software molecule in biology." "So our vaccine is like the software program to the body…."[39]

The conclusion of *Technocracy News and Trends* is as follows. Every citizen on planet Earth should deeply consider the counterfeiting "messianic" implications.

> Technocrats are driving the pandemic as the "Great Panic of 2020" to shut down the global economy to make way for the Great Reset [New World Order] into Sustainable Development, aka Technocracy. Transhumans are piggybacking their own goals on to the pandemic to trigger Humans 2.0.

> "Technocracy is to society what Transhumanism is to humans that live in it." Both are extremely dangerous for all humankind and must be rejected before it is too late to stop them.[40]

Reader beware! A counterfeit pseudo-messiah is being readied to pre-empt the coming of the long-awaited Mashiach, the "Hope of Israel" and the growing hope of humanity worldwide. Unfortunately, the technological chaos being created in feverish pursuit of a human created god and self-immortality, is creating camouflage and cover for godless scientists in their desperate attempt at technological salvation.

Chapter 14

THE GODDESS REVIVAL

"Gaia is immortal...the mother of us all."

EARTH IS A LIVING CREATURE declares the "Gaia Hypothesis" as postulated by British atmospheric scientist James Lovelock and American microbiologist Lynn Margolis, feeding a near-frenzy to embrace and promote a new scientifically-authenticated paganism to undergird the emerging New World Order.[1]

The name *Gaia* refers to the Greek goddess of the earth, goddess of marriage and of death and the hereafter—the firstborn of Chaos and mother of Titans—mother of Uranus (god of the sky).[2] The true spiritual nature of Gaia worship merges a revival of ancient paganism and pantheism with environmentalism, thus undergirding what globalists believe is an essential global belief system to draw all peoples of the planet into a fervor of environmental religiosity fostering an alternative "unity" to that of bringing the world into unity under God as Creator. As atmospheric scientist Lovelock proclaimed, "Gaia is Mother Earth. Gaia is immortal. She is the eternal source of life. She is surely a virgin. She is certainly the mother of us all, including Jesus."[3] Thus, earth spirituality, since 1979, quickly became equated with Gaia worship to the applause of New Age leaders and ultimately by world leaders, including Popes and pastors, pressing for salvation of the planet through a New World Order.

The Deification of Feminism

In order to best understand the spiritual underpinnings and trajectory of Goddess worship and the true spiritual soul of environmentalism, we must begin with a brief, albeit dramatic, display of the feminist movement referred to generally as *feminism*. In the wake of the sexual revolution and rebellion against authority of the 1960's emerged the feminist revolution, rejecting all forms of faith perceived to be cast in male imagery or authority.

While there were reasonable and respectable corrections in male-female relationships connected or confronted at the fringe of the feminist movement, the driving force and energy surging through the soul of the movement was neither reasonable nor respectable but was in radical rebellion against not only men but against all authority not governed by woman…including God as described and revealed in the Bible. And this rebel spirit was vastly contagious, spreading not only through western secular culture but also through the broader "Christian" community. Viruses, whether biological or spiritual, spread rapidly and usually without substantial detection until they ravage the broader populace. This feministic spiritual virus must be accurately diagnosed, which is not difficult.

In essence, we are faced with the resurrection of ancient feministic paganism, now preached as a new "gospel" of feminine deification which is necessary for the ultimate worship of Mother Earth driving the underlying spiritual force of Environmentalism. In order for Mother Earth to save us from our environmental sins, Father God must be removed from human consciousness so that the new global consciousness mandated by the New World Order facilitated by the Great Reset can be achieved, thus manifesting universal salvation.

Consider well the words of Naomi Goldenberg in her 1979 book, *Changing of the Gods: Feminism and the End of Traditional Religions.* Here are her words…

Jesus Christ cannot symbolize the liberation of women. A culture that maintains a masculine image for its highest divinity cannot allow its women to experience themselves as the equals of men. **In order to develop a theology of**

women's liberation, feminists have to leave Christ and the Bible behind (emphasis added).[4]

Jean Shinoda Bolen, author of *Goddesses in Everywoman*, made clear the profound spiritual connection between feminism and the Goddess movement of pagan resurrection, writing that the woman's spirituality movement "is an interior, empowering movement that was being ignored until the concept of the Goddess became more widespread."[5]

Naomi Goldenberg was professor at the Department of Classics and Religion at the University of Ottawa. *Publishers Weekly* described her *Changing of the Gods: Feminism and the End of Traditional Religions* as "going beyond clarifying and explaining" to "what total exclusion from each of the patriarchal religions means." And we need to look no further than to her own words...

The feminist movement in Western culture is engaged in the slow execution of Yahweh (emphasis added).[6]

"Radical Feminism's #1 goal is to replace Judeo-Christianity with their Mother Earth Goddess worship." "The New World Order is coming! Are you ready?"[7] The "execution of Yahweh [Father God]" thus facilitated the global resurrection of universal Creation worship. Since the God of the Bible has been rendered "deceased," Mother Earth will now recover her "rightful" pagan place, embracing humanity in her passionate arms while commanding a corresponding and unifying world-wide passionate embrace to fulfill her promise of planetary salvation.

Thus, the mystical re-emergence of pagan goddess worship under the banner of feminism became the bridge to radical environmentalism as the ultimate "Primitive Religion," declaring man's ultimate "sin" to be not rebellion against the Creator but rather degradation of the environment, thereby condemning us all to earthly damnation rather than to divine judgment. "By playing god to the Earth, humans seek to become as God themselves,"[8] a unifying dogma of collective self-salvation whereby humanity emerges as its own "messiah."

Chapter 15

THE ENVIRONMENTAL DEIFICATION

"It is a battle for the souls of men—MOTHER EARTH vs. FATHER GOD."

IT IS NOT MAN'S BUT EARTH'S DESTINY that now drives the pseudo-religious passions of the planet. "When Earth Day started in 1970, few people would have expected it to become a globally observed religious holiday with its own 10 commandments, including 'use less water,' 'save electricity,' 'reduce, reuse, recycle' and 'spread the word'." As said Robert Nelson, professor of environmental policy at the University of Maryland, "Environmentalism Has Become Primitive Religion."[1]

America's leading environmental historian, William Cranor of the University of Wisconsin, calls environmentalism a "new religion" because it offers "a complex series of moral imperatives for ethical action, and judges human conduct accordingly."[2]

"It is no mere coincidence," declared environmental professor Nelson, that contemporary environmental prophecies virtually echo the same set of calamities warned by God in Deuteronomy for the "worship of other Gods" (Deut. 28:22), now "warning of the earth-rising seas, famine, drought, pestilence, hurricanes, and other natural disasters." "Even without realizing it," writes professor Nelson, "environmentalism is recasting ancient biblical messages to a new secular vocabulary. One radical environmental organization even declared that the most important commandment for beings was to put 'Earth First'!"[3]

It seems the *Endangered Species Act* is the new Noah's Ark of planetary salvation. Earth Day is the new Easter. Environmental religion is a deceptive disguise, and therefore becomes attractive to those resistant to formal theologies and institutional Christianity. It draws and welcomes nominal Jewish and Christian people and nations who think of themselves as "spiritual," while vigorously rejecting any suggestion they should ever belong to a religion.

"Cornerstone For New World Order"

"CLIMATE IS EVERYTHING" declared the cover of *TIME* in its April 28/May 3, 2021 edition. But what does *everything* mean? Is the word *CLIMATE* somewhat of a euphemistic alternative to the term *MOTHER EARTH*, or does it have even greater messianic import? The answer to that question reveals the supreme gravity of the global pursuit of religious environmentalism by pope and politician alike. Environmentalism has become the new "gospel" of planetary salvation, the seductive spiritualized glue to bind humanity in a fear-induced unity, thus seducing mankind in unified worship of creation in hot pursuit of a resurrected "Garden of Eden" utopia to be achieved by a New World Order.

In 1990, Mikhail Gorbachev, communist president of the former Soviet Union, won the Nobel Peace Prize for his work in ostensibly breaking up Communism. In 1992 he came to the United States to establish the International Foundation for Socio-Economic and Political Studies, better known as The Gorbachev Foundation. From his headquarters at a former U.S. military base—the Presidio in San Francisco, he systematically unveiled his blueprint for a world government, involving the manipulation of earth's inhabitants into a new world order in the name of saving the planet from environmental catastrophe. He called for a restructuring of our economic, political and religious views.

"Mirroring this quest for a new spirituality, Gorbachev's website opened with these words: 'We need a new system of values, a system of the organic unity between mankind and nature and the ethic of global responsibility'."[4] Gorbachev spoke as if he were a New Age Leninist, seeking to replace Christianity with a new religious order in which humanism (central to Communism) and pantheism (central to Eastern mysticism) all laced with Christianized terminology, combine to unify the planet for the greater goal of a New World Order. He declared with unmitigated clarity:

"The environmental crisis is the cornerstone for the New World Order."[5]

Here was an "international" issue that involved strong feelings, making it easy to manipulate a naïve and easily misled public, thus fostering international treaties. To that end he fostered an all-encompassing planetary document called *The Earth Charter*. Maurice Strong, the U.N's top environmental activist, referred to The Charter as "a Magna Carta for Earth." Gorbachev went even further, describing The Charter as a new set of rules to guide humanity. He stated, perhaps blasphemously, "My hope is that this charter will be a kind of Ten Commandments, a 'Sermon on the Mount,' that provides a guide for human behavior toward the environment in the next century and beyond."[6]

Paris and Environmental "Prophecy"

The Paris [Climate] Agreement was signed at a special ceremony at the United Nations in New York on April 16, 2015. The heads of 191 nations have pledged their allegiance to its blueprint for global governance in the name of controlling the climate. It was seen as a reboot of the controversial Agenda 21 adopted at Rio de Janeiro in 1992, now to be set for final global implementation by 2030 under the banner of the "2030 Agenda for Sustainable Development."

It is of considerable note that both then U.S. President Obama and then Pope Francis joined hearts and voices for the United Nations adoption of the 2030 Agenda. When Pope Francis spoke to the U.N.

on September 25, 2015, his speech served as the opening address to the 2030 Agenda summit. In introducing the Pope, U.N. Secretary General Ban Ki-moon referenced the papal encyclical on climate change, "Laudato Si," translated as "Praise Be to You." Earlier, at the White House, Pope Francis, embracing President Obama's climate change agenda, declared: "Accepting the urgency, it seems clear to me that climate change is a problem which can no longer be left to our future generation."[7]

As U.N. Secretary General Ban Ki-moon gathered the leaders of 191 nations to sign the landmark Paris [Climate] Accord, he declared: "We are in a race against time." Seven years earlier, Prince Charles, Prince of Wales, warned that nations are "at a defining moment in the world's history." At the Rio de Janeiro Summit, he delivered "his most impassioned and urgent plea yet...for the world to unite to tackle global warming." He told 200 business leaders that the world has "less than 100 months" to save the planet, declaring "we are all fighting for humanity." But "we have less than 100 months before we risk catastrophic climate change."[8]

Race Against Time

Even as Prince Charles warned in Rio de Janeiro in March of 2009 that the nations have "less than 100 months to act" (8 years) to save the planet from inevitable damage due to global warming (euphemistically renamed *climate change*), U.S. President Barack Obama, just nine months later, addressed the Copenhagen climate summit conference declaring "We are running out of time."[9]

"Running out of time" for what...? This is the real and overarching question, the answer to which gives genuine meaning to what appears to be a kind of scientific "gospel" of global salvation that grips the pope and politicians—yes even pastors and priests. Please ponder seriously the actual answer about to be here revealed or unveiled. It changes everything as to why the increasing provocation of a sense of urgency presents itself in a counterfeit of biblical prophecy cloaked in the high-priesthood garbs of "science," compelling all to be true believers and to conform our lives accordingly. Failing to do so is pronounced as the "unpardonable sin," consigning the unbelieving to planetary perdition from which there is no redemption.

But again, why? Why the increasing pressure of urgency seeming to choreograph the world and its leaders into a previously unattainable unity? The answer is actually quite simple. An ulterior and greater motivation or agenda is driving the near-panic driven urgency, actually connected with climate only to the extent it, like COVID vaccines, can be used to accomplish humanity's great goal of the ages...world government. And it must be now pursued with religious fervor for this is history's "messianic" hour.

The word *gospel* means good news. Listen, then, attentively to the carefully-chosen words of former U.S. Vice President Al Gore on July 7, 2009, in Oxford at the Smith School World Forum on Enterprise and the Environment sponsored by *UK Times*.

> "I bring you good news from the U.S.," said Gore. Why? He declared that the Congressional climate bill will help bring about "global governance."[10]

Gore's call for "global governance" echoed that of French President Jacques Chirac in 2000. On November 20, 2000, during his speech at the Hague for the UN's Kyoto Protocol, Chirac declared the Protocol to be "the first component of an authentic global governance." "By acting together, by building this unprecedented instrument, the first component of an authentic global governance, we are working for dialogue and peace."[11]

A few years after the initial Earth Summit, the U.N.-funded Commission on Global Governance unveiled its official plan for implementing the one-world agenda. This U.N. plan called for a World Conference on Global Governance to be held sometime in 1998 for the purpose of submitting necessary treaties for ratification by the year 2000, the turn of the 7th Millennium. The plan, a 400-page report, was titled *Our Global Neighborhood*. These sinister plans were submitted under the U.S. Clinton/Gore Administration, both of which were and are consummate globalists.[12]

The drumbeats of urgency to avert climate catastrophe have reached a screaming crescendo, because, again, the time for true global government and a New World Order is now seen, not as a distant hope, but as a spiritual "messianic" mandate to be consummated gloriously by the year 2030, approximately 2000 years after the death and resurrection of Yeshua the Messiah. Therefore, the perceived competition for global domination, either by man or a returning Messiah, is intense. As reported by a *New York Times* columnist in July 2021, "Now Democrats have only 1 year to save the planet." "A century from now," he claims, "our descendants may look back on next year or so as a hinge of history."[13]

Does Climate Matter?

Of course climate matters! Climate is a significant part of our human environment and has been since creation. But mankind did not create either the earth or its climate. Neither can mankind gain messianic power or authority to save mankind by "saving" the climate or environment. We are ordained by the Creator as caretakers, not as saviors.

The Creator's declared vision was that the earth and universe were created for man, not man for the universe or planet. To attempt to reverse these roles inevitably places the creature in competition with the Creator for ultimate governance, hence environmentalism has progressively emerged as an alternative religion, with its own self-generated dogma, prophets and priests.

The emerging reality is that environmentalism has become a pseudo-scientific messianic movement being utilized for a greater globalistic goal, dismissing the Creator and usurping all power and glory for the created man, thus fulfilling Satan's (Lucifer's) long-declared intent to be equal with the Creator. Since "pride [always] goes before destruction and a haughty spirit before a fall," environmental deification has become an integral part of the end-time battle for the souls of men.

The Not-So-Subtle Shift

It has been said that the earth beneath our feet is shifting. That has been true historically and is increasingly true at our historic and prophetic moment in time. Seismologists confirm that the tectonic plates of the planet are showing increasing movement, often in somewhat unsuspecting places but concentrated along the major fault lines, particularly emanating from the global "ring of fire."

These events were clearly foretold by Jesus, who claimed to be the Messiah, as demonstrating "birth pangs" preceding the culmination of history before His prophesied "Second Coming" (Matt. 24:7). In reality, the Bible warned that at the end of the age "everything that can be shaken will be shaken" (Heb. 12:27), referring not only to earth's surface but also to our more fundamental trust.

Both the earth and the heavens are being shaken as prophesied, and will increasingly be shockingly shaken. In fact, the earth itself is actually tilting warningly on its axis, threatening to reverse poles. So why the intense focus on a changing climate, when climate has always been in flux, experiencing both unanticipated variety over months, years and decades but also epochal changes verified by geologists and meteorologists. There is a reason that involves perhaps a more serious shift—a spiritual shift.

The Emerging "Spirit of Earth"

It may be baffling to many, but a new story of spirituality is spreading like a virus throughout the planet. It is being manifested in a variety of discernable symptoms, but has been called "the spirit of the Earth."[14]

The phrase was the thought-product of Pierre Teilhard de Chardin, a French Jesuit and paleontologist, whose famous philosophical cogitations underlying the New Age movement resulted in conclusions and projections concerning the interrelationship between "religion and science, religion and evolution, and spirit and matter."[15] His observations were deemed both profound and prophetic so much so that an entire quasi-spiritual following developed called "The American Teilhard Association, " that periodically publishes commentaries on his spiritual conceptions portraying the evolutionary developmental progression of the "spirit of the Earth." These underlying convictions, prophetically prompted, have been described as "The New Story."[16]

Neither time nor space here permit an extensive presentation of this "New Story," so we will allow to suffice the words of Thomas

Berry, former president of the Teilhard Association, giving it a home in the 1980s and 1990s at the Riverdale Center for Religious Research in New York City. Contemplate these words carefully, for they are pregnant with prophetic implications.

> It's all a question of story. We are in trouble just now because we do not have a good story. We are in between stories. The Old Story—the account of how the world came to be and how we fit into it—is not functioning properly.

> Today, however, our traditional story is nonfunctional in its larger social dimensions even though some persons believe it firmly and act according to its dictates.

> The basic elements in the religious community of the modern world have become trivialized. What we offer our society serves only a temporary function.

> We in America who remain members of the believing redemptive community represent the most modern phase of this tradition. We have kept this Christian story and shaped our world accordingly.

> The American version of the ancient Christian Story has functioned well in its institutional efficiency and in its moral efficacy. But it is no longer the Story of the Earth, nor is it the integral Story of Humankind. At its center there is an intensive preoccupation with the personality of the Savior, with the interior spiritual process of the faithful, and with the salvific community. It is little wonder that we now discover that our story is dysfunctional in the larger cultural, historical, and cosmic perspectives. As with every isolated life system…the believing community is in an entropy phase of its existence.

> The Christian redemptive mystique is little concerned with any cosmological order or process, since the essential thing

is redemption out of the world through a relationship with a Savior that transcends all such concerns.

But now this excessive redemptive emphasis is played out. It cannot effectively dynamize activity in time because it is an inadequate story of time. The redemptive story has grown apart not only from the historical story but also from the Earth story.

The Story of the Universe is the story of the emergence of a galactic system in which each new level of being emerges through the urgency of self-transcendence.

The human being emerges not only as an earthling but also as a worldling. Human persons bear the universe in their being as the universe bears them in its being.

If this integral vision is something new both to the scientist and to the believer, both are gradually becoming aware of this view of reality…. It might be considered a new revelatory experience. Because we are moving into a new mythic age…a kind of mutation is taking place in the entire Earth-human order. A new paradigm of what it is to be human emerges.

One aspect of this change involves the shift in Earth-human relations, for the human now in large measure determines the Earth process that once determined men and women… we could say that the Earth that controlled itself directly in the former periods now to an extensive degree controls itself through human beings.

Formerly values consisted in the perfection of the earthly image reflecting an eternal Logos in a world of fixed natures; values are now determined by the sensitivity of the human responding to the creative urgencies of a developing world.

The scientific community is possibly more advanced than the religious community in accepting the total dimensions of the New Story.

The believing redemption community is awakening only slowly to this new contest of understanding.

A new sense of the Earth is arising in the believing community. The dynamics of creation are demanding attention once more in a form unknown to the orthodox Christian for centuries.[17]

The Story of Environmental Salvation

"Follow the science," we are told. And so, in compliant obedience, we will briefly do that, since the secular belief system declares "science will save us." For the secular mind, scientism has become the new spirituality. It is a belief system supplanting a Creator with an ever-evolving Mother Earth or Nature.

The creature or creation has thus evolved into a modern idol to be worshipped. Unfortunately, while Scripture declares that God as Creator "changes not," climate changes through eras and epochs, seemingly at its own whim—a whim best explained by ever-evolving scientific theories preached as dogma. As the western world once acknowledged "Nature's God," God has been supplanted by Nature that will lead us to a utopian nirvana of universal peace and oneness.

"Democrats have only 1 year to save the planet" declared a New York Times columnist in July 2021. This could be the "turning point," he said triumphantly, "to curb the worst effects of a climate barreling toward catastrophe."[18] Interestingly, President Biden's new "Environmental Czar," John Kerry, recently claimed that the world has only nine more years to "avert the worst consequences" of the climate crisis.[19] So is the "divinely-declared" limit for scientific salvation one year…or nine? Just three years earlier, scientists warned we had 12 years to escape environmental hell. But then in 1992 at the Rio Climate Summit, activists made clear we had only 10 years to get global warming under control.

In reality, the Earth has been given a 10-year survival warning for at least the last fifty years, serially doomed by either global cooling or global warming. And so the story of environmental salvation continues, awaiting the First Coming of a global savior who, through his one-world-government wisdom, will unite the planet through despotically-enforced environmental dogmas bringing all then-remaining denizens of earth into salvific compliance. His descriptive name is Antichrist, a scientifically-imposed Imposter savior messiah.

Never has a changing climate been seen as a man-devised "sin" until science decided to confederate with the political councils of the New World Order so as to seize this moment for establishing the Great Reset destined for world domination by the year 2030. It should captivate the interest of any serious-minded person that the year John Kerry has determined for ultimate environmental salvation corresponds precisely to the year declared by the World Economic Forum for effectuating the world-changing Great Reset. That date, corroborated by the United Nations for culmination of its own globalist agenda, was also apparently known and embraced by scientists who, in 2015, together with Pope Francis and the United Nations General Assembly of 193 nations, unanimously adopted the "2030 Agenda for Sustainable Development" …a euphemism for environmental salvation…which was noted as a news item with the title: "U.N. Advances Global Governance with Climate Accord."[20]

A brief modern history of scientific monitoring and messaging of Earth's evolving climate is in order so as to grasp the ostensible "scientific" willingness to embrace "scientific" conclusions that correspond to the political goal of a New World Order by 2030. First came severe warmups of a coming miniature ice age. Then, after about two decades, emerged a growing chorus of ominous warning of global warming, which advanced over another two decades. Perhaps, not all that surprising, came the next iteration of scientific revelation that, in the face of diminishing warming, we earthlings faced global-threatening "climate change." Which of these, if any, were driven by science, or did scientific observations just change as observable measurements changed, which world climate history confirms is the norm rather than the exception?

As we approached the seventh millennium, it became increasingly apparent that the ever-changing climate patterns could be seized upon for political purposes, thus enabling the commandeering of global economies, law and even religious persuasion to embrace a global enterprise to save the planet because environmental "hell" was on the immediate horizon. We therefore must be "saved," and godless, global powerbrokers preached a "gospel" of fear, stoking the engines of a hyperventilated environmentalism to evangelize the world into a pseudo-religious unity to undergird the goal of a Great Reset (New World Order) by 2030.

The reasoning was simple, giving only the illusion of genuine scientific conclusion. First, in the global cooling stage in the 1960s and 1970s, it was reasoned that mankind must be causing the cooling, so it was attributed to aerosols in the air. When things then began to warm, humans were again concluded to be at fault through infusion of greenhouse gases. Then again, when warming began to wane, the politically needful engines of environmentalism had to be fed to enforce global fear of impending doom…unless of course a New World Order could be reached by 2030 to save us by means of elitist human "messiahs."

The preached dogma was that climate change was caused by humans and must therefore be solved by humans, notwithstanding the "Inconvenient Truth" that climate has periodically changed throughout history regardless of man's presence or intervention. That inconvenient truth could not be allowed to trouble the masses, since it would undermine the real agenda to surreptitiously engineer a long-desired global government by means of a deceptive and intentional perversion and use of science as a tool rather than as a genuine path to truth.

In order to explain away previous "scientific" climate observations and conclusions that no longer served the globalist agenda as climate continued its inexorable changes over decades, previous scientific measurements and conclusions were now labelled "conjectures."[21] And so the entire scientific history of global cooling was debunked by increasingly politicized science. When global cooling became global warming, and when that iteration of climate also began to change, globalist "science" could not resort to "debunk" warming, and so resorted to the term *climate change* that would serve their purpose regardless of which way the wind would blow to drive the engines of political unity toward a One World Order.

Where lies reality? The real issue is not whether climate changes. It does, and always has. Has humankind caused these changes, historically? Can humanity, or its globalist ideology, change the climate or save humanity from climate changes? And will climate then stop changing? Perhaps it is time for fear-driven homo-sapiens to rethink and reconsider to what extent any human or amalgamation of humans can truly change the climate. But our thoughts in this regard unfortunately reveal where we put our trust. And trust is at the very heart of any discussion of a messiah.

Here, however, is the latest scientific-sans-politics-developing view for the foreseeable future. "After a period of gradual global warming, the Earth is poised to enter a 'Cold Dark Winter'." A 206-year cycle of solar and planetary warming and cooling has been established through historic research and climate science. Some climate researchers and scientists are now warning we reached the ends of a long cyclical warming trend and are entering a 30-year cooling trend. But "their warnings are being suppressed by the highly politicized and profitable climate change industry."[22]

Even the foremost expert on climate science, Valentina Zharkova, provided this understanding in November 2019 to a group of leading solar physicists. This conviction is based on very diminished Sun-spot activity known as "Cold Sun" or "Grand Solar Minimum." Furthermore, the biggest driver of the Earth's climate is the Sun, not carbon emissions. The Sun controls 99.5% of climate, not trace CO_2. Hence the current conclusion, "the Earth is on schedule for a 30-year cooling trend," several periods with "virtually no Sun-spot activity…." The "bottom line is that the planet is on the cusp of a Cold Sun phase, which will last at least a quarter of a century and lead to a global food crisis. The ramifications are immense." This "could equate to up to a 30% crop loss per year."[23]

In response, a further observation may be here in order, since our over-arching consideration is that of unveiling the messianic mystery of the ages. One Jesus of Nazareth, two days before his crucifixion, warned his disciples that in the increasingly terrifying latter days before his Second Coming, "there shall be famine and pestilence" in many places (Matt. 24:7). Is this not precisely what such a massive crop loss might suggest?

"Meet the Church of Global Warming"

When science becomes "religious," demanding belief in its theories as dogma and in its prognostications as prophecy, it has actually become a new "faith" system. Unfortunately, this scientific "faith" and its precepts are not permitted to be accepted by free will but by force, threat of force, or by fear. And when the proposed gospel of global cooling was no longer persuasive, a new and more persuasive message given cultural and climate changes became necessary, hence the "Church of Global Warming."[24] Not surprisingly, however, the alleged facts of global warming began to wane, leaving the new scientific religion without a currently-compelling message, and thus, for scientific "church growth," an irresistible alternative was conceived under the seemingly righteous rubric of "Climate Change." All of this became necessary in the face of the profoundly deceptive University of East Anglia scandal where their Climate Research Unit "cooked the books" on temperature data from around the world when those data didn't reflect their global-warming agenda.[25]

Perhaps the best way—maybe the only way—to comprehend a belief system requiring faith to embrace ever-changing and contradictory "facts" is reflected in the recent televised declaration of globalist president Joseph Biden who without shame, declared, "We believe in truth, not facts," where "truth" is whatever I need or want it to be to best achieve my preconceived and pre-ordained agenda to rapidly advance the long-desired New World Order that will save us, at last, from our destiny-destroying environmental sins.

Ian Plimer is a geologist and professor at Adelaide University in Australia. As the popular world of scientific theorism was making it shift from "global warming" to "climate change," he challenged the new scientific claims of man-made climate change which he called the "current environmental orthodoxy" of the new religion. He made abundantly clear the religious fundamentalism of the movement, as described poignantly by the *Vancouver Sun* July 28, 2009.[26]

> Purging humankind of its supposed sins of environmental
> degradation has become a religion with a fanatical and often

intolerant priesthood, especially among First World urban elites.

…anthropogenic global warming is little more than a trick on the public perpetuated by environmental fundamentalists and callously adopted by politicians…who love nothing more than an issue that causes public anxiety.

The dynamic and changing character of the Earth's climate has always been known by geologists. These changes are cyclical and random. They are not caused or significantly affected by human behavior.

The Re-Deification of Earth

It is one thing to respect and protect the Earth and the environment as our servant. It is quite another when it becomes our master. When, in the name of science, we reverse the role, Earth itself becomes a pseudo-messiah that, rather than saving us, actually enslaves us. This has been the trajectory of Nature worship throughout history.

Perhaps no one has grasped and revealed the spiritual roots, reality and ultimate goal of this pantheistic movement more understandably than Gary Kah in his *The New World Religion* wherein he unveils this resurrected, dogmatically and evangelistically promoted pseudo worship of Mother Earth as "The Spiritual Roots of Global Government."[27] We will conclude this sub-section with lengthy excerpts from the final pages of his chapter titled: "The Environmental Agenda."

A few years after the initial Earth Summit, the U.N.-funded Commission on Global Governance unveiled its official plan for implementing the one-world agenda. This U.N. plan called for a World Conference on Global Governance to be held sometime in 1998.

As a result of an effectively waged environmental campaign, humanity has been whipped into a near frenzy over the "deteriorating" condition of the planet.

But what if the "problems" of global warming, deforestation, and depletion of the ozone are deliberately being overplayed to convince humanity of the need for world government.

If *The Earth Charter* and its supporting programs are implemented, sovereign nations would no longer exist. Private property and the ability to choose what to do with your land would be severely limited. The right to decide your child's schooling, and what your child is taught—even at home—would be restricted. This state control would also extend into the realm of personal beliefs. Christianity—saying that Jesus Christ is the only way of reconciliation to God—would not likely be tolerated, in fact, it might be made a crime.

So why is humanity falling for this deception? The answer is simple—the majority of people have rejected the truth of God for a lie. Seeking to "liberate" themselves from a moral God and His holy commandments, most of earth's inhabitants have embraced humanism or pantheism as their world view…inevitably resulting in the direct or indirect worship of man or nature.

Nature worship—the elevation of nature (creation) above God (the Creator)—is nothing new. In fact, it was prevalent among the Lucifer-inspired mystery religions of the Old Testament Era.

Throughout history, whenever man chose to worship himself or the pagan deities of nature in place of God, the consequences were severe. Pantheism, with its earth (or Gaia) worship, has inevitably had the effect of enslaving man. Whether it was the version presented by the Pharaohs of Egypt, the Brahmins of India, or the Caesars of Rome, the result of earth-centered religion was always the same—the enslavement of man under a ruthless, occultic system.

Unfortunately, most leaders of today's environmental movement hold a similar and equally militant world view.

According to this view, those who believe in a personal Creator—refusing to make creation their god—are a threat to nature and must be eliminated. Only "enlightened" man… can evolve to a higher spiritual state, taking the quantum leap into "Godhood" and the New Aquarian Age. In pursuing this goal New Agers falsely believe they are "saving" themselves and the planet.

There are some legitimate concerns over the environment that need to be addressed, but we do not need to unite under a world government to do so. If only people would apply God's wisdom, they could avoid Satan's deception and the resulting consequences![28]

Unveiling A Counterfeit

You perhaps missed the historic vote at the United Nations that took place on September 25th, 2015.

The 193-Member United Nations General Assembly formally adopted the 2030 Agenda for Sustainable Development, along with a set of bold new Global Goals, which Secretary-General Ban Ki-moon hailed as a universal, integrated and transformative vision for a better world.

In other words, the United Nations which represents the nations and people of the world, came together and agreed upon what they have termed "Agenda 2030"—a set of goals for the entire planet that will be universally binding on everyone, everywhere…the UN intends to impose new laws, rules, regulations, programs, and initiatives upon every human being in the world in an effort to accomplish a series of 17 goals that they feel are in the best interests of the planet which they lump under the term "Sustainability".

The concept of "sustainability" or "environmentalism" is the one subject/initiative that all peoples from all cultures, of all faiths, and all political ideologies should be able to support, [they contend]. In other words, rallying all of the people of Earth together to accomplish sustainability leads toward a specific outcome…global unity.

When the time comes for the [great world leader] to be revealed, he isn't going to appear on the world stage and then try to build the New World Order. The NWO will already be prepared and ready to go for his arrival so that when he takes his place as leader of the world, he will immediately have control of a unified planet. Thus, it is necessary for all of the structures to be put into place first in order to usher in [this counterfeit messiah].

Ever since the United Nations enacted Agenda 21 (basically a first draft of Agenda 2030) in 1992 at a meeting in Rio de Janeiro, it has been grabbing more and more power at a faster pace, and this latest round of global goals is pushing things into high gear. There are 17 goals outlined in Agenda 2030.

On the surface these goals sound great. But the problem is what they are really intended to do and that is to give more control over every human being's life to the UN. These goals will lead to laws that will allow a global government, the NWO, to gain control into almost every aspect of our lives. It's the perfect way to lay the ground work for a one world government.

The New World Order has been in the works for a very long time and we are quickly approaching the final stage where all of the pieces have come into place. Trade agreements have been signed, new central banks have been established, people of various faiths are becoming…unified.

As the UN begins to start acting on the goals outlines in Agenda 2030, be prepared to see a rapid erosion of freedoms and the replacement of the U.S. Constitution with a Global Constitution. Then it will only take some sort of catalyst such as war, economic collapse, famine, disease, terrorism, or some other method to create a state of chaos that will lead the people of the world to cry out for the official establishment of the NWO along with a global leader…the one known in the Bible as the Antichrist.[29]

The Unifying Power of Earth Faith

Who actually wants to defile and destroy the Earth and make the environment uninhabitable? Probably no one. On the other hand, what percentage of the planet's people want to and do worship the Creator of the Heavens and Earth. Surely less than half. And what percentage of those leading the world's systems of government, education, science, economics, law and media have dedicated their lives to worship and serve the Creator. Precious few! Hence the perceived unequalled unifying power of Earth Faith and the activating ISM that enforces that faith known as environmentalism.

As we close out this chapter, it is necessary, much as a lawyer makes a closing argument to a jury, to re-emphasize and re-state the purpose and power of Earth Faith and its emerging force to propel the citizens of our planet toward the final prophesied events culminating the end of the age.

Perhaps the term *Earth Faith* is confusing. Let's take a brief look from the viewpoint of Larry L. Rasmussen, professor of Social Ethics at New York's Union Theological Seminary. He speaks and writes authoritatively on behalf of the World Council of Churches. In his book titled: *Earth Community, Earth Ethics*, Part II is called "Earth Faith" in which he makes the following claim.

"Earth Faith" is about renewable "moral spiritual energy" in the "inner recesses" of humanity's "mysterious, uncompromising, unfathomably, and divinely inspired soul…as directed to an earth-honoring faith.

Earth Faith…is incurably religious and moral, the stimulus is less the nature of human nature than the prospect of intensified unsustainability.[30]

In effect, Dr. Rasmussen is saying that it is not humankind that needs salvation in its relationship to the God of Creation but rather it is Earth that needs salvation from the ravages of man. This cause he deems as the ultimate "ecumenical" cause to draw all peoples, all races, all nations, all religions and all politics into global oneness for a new ecumenical [unifying] redemption, speaking of "this ecumenicity and the moral imperative of whole-earth justice."[31]

He writes with passion concerning the World Council of Churches and its World Convocation of Justice, Peace, and the Integrity of Creation held in Seoul, Korea in 1990. He exults in the "closing worship" in which a replica of the planet was presented so that "the entire assembly, representing most of historic Christianity and every race and region, was invited to come forward and lay hands quietly on the earth. He describes the turn to earth as "an imperative of Christian faith itself." To turn toward God now meant not to return to God but to turn toward Earth.[32]

And so, Dr. Rasmussen describes this new Earth-forward ecumenicity that will draw all faiths and ethics into one unified "grace through faith" with the final call to "global unity."

> All citizens, bar none, are invited and urged to love earth
> fiercely and vow fidelity to it, to display sacramental sensibili-
> ties and covenantal commitments.[33]

Apparently, this concept of the vow of fidelity to Mother Nature is a holy mandate within the global ecosphere and truly taken to heart. On May 24, 2016, a philosophy professor at Santa Monica College led a "married to the ocean" wedding to encourage a deeper love for the planet through "ecocentric passion and even lust." It was promoted as an "EcoSexual Sextravaganza."[34] No such love or passion was encouraged, however, for the Creator of the oceans. That would be heresy to fundamentalist ecumenical earth worshipers.

In conclusion, it might be instructive to know where the Pope and the Vatican stand in this evangelistic push for environmental ecumenicity. To that end, the Vatican held a special conference in the manicured Vatican Gardens on April 28, 2015, to which Pope Francis summoned scientists, government officials and religious leaders. The conference was held under the auspices of the Pontifical Academy of Sciences to prepare for a special papal encyclical soon to be published. The author of *The Vatican Diaries* noted that the pontiff's action on climate change "is the most aggressive of any pope." The "secret" encyclical was ultimately released as Laudato Si', and as the promotion of the conference's goal was made clear, it was to build "a global movement across all religions for sustainable development." The word *sustainable* is the ecocentric-correct buzzword encompassing the vision of environmental globalism soon to be imposed under the mantra "Build Back Better" for world-wide salvation. As Jesuit Father Thomas Reese, senior analyst with the *National Catholic Reporter* emphasized: "The pope wants to make the environment one of the signature issues of his papacy."[35] Of perhaps further interest is that Dr. Rasmussen's *Earth Community and Ethics* was actually published by the Catholic Foreign Mission Society of America.

And in final perspective, the *New York Times* reported that top Vatican officials were on a "campaign aimed at promoting Francis' effort to persuade the world to pass climate-change laws…" at the then-upcoming Paris Accord conference. But the president of the Heartland Institute warned that "The Holy Father is being misled by 'experts' at the United Nations who have proven unworthy of his trust." "…he would do his flock and the world a disservice by putting his moral authority behind the United Nations' unscientific agenda on the climate."[36]

Our Destiny-Determining Dilemma

Is Climate Change the end-of-the-age nouveau gospel that alone can unify the world and bring salvation, hope and redemption? Or is this just the ecumenical religion du jour enabling all with a self-righteous straight face to substitute an alternative "sin" for the biblically-described sins of the heart from which the Scriptures call to repent? With the one we save ourselves. With the other we need a savior messiah. Our decision looms alluringly ahead.

Chapter 16

THE EVOLUTIONARY "CHRIST"

*"Your hope for human salvation and
choice of a 'messiah' lies straight ahead."*

"MATTER IS THE MATRIX OF SPIRIT," declared Teilhard de
Chardin.[1] For de Chardin, all of matter is evolving toward higher
forms of complexity-consciousness.[2] For Teilhard, "the ultimate
human adventure is to bind one's energies with evolution and to unite
one's personhood with that animating center that is drawing forward
all creation."[3]

"The final threshold is when evolution moves toward the highest
form of personalization and spiritualization in the Cosmic Christ of
the universe."[4] "…spirit-matter simultaneously arrives at the end that
was its beginning—its Omega point."[5] Teilhard is the foundational
"theologian" of New Age "faith," which, as should be apparent, is predicated on the evolution of humankind into godhood. This divine evolution ultimately finds its true roots in the deification of Earth.

The "Depths of Mystery"

"There is a communion with God, and a communion with earth,
and a communion with God through the earth," declared de Chardin.
He eventually (evolutionally) came to the conclusion "that human
participation in this communion experience brought one into the

depths of mystery." As Teilhard expressed it, "I see in the World a mysterious product of completion and fulfillment for the Absolute Being himself." "And convergence of cosmic, planetary, and divine energies in the human."[6] Thus the collective messiahship of humanity emerges in evolutionary glory.

The collective consciousness and action of humans now emerging through the evolutionary process was something that Teilhard believed had enormous potential for creating a global community. Thus, Teilhard saw a need for increased unification, centralization, and spiritualization.[7] This vision of global community is now evolving with intentionality into a New World Order of global governance.

Teilhard "dramatically shifted theological agendas from an exclusively redemptive focus on the historical person of Jesus of Nazareth toward one cognizant of the dynamic [ever changing] picture of creation given by the evolutionary sciences." "Teilhard inherited the modern faith in progress and in human ingenuity that was a particular legacy of the [God-rejecting] French Enlightenment. This accounts for his optimism with regard to the human capacity to 'build the Earth'."[8] This "build the Earth" vision was ultimately embraced by the global leaders of the Great Reset (AKA, New World Order) with the mantra "Build Back Better" plagiarized by the Biden administration as its globally-uniting purpose.

Scientific Salvation

Science can be deceptive. In fact, science can be and is seductively deceptive precisely because of how people popularly perceive it. Also, contrary to popular notions, science has profound spiritual implications and applications. In reality, "pure" science is not pure.

To use the term "pure science" is a virtual oxymoron. The reason is that every scientist, wittingly or unwittingly, brings to his or her "scientific" endeavor a host of isms and viewpoints that can either overtly or covertly affect the choice of projects promoted, the plan of inquiry, the perception for interpreting data, and even pre-conceived conclusions. The public is not usually privy to these hidden and undisclosed pre-conceptions and false-real conclusions. Hence, "pure science" is not truly *pure*.

The pretense of scientific purity is what prevails in the public mind. It is the *pretense* of purity that seduces the unsuspecting to sacrifice true principles, practices and profound beliefs on the altar of science.

Scient-ism—A Modern Belief System

"Scientism" is the collection of attitudes and practices considered typical of scientists. It is based on the belief that the investigative methods of the physical sciences are applicable to all fields of inquiry, including the spiritual. The "scientific method" is the systematic procedure for scientific investigation involving observation of phenomena, experimentation to test the hypothesis, and a conclusion that validates, modifies, or rejects the hypothesis.

Scientists, using the scientific method, have brought and continue to bring amazing advances to modern life in nearly every field of genuine scientific exploration. Yet science has its limits. It can be used for good or for destruction. It can serve us or enslave us.

Science itself has become a modern ism. It has come to be seen in the modern and post-modern mind not just as a *means* of finding truth but rather as the *mediator* of truth. Rather than being our servant, it has become our master. The Spirit of the Creator which once governed and inspired the mind to legitimate and humble inquiry has been supplanted by the spirit of science which, in pride and illegitimate pursuit of power, seeks to silence the voice and remaining vestiges of the Creator.

Science itself becomes a false gospel. It presents itself as a false gospel when it presents its theories as "gospel truth." When a theory is presented and marketed to the public as an idea or concept to be accepted without question and without proof, science has breached the wall of its own self-limitations, taking on the extra-scientific aura of philosophy and religious belief. Science has thus, since the middle of the nineteenth century, "evolved" into a new ism...a virtual "religious" belief system with its own dogma and high priests.

A Serious Dilemma

The ultimate issue subject to scientific exploration and hypothesis is the origin of all things, more particularly the origin of living things. The crown of this scientific conundrum is the origin of man. The potential answer to the question of origin of things material, life, and ultimately humankind poses a profound problem for the world of science, and indeed, for the entire world.

The explanation of origins presents a serious dilemma of monumental proportions, indeed eternal proportions, for it thrusts the theories of science into a no-holds-barred, battle-to-the-death confrontation with the biblical proclamation of truth as to the origin of all things, including man. You and I, indeed the inhabitants of the entire planet, are caught in the cross-fire of this war. Most have taken sides. Ultimately, it is a battle for the mind and heart of every man, woman and child. As with many (perhaps most) wars, it's true underlying motivations are camouflaged by the now-sacred robes of science.

Lurking within the question of origins are fundamental questions over which the battle lines are drawn.

- Was mankind created, or did he evolve naturally?
- Does mankind have a greater purpose than do animals?
- Is mankind accountable for his attitudes and actions? If so, to whom or what…and when?
- Does mankind have any hope beyond the grave?
- Wherein, and with whom lies that hope?

A Confluence of Isms

Historically, scientists, while pursuing answers and explanations in the natural world, did their investigative work with an over-arching consciousness that the secrets of this amazingly ordered world could only be truly uncovered because there was an originating intelligence that designed it. A distinct element of humility and increasing awe graced the scientist's exploration. But gradually, as the nineteenth century progressed, the "spirit" of science and scientific endeavor began to change. A search was on to explain the origin of things, in particular man, outside of the revelation of Biblical Scripture. That change was merging with emerging new isms in other fields of thought.

A new, virulent "humanism" exploded upon the world stage through the French Revolution; erecting the "Goddess of Reason" while purporting to topple the God of the Bible and all legitimate authority of faith and family.

Into this vacuum of authority came new political, social and religious isms. George Friedrich Hegel, abandoning traditional concepts of biblical spirituality, sought to explain the material world through "spiritual" principles, a dialectic or method of reasoning of: thesis, antithesis and synthesis. He envisioned a political utopia that could be synthesized by a kind of political evolution called Hegelianism. Karl Marx merged the method of Hegel with a message of "scientific socialism," luring one-third of the world's people into a man-centered, God-defying "communism."

It should not come as a historical surprise, then, that into this hot bed of radical new isms should come the modern and post-modern world's "synthesis" of origins, called "Darwinism."

Charles Darwin introduced his *Origin of Species* in 1859, in which he proposed his theory of natural selection. "He knew full well what he was up to," notes *NEWSWEEK*. "As early as 1844, he famously wrote to a friend that to publish his thoughts on evolution would be akin to 'confessing a murder'." "To a society accustomed to searching for truth in the pages of the Bible, Darwin introduced the notion of evolution…rather than as Genesis would have it."[9]

By 1871, Darwin released his *Descent of Man*, claiming that man and ape could have evolved from the same ancestor. The shock waves swept the world, eventually reforming the viewpoint of pastors, presidents, popes and most people as to the origin of all things, including man. It was not by the hand…or voice…of God, but by natural selection. "To a world taught to see the hand of God in every part of Nature, he suggested a different creative force altogether, an undirected, morally-neutral process he called natural selection."[10]

If God did not create as stated in Genesis 1, does God exist? If Genesis 1-11 is not true, can any of the rest of the Bible be believed? Does Scripture carry any moral or spiritual authority? If Scripture has no ultimate authority and if God does not exist or did not create, who has authority in our lives and in our world? Is there a "messiah" who can deliver from human despair, or is there no hope beyond the grave?

Dr. Douglas Patina, author of an anti-creationist book, as quoted by Henry Morris, writes, "Creation and evolution between them exhaust the possible explanations for the origin of living things. Organisms either appeared on earth fully developed or they did not. If they did not, they must have developed from pre-existing species…. If they did appear in a fully developed state, they must indeed have been created by some omnipotent intelligence."[11] It is CREATION vs. NATU-RALISM. This is where science and biblical faith collide. Ultimately, it is not science at stake, but your soul. The real question remains… "Hath God said…?" Scientists well know the consequences. Do you?

NATURALISM vs. CREATION

Here is a clear-cut choice. The culture would seek to overlay the simplicity of this choice with a blanket of alleged complexity, spewing pseudo-science to create a fog of obfuscation and confusion. In a world where the majority are convinced that "science does not lie" and that scientists have no ulterior motives for their projects and papers, natural-ism wrapped in the concealing robe of "science" is both seductive and deceptive. The consequences of your choice are vast, beyond imagination. *VIEWPOINT DETERMINES DESTINY!* Your hope for human salvation and choice of a "messiah" lies straight ahead.

Naturalism is a belief system. Just as it requires an element of faith to believe in CREATION, so it requires faith to believe in natural selection. In fact, it requires massive faith…irrational faith…to believe that nature, the physical world, has created itself from nothing.

Naturalism defies the most basic, accepted laws of science. The Second Law of Thermodynamics, called the Law of Entropy, declares that all matter and energy, all of the physical world, is in the process of steady deterioration and that such deterioration is inevitable and cannot be avoided, just as the Bible declares. Sir Isaac Newton gave us the accepted and unrefuted "Laws of Motion." They include:

1. A body at rest tends to remain at rest until acted upon by some outside force.
2. A body in motion tends to remain in motion until acted upon by some outside force.

Using simple logic as a reasonable person, it should be obvious that if a body, or matter, including an atom, molecule, neutron or proton, will not advance, progress, or move in a developing direction unless acted upon by an outside force, that it would be even more difficult for something that does not exist at all to take on existence, either suddenly or gradually, unless and until acted upon by some outside force. That problem leads inevitably to a discussion of "First Cause." What caused the first thing, whatever it was?

For this question, science has no genuine answers. The scientific world is filled, however, with multiplied unproved "hypotheses" which change with every decade and generation, all of which amount to nothing more than speculation and hyper-ventilated imagination wrapped in the protective aura and mystique of "science." The Bible speaks simply to this conundrum: "The fool hath said in his heart, There is no God" (Ps. 14:1, 53:1). In other words, only a fool could come to the conclusion that there is no Creator God because of the manifold evidence to the contrary, obvious to any truly honest man. As the apostle Paul noted, the very existence and operation of the material world that can be observed and experienced is sufficient to conclude any man or woman without excuse as to the existence and eternal power of God (Rom. 1:20). James goes further, stating that even the devils believe in God and tremble (Jam. 2:19).

Why then is the nineteenth century conception of Darwinism and the militant march of naturalism presented not as theory but as dogma? Why did the British *the Independent* announce, "World scientists unite to attack creationism?" Why did the national science academies of 67 countries warn parents and teachers to ensure that they did not undermine the teaching of evolution?[12] Why did they warn parents and teachers not to teach the concept of creation? What is driving this growing belligerence? Why are professors and researchers who even suggest the idea of "intelligent design" being fired and blacklisted worldwide?

The answer is quite simple. "It was apparent to many even in 1860—when the Anglican Bishop Samuel Wilberforce debated Darwin's defender Thomas Huxley at Oxford—that Darwin wasn't merely contradicting the literal Biblical account of a six-day creation…."

As *NEWSWEEK* noted, he "appeared to undercut the very basics of Christianity, if not indeed all theistic religion." Was this "undercut" the natural consequence of a legitimate scientific fact or the promulgation of a theory intentionally designed to avert the implications of an omnipotent Creator for modern man? If there is no intent to foreclose honest inquiry, why then did the Quebec Ministry of Education tell Christian evangelical schools that they "must teach Darwin's theory of evolution and sex education or close their doors…?"[13]

The Religion of Evolution

The true answer is that Naturalism is a non-theistic religion and belief system requiring immense faith, and is led by a passionate priesthood teaching and preaching the dogmas of Darwinism and humanism. It is an alternative faith to Biblical Christianity and orthodox Judaism, with its own "authoritative" teaching on the origins of all things material, shifting ultimate allegiance from a Creator God to Man as his own god.

Eminent scientific philosopher and ardent Darwinist, Michael Ruse, even acknowledged that evolution is their religion!

> Evolution is promoted by its practitioners as more than mere science. Evolution is promulgated as an ideology, a secular religion—a full-fledged alternative to Christianity…. Evolution is a religion. This was true of evolution in the beginning and it is true of evolution still today.[14]

Revealing the massive deception perpetuated upon an often unsuspecting, yet willing public, Richard Levontin of Harvard, left no doubt.

> We take the side of science in spite of the patent absurdity of some of its constructs…in spite of the tolerance of the scientific community for unsubstantiated commitment to materialism…. We are forced by our *a priori* adherence to material causes to create an apparatus of investigation and set of concepts that produce material explanations, no matter how counterintuitive, no matter how mystifying to the

uninitiated. Moreover, that materialism is absolute, for we cannot allow a Divine foot in the door.[15]

This pseudo-scientific deception has seduced most of the academic world as well as the common man who bows at its shrine. Speaking of the trust students naturally place in their highly educated college professors, physicist Mark Singham blatantly admitted the intentional abuse of that trust by professors.

And I use that trust to effectively brainwash them…our teaching methods are primarily those of propaganda. We appeal—without demonstration—to evidence that supports our position. We only introduce arguments and evidence that supports the currently accepted theories and omit or gloss over any evidence to the contrary.[16]

Evolution is a religion…a religion without God. Julian Huxley, primary architect of Neo-Darwinism, called evolution a "religion without revelation" and wrote a book by that title. In that book, he argued passionately that we must change "our pattern of religious thought from a God-centered to an evolution-centered pattern."[17] Huxley then boldly declared the underlying motivation behind the dogma of evolution or naturalism that demands its tenets be preached. Please try to absorb the sheer arrogance of this deception.

"The God hypothesis…is becoming an intellectual and moral burden on thought." "We must construct something to take its place."[18]

The Heart of Deception

At the heart of deception lies a deceptive heart. The promulgators of evolution have chosen deception because they considered the alternative "religiously" intolerable. Robert Muller, a leader of the New Age movement and former assistant secretary general of the United Nations, said, "I believe the most fundamental thing we can do today is to believe in evolution…evolution is not merely a peripheral matter… its basic in everything."[19]

Why is evolution considered "basic in everything" and "the most fundamental thing we can do"? The reason is quite simple. Evolution is not science but a philosophical and religious world view that precludes a Creator God who would have the authority to hold His creatures morally accountable to His own will. This is why Julian Huxley stated, "The God hypothesis is becoming an intellectual and moral burden." If the world is to create a global, godless system, defining its own "moral" standards rooted in sexual promiscuity and utopian unity that rejects the revealed truth of sin and salvation, the only alternative is naturalistic evolution to explain our existence.

In order for those intentionally self-deceived promoters of evolution to somehow live with themselves and promote their greater agendas, they need you to join them. If they can dupe the masses to democratically join them in the absurdity of their own deception, it somehow breathes legitimacy into a system that not only defies intellectual logic and mathematical probability but the most fundamental laws of science itself. Do we truly believe we can democratically overrule the laws of creation and the Creator by devising an artificial explanation for our existence, doubly deceiving ourselves by pretending it to be scientific? If you will believe this fundamental lie, what other lies are you prepared to believe built upon this lie?

Foundation of the Global Order

Evolution does not stand alone. It is, as the former assistant secretary general of the United Nations noted, "the most fundamental thing we can do" … "to believe in evolution" as "basic in everything." To what is evolution so "basic"? It is basic to a new vision of man. It is basic to a vision of a global utopia, man-centered rather than God-centered. It is a satanic "salvation" being prepared for the world as an "acceptable" alternative to the hope of salvation in Jesus the Messiah.

The *Humanist Manifesto II* gives us a preview of the thinking undergirding this New World Order now exploding boldly into the Brave New World. Take thoughtful heed.

Traditional moral codes…fail to meet the pressing needs of today and tomorrow. False "theologies of hope" and messianic ideologies…cannot cope with existing world realities. They separate rather than unite peoples.

Humanity, to survive, requires bold and daring measures. We need to extend the uses of the scientific method…in order to build constructive social and moral values. Humanism can provide the purpose and inspiration that so many seek; it can give personal meaning and significance to human life.

We believe…that traditional dogmatic or authoritarian religions that place revelation, God, ritual, or creed above human needs and experience do a disservice to the human species. We can discover no divine purpose or providence for the human species…humans are responsible for what we are or will become. No deity will save us; we must save ourselves.[20]

Atheism in Disguise

Evolution is atheism in disguise. It is a religion in which man, having denied a Creator God, declares himself "god." Evolution is foundational to all fields of thought undergirding the rapidly advancing global evolutionary "church." The members of this "church" embrace man as the center of the universe and natural selection as their "creation story." This is the tale of Teilhard de Chardin. Their priests are scientists and science teachers who have prostituted the legitimate purposes of science for an ulterior agenda. They preach their doctrine dogmatically, and will brook no opposition from within the ranks of science, labeling any who dare to suggest "Intelligent Design" or a Creator as a scientific "heretic," excommunicating them, burning their reputations at the stake.

Why the vengeance if this is science? It is because much more is at stake. Evolution is atheism in disguise, and those who promote it are at war with God. The atheistic nature of evolutionary thought is admitted, even insisted upon by most of its leaders. Ernst Mayr, for example, says that "Darwinism rejects all supernatural phenomena and causations."[21] A professor in the Department of Biology at Kansas State University made clear:

> Even if all the data points to an intelligent designer, such a hypothesis is excluded from science because it is not naturalistic.[22]

Evolution is, indeed, the false scientific basis of religious atheism. Will Provine at Cornell University frankly admits it. Consider the implications for your life, family and congregation.

> As the creationists claim, belief in modern evolution makes atheists of people. One can have a religious view that is compatible with evolution only if the religious view is indistinguishable from atheism.[23]

A Choice for Destiny

Evolution or naturalism is not simply a scientific viewpoint or theory that one can idly choose. The consequences of this choice are both temporal and eternal.

In the temporal realm of man's ongoing experience on this planet, evolutionary thinking has invaded and now pervades virtually every field of thought and endeavor, including the law. Nothing is deemed fixed or anchored in truth. Even the very concept of *truth* has largely vanished. "Truth" now is whatever I want it to be, morphing or "evolving" to suit the agenda *du jour*.

This abandonment of truth is leading inexorably to the embracing of a new evolving humanistic "truth," the revision of history, and the construction of a New Age utopian global order ostensibly to bring "salvation" to mankind and peace on earth through the New World Order announced over two hundred times by George Herbert Walker Bush during his presidency. At root is the religious belief of evolution. Julian Huxley, the first director general of UNESCO, could not have made it more plain.

We must develop a world religion of evolutionary humanism.[24]

The choice of evolutionary humanism as the world's religious belief system will culminate in a counterfeit (fake-real) messiah promising peace on earth. That temporary peace, enforced by compelling every man, woman and child to submit, will explode in the greatest devastation and reign of terror ever experienced or conceived by man, for without God, every man does that which is right in his own eyes. He has become "god."

The most devastating consequence remains. Eternity lies in the balance. One cannot embrace naturalistic evolution and the Word of God. They are mutually exclusive as clearly stated by evolution's strongest proponents. You must make a choice.

To choose evolution is to reject the God of Creation, the God of the Bible. The Bible declares that Yeshua created all things (Eph. 3:9, Col. 1:16). To embrace evolution is to reject Jesus and to shift your worship to man. God's final warning to mankind before the outpouring of His wrath on the "children of disobedience" (those who refuse to humbly obey him) is a clear confrontation on the issue of creation. The book of Revelation states that God will dispatch an angel to make one final plea to those on the earth, having "the everlasting gospel." Here is what the angel will say with a loud voice:

*Fear God, and give glory to him; for the hour of his judgment is come: and **worship him that made heaven, and earth**, and the sea, and the fountains of waters (Rev. 14:7).*

Shocking Papal Evolution

Darwin's theory—that humankind was the product of a slow, evolutionary process from early forms of life—conflicts with the literal biblical account of creation. Notwithstanding, on October 23, 1996, Pope John Paul II declared that now knowledge confirms the theory of evolution to be "more than a hypothesis." The Vatican is evolving, again, from the authority of Scripture to the authority of the Pope.

On February 9, 2009, the Vatican under Pope Benedict XVI, "admitted that Charles Darwin was on the right track when he claimed that man descended from apes," also declaring Intelligent Design to be but a "cultural phenomenon" rather than either a scientific or theological issue. It appears that the pope, claiming to be the "Vicar of Christ," has arrogantly supplanted the viewpoint of the Creator in order to ingratiate the papacy to prevailing evolutionary scientism.

A Destiny-Determining Decision

Whom you worship will determine your destiny. Those who believe in naturalistic evolution, by definition, cannot truly be worshipers of the God of Creation as revealed in the Scriptures. Will you worship man…or the Creator, God? Your viewpoint will determine your eternal destiny, if indeed there is a coming Messiah who will judge the world in righteousness (Ps. 96:14; 98:9; Acts 17:31).

A Faith Beyond Hope

Evolution is a hopeless faith. It requires a preposterous level of faith that defies the fundamental laws of science. True science is predicated on the principle that an ordered and orderly Creation can be discovered. That principle has been perverted so as to avert or avoid ultimate accountability to a Creator, thus creating the illusion that humankind, in collectivized wisdom over enough time, can self-create a utopian civilization of self-salvation, hence a New World Order for the ages. Truly there is no real mystery here but manipulation of mind such that mankind can envision and declare himself "messiah." It should be patently obvious that such is hopeless and self-deceptive endeavor, for nothing has ever self-created itself.

Chapter 17

THE MARXIST MESSIAH

*"While promising messianic hope, it devolves
into despair, hopelessness and horror."*

"THE MATERIALIST MESSIAH" is the label affixed to Karl Marx titling a book on his life.[1] Walter Benjamin and Ernst Bloch believed that "Marxism is a secularization of Judeo-Christian Messianism." "Marx has secularized the messianic time in the conception of the classless society," wrote Benjamin. And observed Bloch in his *Atheism in Christianity*. "Messianism is the real secret of every revolutionary...."[2]

The "Messianic" Manifesto

The identity of Marxism and socialism has been one of the most observable facts in the whole range of socialism phenomena. Marx is seen as "the prophet" of all socialist factions, to whose teachings much of the modern world has bowed, in whole or in part. While some socialists attempt, at least for public face, to distance themselves from Marx, the fruit of their secular faith reveals the actual root.

During his lifetime, as even now, many of Marx's disciples regarded his theoretical manifesto, *Deas Kapital*, as the "Bible of the proletariat." With religious passion thousands of working men read and studied it. It was, to them, an "impregnable rock of Holy Scripture."[3]

The Non-Religious Religion

Karl Marx despised religion, calling it "the opiate of the people." Yet he, in effect, reduced socialistic communism to a secularized form of eschatological (end-times hope) religion defined by his own dogmas.

Perhaps Ludovico Lalli best captured the religiously covenantal concept of Marx's "theology" absent God.

> The Prophet, Karl Marx arrived with the aim to save the least of society, the proletarians [workers], through the establishment of the New Covenant, the dictatorship of the proletariat.
> The dictatorship of the proletariat is that eschatological meaning driving the Marxist credo…the establishment of a new material and moral order.
>
> The communist revolution represents an operative and cultural event that is perfectly comparable to the process of Christian evangelization, while the dictatorship of the prole-tariat is the ultimate goal, the supreme materialization of the Marxist political thought.
>
> Marxism does not only resemble a religion; it is a clear reli-gious account based on hope, the recurrent form of religious commitment.[4]

While Marxist sociology and economics make no assertion about religious issues other than to, in practical effect, seek to supplant reli-gious implications, Marxist philosophy is the "theology" of God-deny-ing atheism, pursued religiously. Liberation theology is a Christianized offshoot of Marxist philosophy that emerged politically in Latin America in the 1950s and 1960s. It has since spread throughout the world, including the United States, in so-called "black theology."

Liberation theology looks not primarily to salvation of the soul or spirit but rather to a practical liberation of the poor, thereby revealing its Marxist roots, embraced in significant measure by Pope Francis who is well-known for his deeply embraced Marxist/Liberation theology preachment and practice.[5] This perspective renders the pope a primary agent to advance the cause of the emerging neo-Marxist New World Order or Great Reset promoted by the Vatican as a "Christian" manifestation of world-communism in the pope's war against capitalism.

This neo-Marxist movement is, in the words of a Norwegian commentator, "strangling America." It is shifting both American and Western culture to cannibalize itself by stirring hatred towards traditional values. She reveals that this neo-Marxist left-wing ideology "came out of the Frankfurt School in Germany. Its apostles such as Herbert Marcuse and Theodore Adorno spent years redefining Western values to fit the Marxist view. They openly called themselves neo-Marxists or Marxists, introducing the term for the 'new left' hippie movement that completely engulfed Western universities from the 1960s onwards. "The Marxist movement in the United States transformed society during the past decades, which is now obvious to the international world watching the dramatic cultural decay as the country is turning into a third-world tragedy."[6]

Thus, the world's sole remaining bastion for not only freedom and liberty but for biblically-based values and Christian convictions has been overwhelmingly, yet somewhat surreptitiously, invaded by the advance of Divine-denying Marxism so as to finally merge America and Israel into the Marxist messianism of the New World Order, no shots having been fired. Is this not a demonic coup to usher in the utopian vision for global salvation without divine intervention? We must all decide.

Yet why is Marxist socialism so deceptive? Why is it so easily received by an increasingly non-Christian and non-Torah observant world? We explore that answer next.

The Seduction of Socialism

Political and economic isms are deceptive, as with all other isms, precisely because they are wrapped around an element of truth. Political and economic isms tend to extract authority from humanism and/ or naturalism, making specific application in the realm of government and economics which affect untold millions or billions of people on our planet. We will now inspect the more prominent of these isms, seeking to identify the spiritual sleight of hand which enables deception to be woven around a thread of truth.

Socialism is rooted in Marxism and is powerfully persuasive and almost solemnly seductive to the natural mind. It carries with it somewhat of a spiritual aura of "doing good to all men" (Gal. 6:10). In fact, its proponents, while denying the authority of Scripture and the existence of a Creator, will often argue the authenticity of socialism by appealing to the Bible for authority.

GOOD REPLACES GOD

Social reformers love socialism. Socialism is a systemized substitute for the unselfish love and compassion God desires to flow from every human heart to his fellow made in God's image. The Apostle Paul exhorts, "...let us do good unto all men, especially to them who are of the household of faith" (Gal. 6:10). The unregenerate or biblically unbalanced human mind rationalizes in response, thinking...*If we should do good to all men, why not devise a society to **compel** all to "do good" so as to achieve a "just" society?*

COMPULSION REPLACES CONVICTION

Socialism, while seemingly driven by principles, is in reality driven by pragmatism. The purported "good" ends justify ignoring the heart-driven means which, from God's viewpoint, are as important as the ends. For the socialist, force supplants faith. Compulsion replaces heart conviction. Political freedom and spiritual liberty driven by conscience becomes the inevitable casualty.

A SHIFT OF TRUST

It should be noted that the farther both America and the entire West have drifted from our biblical roots and Judeo-Christian conviction, the more we embrace socialism as a deceptive substitute to accomplish care in the social order. Inevitably, the source of trust for care of others is shifted from God to collective government. This issue of *trust* is truly significant. It will become the defining "truth" of end-time worship as the ultimate world care-giver, a counterfeit Christ, seeks to provide peace and safety to the world through a counterfeit salvation, compelling all inhabitants of earth to receive his mark to secure the final utopian provision. It will truly test your trust, as is even now becoming apparent in the global suppression of the free choice of conscience ostensibly in radical pursuit of the claimed "common good."

LOVE IS LOST

Yet many will argue, "Didn't the early church sell what they had, holding things in common, so that the needs of all were met (Acts 2:44-47)? Truly they did. However, their action was not driven by external compulsion but by internal conviction. Their genuine love of the Lord birthed a love for one another. The fruit revealed the root. "Behold how they love one another" became the living "marketing" motto in a pagan world to advance the message of salvation, turning man from a heart of sinful rebellion.

GOVERNMENT REPLACES GOD

Why should we be surprised at Satan's counterfeit in socialism? Why should we be shocked that the early seeds of socialistic utopianism revealed in Plato's *Republic* and Sir Thomas Moore's *Utopia* should be brought into focus by French revolutionary thinking in the rebellion of "Enlightenment" and be brought to full birth by Karl Marx and Friedrich Engels through the *Communist Manifesto* even as naturalistic Darwinism, a creation substitute, was also being born. Should we really be surprised that by the early 20th century, socialism had become the most potent political force in formerly "Christian" Europe and even now in America?

A DRAMATIC DRIFT

As America drifts dramatically away from her godly roots and righteous ways, the conviction grows that a new society can be created that will improve mankind. God and His heart-driven gospel is being replaced by a man-centered "gospel." Longing for Heaven wanes in pursuit of heaven on earth. Capitalism must be destroyed, declare socialists, because it is fundamentally unjust. We must trust the saving and caring power of government to re-distribute wealth through taxes, nationalized health care, and cradle-to-grave social benefits.

As the Church and the Jew renege on their biblical call to "love one another," embracing the self-serving cry of the godless culture, democratically-driven government increasingly fills the gap, leading inexorably toward a final shift of trust, paving the way for a global governmental "savior."

Have you been seduced? Where do you truly put your trust? Are you willing to be part of a re-birth of New Testament Christianity or of the spirit of the Torah for the 21st Century where it can be truly said, "Behold how they love one another?"

Perhaps this is why the Apostle Peter warned, "But the end of all things is at hand...and above all things have fervent charity among yourselves...use hospitality one to another without grudging" (I Pet. 4:7-9). Let the love of Messiah constrain you.

Communism – A Synthetic Community

Even as socialism is a synthetic substitute for "loving your neighbor as yourself," so communism (commune-ism) presents a synthetic utopian government to enforce the perceived wonders of synthetic love through socialism on nations and the world. The driving motivation, at one level, almost seems biblical. After all, didn't the book of the Acts of the Apostles say that they "had all things in common," selling their possessions, parting them "as every man had need" (Acts 2:44-45)?

Where, then, is the deception? How does communism present a counterfeit? And why is and has that counterfeit been so persuasive, dominating nearly one-third of the planet's population, despite its abject failure?

SANCTIFIED CHURCH REPLACED BY SECULAR COMMUNITY

Broadly speaking, communism is a governmental belief system in which property used for production of goods and services is owned by a community or group instead of an individual. Such groups are frequently known as *communes* or cooperatives or, as in the early days of reborn Israel, the kibbutz. The ancient Greek philosopher Plato in his *Republic* and Sir Thomas Moore in his *Utopia* (1516) advocated forms of communism. Communism effectively becomes a secular, surrogate church, a secular congregation. It is this vision that defines the direction of the Great Reset ushering in the soon-to-be-revealed One World Order.

FORCE REPLACES FAITH

But communism, as more commonly discussed, finds its expression in what is called Marxism-Leninism. Karl Marx and V.I. Lenin contributed most to establishing Communist doctrine. During the latter part of the 19th century, as Darwinian naturalism had taken hold to present a godless explanation for men's existence, Karl Marx and Friedrich Engels advocated communism as a way of remedying the ills of society by replacing capitalism with a system where all the means of production were owned in common. The only way to achieve this grand utopian accomplishment, they concluded, was through violent revolution. Capitalism, they advocated, must be overthrown by force and must be replaced by a tightly controlled elite who would administer the system by totalitarian force. Communist doctrine was rooted in the *Communist Manifesto* (1848) just as evolution, an alternative "creator," was about to be presented to the world.

GOVERNMENT SUPPLANTS GOD

Interestingly, all Communist governments are officially atheistic. The Communist ideal is that all property is owned by the state and that everyone works for the common good at equal wages. The state becomes the ultimate and grand expression of "community" which is to be served as a veritable act of worship, not by free will but by threat of force.

UNIFIED BY COMMON GOOD RATHER THAN GOD

Communism ostensibly seeks the "common good" for the "community," but, having denied a Creator God, also fails to recognize man's sin nature, necessitating totalitarian government to compel men to do what God desires from the heart. Rather than elevating humankind as made in God's image, Communism oppresses man's spirit, and suppresses his desire and will to be productive, either for himself or anyone else. Incentive to be and become all that God makes available is stolen by the worshipful demands of the state. The government becomes a surrogate god, promising to meet all human need, with equality (now defined as "equity") for all.

HOPE BECOMES HORROR

Social-ism thus merges with commune-ism to create one of mankind's greatest efforts to be governed without God. While giving the theoretical appearance of pursuing an equitable and just society, it denies the fundamentally sinful nature of man, necessitating replacement of mercy with merciless totalitarianism supported by secret police. False worship of the state coupled with lack of capitalistic incentive inevitably reveals the synthetic authenticity of socialistic communism. Hope is replaced with horror.

A Fundamental Flaw

Without acknowledging and submitting to a Creator God, man becomes his own messiah, his own ultimate deliverer. Therefore, motivation of the heart becomes essentially irrelevant, for the only value or truth is perceived to be the global salvation. Thus, the ends always justify the means.

In contrast, the Creator God is not only concerned with actions producing a desired result but is equally concerned with the attitudes of the heart that motivate toward a good or godly end. The current redefinition of equality reveals the underlying flaw driving the globalist agenda and Marxist "theology." Now, equality of opportunity has been replaced with a new demand for equity, which requires by Marxist definition absolute equality of outcome, thus reducing economics and therefore political policy to forcibly take from those perceived to "have" and give to those perceived to "have not" or have less.

Freedom of the will, motivation of the heart to freely give and the right to ownership of the fruit of one's labors is stripped from human life and endeavor. While promising messianic hope, it devolves into despair, hopelessness and horror.

The Western world must make a choice of messiahs. And what we, you, I do, we must do quickly, for the Great Reset is just ahead, scheduled for the year 2030.

Chapter 18

THE MASONIC MESSIAH

"The Masonic Oath initiate has, in effect, sold his soul to a spiritually fraternal bond in a counterfeit messianic movement to unite the world in a New Order of the Ages."

FREEMASONRY IS NOT FREE. In truth, to truly be a freemason will demand your ultimate worship, a fact that is secretly kept from the new adept as he is progressively discipled through the ever-ascending degrees led by worshipful masters toward the ultimate unveiling of the glorious goal of the craft.

Freemasonry is Seductive

Why are men worldwide drawn into the receptive waiting arms of Freemasonry? The answers are several but simple. Men want to belong to something they deem bigger than themselves. That craving to belong is both deeply engraved in the human soul and in history. When that yearning for a sense of brotherhood is perceived to be wedded in some way to a seemingly spiritual environment, two essential needs are met.

In effect, the local and global gatherings of the members become a surrogate "church," or synagogue to which one must ultimately pay his vows or suffer not only excommunication but loss of life itself. The membership thus, in reality, becomes a quasi-spiritually-bonded band of blood brothers committed, without reserve, to an ultimate cause the truth and depth of which is perpetually cloaked in secrecy and mystery until the final unveiling, the perhaps shocking truth of which we must uncover in order to see its global "messianic" significance.

A Universalist Fraternity of Faiths

"The secret fraternal (men-only) order of Free and Accepted Masons [is] the largest worldwide secret society." It was "spread by the advance of the British Empire." Estimates of the worldwide membership of Freemasonry in the early 21st century ranged to more than six million.

"Freemasonry evolved from the guilds of stonemasons and cathedral builders of the Middle Ages." "With the decline of cathedral buildings, some lodges of operative (working) masons began to accept honorary members." From a few of these lodges developed modern symbolic or speculative Freemasonry, which particularly in the 17th and 18th centuries adopted the rites and trappings of ancient religious orders and brotherhoods. "In 1717 the first Grand Lodge, an association of lodges, was founded in England."

However, the legend of Hiram Abiff purports to make Masonry of Biblical origin. Hiram Abiff is the central character of an allegory presented to all candidates during the third degree in Freemasonry. Hiram of Tyre is presented as the chief architect of King Solomon's Temple. He is murdered inside this Temple by three ruffians after they failed to obtain from him the Master Masons' secret passwords. The themes of the allegory are the importance of fidelity and the certainty of death, which are then translated into the Masonic Oath of the Third Degree by the initiates to the incremental higher degrees until, by the 33rd degree, one has, in effect sold his soul to a spiritually fraternal bond in a counterfeit messianic movement to unite the world in a New Order of the Ages.

"Freemasonry is not a Christian institution, though it has often been mistaken for such. Freemasonry contains many of the elements of a religion; its teachings enjoin morality, charity, and obedience to the law of the land." The applicant for admission is required to believe in the existence of a Supreme Being and in the immortality of the soul.

"Freemasons are divided into three major degrees—entered apprentice, fellow of the craft, and master mason." In many lodges, there are numerous degrees superimposed on the three major divisions. Female relatives of master masons may join the Order of the Eastern Star, boys may join the Order of DeMolay and girls may join the Order of Job's Daughters or the Order of the Rainbow.[1]

"The only belief requirement is not that one must believe in the True and Living God, but rather, that one must believe in the existence of a "Supreme Being," which includes the "gods" of Islam, Hinduism, or any other world religion. The unbiblical and anti-Christian beliefs and practices of this organization are partially hidden beneath an outward appearance of a supposed compatibility with the Christian faith." "The very process of joining the Lodge requires Christians to ignore the exclusivity of Jesus Christ as Lord and Savior", but rather to embrace "The GREAT ARCHITECT of the Universe."

The Masonic view is that "the Bible is only one of several 'Volume(s) of Sacred Law,' all of which are deemed to be equally important in Freemasonry. The Bible is an important book, only as far as those members who claim to be Christians are concerned, just as the Koran is important to Muslims. The Bible is not considered to be the exclusive Word of God, nor is it considered to be God's sole revelation of himself to humankind." "Freemasonry invites people of all faiths, even if they use different names for the 'Nameless One of a hundred names,' they are yet praying to the one God and Father of all," thus establishing the syncretic foundation for unifying all religions into mutual embrace for global unity. For the true Mason "there is no exclusivity in Jesus Christ or the Triune God who is the Father, Son and Holy Spirit; therefore there is no doctrine of the deity of Jesus Christ. It is deemed to be un-Masonic to invoke the name of Jesus when praying, or mention His name in the Lodge. Suggesting that Jesus is the only way to God contradicts the principle of tolerance. The name of Jesus has been omitted from biblical verses that are used in Masonic rituals. Jesus is on the same level as other religious leaders."

"Through symbols and emblems, Masons teach that man is not sinful, just 'rude and imperfect by nature.' Human beings are able to improve their character and behavior in various ways, including acts of charity, moral living, and voluntary performance of civic duty. Humanity possesses the ability of moving from imperfection toward total perfection. Moral and spiritual perfection lies within men and women. When a Christian takes the oath of Freemasonry, he is swearing to the following doctrines that God has pronounced false and sinful":

1. That salvation can be gained by man's good works.
2. That Jesus is just one of many equally revered prophets.
3. That they will remain silent in the Lodge.
4. That they are approaching the Lodge in spiritual darkness, when the Bible says Christians are already in the light.
5. By demanding that Christians or Jews take the Masonic oath, Masonry leads Christians and Jews into blasphemy and taking the name of the Lord in vain.
6. Masonry makes Christians take a universalist approach in their prayers, demanding a "generic" name be used so as not to offend non-believers who are Masonic "brothers."
7. By swearing the Masonic oath and participating in the doctrines of the Lodge, Christians are perpetuating a false gospel under oath, committing to Masonry's plan of salvation to get to heaven. By their very membership in such a syncretistic type organization, they have severely compromised their witnessing as Christians.[2]

Blood Oaths of the Brotherhood

A heavy burden is placed upon the shoulders of a Mason when he joins the lodge. He is no longer his own man and must obey unseen powers set above him, whether he agrees or not, or else he pays a penalty, even death. He enters into a blood covenant, which if he blatantly breaks, he meets a most gruesome death which he has already pronounced against himself. It is not breaking covenant with God that damns him but breaking his oath to the lodge. Masonry thus becomes either his savior "messiah" in which he trusts or his ultimate judge.

For the uninitiated, perhaps reading the oath of the Blue Lodge Mason (degrees1-3) will provide shocking insight to the quasi-religious bondage of the Masonic brotherhood which mandates commitment to never reveal any of the secret arts or hidden mysteries of

Freemasonry. This covenant with death requires not that the Mason believe and obey God but that he obey, without question, the mandates of the superseding degrees in whom he must place unswerving trust.

> All this I most solemnly and sincerely promise and swear, with a firm and steadfast resolution, to keep and perform the same without any equivocation, mental reservation or secret evasion of mind whatever, binding myself under a no less penalty than having my throat cut across, my tongue torn out by its roots and buried in the rough sands of the sea at low water mark, where the tide ebbs and flows twice in twenty-four hours…having my breast torn open, my heart plucked out and given as a prey to the beasts of the field and the fowls of the air…having my body severed in twain, my bowels taken from thence and burned to ashes, and the ashes scattered to the four winds of heaven, that no trace or remembrance may be had of so vile and perjured wretch as I, should I ever knowingly violate this my solemn obligation of an Entered Apprentice Mason…Fellow Craft Mason. So Help me, God, and keep me in performance of the same.[3]

From 1813 until our day, the name of Jesus Christ has been forbidden to be uttered in Masonic lodges, claiming it to be divisive and exclusionary in achieving the global unifying of all faiths. In the United States, the rapid expansion of Freemasonry became a matter of public pride. By 1826 broad public congratulatory speeches were given at public events. A Mr. Bainaird announced that "Masonry was exercising its influence in the sacred desk [pulpits] in the legislative hall, and in the bench of justice."[4]

In order to grasp the severity of the quasi-religious Masonic oath, we must highlight the classic historical and horrific case of William Morgan. After thirty years as a Royal Arch Mason, he accepted Jesus as Messiah, Savior and Lord of his life, renounced Freemasonry and resigned the Lodge, and contracted to print a book revealing his grave concerns that Masonry was "highly injurious to the cause of Christ, and eminently dangerous to the government of our country." Morgan disappeared and his badly decomposed body was found a year later in Oak Orchard Harbor.[5] Morgan unsealed the truth that had been hidden by publishing his pamphlet titled *Illustrations in Masonry*, sacrificing his own life.

Confession to that oath-bound murder was made as recorded in 1848 in a pamphlet titled *Confession of the Murder of William Morgan*, taken down by Dr. John L. Emory from Henry L. Valance who acknowledged being one of the three men selected to make final disposition of the ill-fated victim of Masonic vengeance.[6]

The Religious Fabric of Freemasonry

"In the ceremonies connected with the degree of 'Grand Elect, Perfect, and Sublime Mason,' the master says: 'I will now give you the true pronunciation of the name of the Deity as revealed to Enoch' [engraved letters on a triangular plate of gold hidden for many ages]. In this engraving the vowel points are so arranged as to give the pronunciation thus, YOWHO. This word, when thus pronounced, is called the Ineffable word…and the degrees are called, on account, Ineffable degrees."[7] Jews claim the "ineffable name" to be YAWEH but Masons insist it is YOWHO.

Is this not a religious claim and declaration of the highest order? And this ostensible "true name" of God is then, by Masonic oath, to be preserved as a Masonic secret not to be disclosed to the uninitiated masses of humanity. Hence, Freemasonry is, at its heart, a secret religion, but how wide and deep are its roots and implications in this messianic era? "Masonry claims that, to this day, none but Freemasons know even the true name of God."[8]

It is indeed fascinating that while Freemasonry is established in and through every religion and even among pagans, yet it claims its own exclusive means of salvation through benevolent works under the all-seeing eye of the Architect of the Universe whose will is determined and dispersed by the exalted degrees of the Masonic Masters. Yet Salem Town wrote: "The principles of Freemasonry have the same coeternal and unshakeable foundations…and propose the same ultimate end, as the doctrines of Christianity (p. 53)."

And again Salem Town says, "In advancing to the fourth degree, the good man…has a name which no man knoweth save him that receiveth it." "…he knows full well that the great Master-builder of the universe, having chosen and prepared him a lively stone in that spiritual building in the heavens, will bring him forth in triumph, while shouting grace, grace to the Divine Redeemer. Then the Freemason is assured of his election and final salvation. Hence, opens the fifth degree, where he discovers his election to, and his glorified station in, the kingdom of his Father."

"With these views, the sixth degree is conferred, where the riches of divine grace are opened in boundless prospect." "Then he beholds in the eighth degree, that all heavenly sojourners will be admitted within the veil of God's presence, where they will become kings and priests before the throne of his glory forever." (pp.79-81).[9]

Consider the words of the Masonic commentator Stearns from his *Stearns on Masonry* (p. 28) referencing Preston, another revered Masonic historian/commentator on his book titled *Illustrations of Masonry*. On page 30 of his book he declares, "The universal principles of the art unite in one indissoluble bond of affection men of the most opposite tenets, of the most distant countries, and of the most contradictory opinions."[10]

It is clear, then, that Masons are to embrace the prevalent religion, whatever it may be, and accept whatever is claimed in any country they may reside, *to be the law and will of God*. Charles Finney, in his observational work on Freemasonry, then asks a probing question: "Now if this is so, how can Freemasonry be the true religion, or at all consistent with it? Multitudes of Universalists and Unitarians, and of errorists of every grade are Freemasons; and yet Freemasonry itself claims to save its disciples, to conduct them to heaven!" "In a Christian nation it professes to receive Christianity as a true religion; in Mohammedan countries it receives the Koran as teaching the true religion; in heathen countries it receives their sacred books as of as much authority as that which is claimed in Christian countries for the Bible."[11]

Charles Finney, former Mason and nineteenth-century American revivalist, wrote passionately of what he perceived as the despotic and massively deceptive depths of Freemasonry, declaring that

"Freemasonry is the most anomalous, absurd, and abominable institution that can exist in a Christian country." "Have we an institution, the ramifications of which are intertwining themselves with every fiber of our government and our institutions, our civil and religious liberties, of which the whole country is so much afraid that they dare not speak the truth concerning it?" "But again, it should be considered that Masonry is an institution of vast proportions, and of such nature that it will not allow its principles to be discussed. It works in the dark."[12]

The Darkness of Enlightenment

Neither time nor space suffice to reveal the full and entangled extent of the darkness of the purported enlightenment of Freemasonry, both past and present. A brief overview must suffice.

We are getting a bird's-eye-view of a secret, yet pervasive, system framed as providing the hope of Masonic salvation for the initiated only, yet promising global inclusiveness for those of any or no religious persuasion. Perhaps the best way to interpret its incipient deception is to see Masonry as a reverse reflection of the Christian Gospel that is inclusive to all who believe Jesus as savior, regardless of nationality, yet still exclusive only to those who are true disciples. Perhaps it might be aptly described as satanic mimicry, requiring no salvation from sin but self-salvation through progressive exaltation to ever higher degrees of Masonic revelation of the true spiritual nature of the craft. This is precisely the plan Lucifer declared for himself from the beginning (Isa. 14:12-14).

Regrettably, Freemasonry progressively defined and directed much of the early political formation of the United States, first imported from England followed by French Freemasonry under the name Scottish Rite Freemasonry in the mid-1700s. George Washington became a Mason at age 21 and continued his alliance to his death. On September 18, 1793, he laid the cornerstone of the Capitol Building wearing his Masonic apron, and in 1795 he assisted in laying out the streets of the Capitol in the shape of Masonic symbols.[13]

When Washington referenced God, he used the Masonic term "Grand Architect of the Universe." Masonic scholar William H

Stemper wrote: "Freemasonry was Washington's political theology." He was so revered by American Masons that some moved to make him Grand Master of all U.S. Masons.

When the Revolutionary War was over, Masons occupied every dominant position that militarily protected or politically governed the fledgling nation. Of the 56 signers of the Declaration of Independence, 53 were claimed by Freemasonry to be Master Masons. Masonic partiality paved the way to the White House for both Washington and his vice president, John Adams.[14] These facts are not meant to demean the vast contribution of these men but rather to reveal roots that produced, through the viral influence of French Illuminati, a dramatic and continuing anti-Christian force that, unbeknown to most, infiltrated every aspect of America's institutions that has defined the trajectory of American government, law, education, economics, and even churches.

So great was the concern, that upon the election of John Quincy Adams, the 6th president, when he learned of the odious Masonic obligations and partialities, he united his National Republican Party with the Anti-Masonic Party, which ultimately became the Whig Party in 1838. In 1845, Adams wrote of Freemasonry, "A more perfect agent for the devising and execution against church and state could scarcely be conceived."[15]

(Note to the Reader: In order to more freely understand the vast import of the goals of Freemasonry and the amazing implications for the present hour of American and world history, you are directed to the analysis of Investigative Journalist, Paul Fisher, in his book, *Behind the Lodge Door*, (Washington, D.C.: Shield, 1998, p. 40).

Unveiling the Masonic "Light"

Light dispels darkness. But when that which purports to be light, and in the name of "light" brings darkness, how great then is that darkness! This describes the spiritually dangerous deception of Freemasonry. First, it does not make a man free as purported but brings him into the terrifying bondage of a death oath. Secondly, it purports to provide a false salvation if a man embraces the messianic hope defined by Masonic theological doctrine as defined and determined by the high priests of the 33rd degree.

In order to comprehend the pursuit of the "light" that is darkness in Masonic messianism, we must "connect the dots" that elude the earlier degrees of Freemasonry—the deeper secrets of Masonic spirituality and promised salvation. We begin with 33rd degree Mason Albert Pike, the most important Masonic figure of the 19th century, who confirms that the rituals of the Scottish Rite from the 4th degree to the 33rd degree were acquired from the mysticism of the Jewish Kabbalah. In his famous 1871 Masonic publication, *Morals and Dogma*, he writes:

> All truly dogmatic religions have issued from the Kabalah and return to it: everything scientific and grand in the religious dreams of all the illuminati [Enlightened Ones]…is borrowed from the Kabalah; all the Masonic associations owe to it their secrets and symbols.

> The Kabalah alone consecrates the alliances of the Universal Reason and the Divine Word… it alone reconciles Reason with Faith, Power with Liberty, Science with Mystery; it has the keys of the Present, the Past, and the Future.

> Masonry is a search after light. That search leads us directly back, as you see, to the Kabalah. In that ancient and little understood medley of absurdity and philosophy, the Initiate will find the source of many doctrines….

> Thus was a second Bible born, unknown to, or rather uncomprehended by, the Christians….[16]

The messianic confusion continues. Since the rituals of Scottish Rite [French Illuminati Freemasonry] came from the Kabbalah, it is known as the Jewish Rite of Freemasonry. The second great Masonic authority, Mackey's *Encyclopedia of Freemasonry*, confirms the Jewish character of Gentile Masons.

> Each Lodge is and must be a symbol of the Jewish Temple; each [Masonic] Master in the chair representing the Jewish King; and every Freemason a personation of the Jewish Workman.[17]

An interesting question then arises. Is the Masonic Lodge a counterfeit synagogue? Is this counterfeit synagogue a Satanic order? Is this the group warned of by Jesus addressing the Philadelphia Church in the book of Revelation's the Apocalypse...meaning "Unveiling," where it is written, "Behold, I will make them of the synagogue of Satan, which say they are Jews, and are not, but do lie; behold I will make them to come and worship before thy feet, and to know that I have loved thee" (Rev. 3:9)? Are then professing Christians who take the Masonic oaths permitting themselves to be deceived? In alleged pursuit of Light, are they enveloping themselves progressively in blinding darkness?

Yet the proclaimed pursuit of Light persists. Enter now the world of the mysterious Illuminati—the ultimate "enlightened" ...en-light-end... Freemasons driving the global, geo-political and cultural confines of a New World Order of the Ages. The unveiling of this historical, quasi-spiritual messianic endeavor to provide Masonic salvation to an illuminated remnant of Masonic adepts for global government is about to be revealed. This is not conspiracy theory but is rapidly becoming consummated reality

The Darkness of the Illuminati

To be clear, no effort is made here to claim that all Freemasons embrace the secret society of the Illuminati... or even are actually aware of its insidious inroads into the soul...the life, promises and purposes of the Masonic Masters. Nevertheless, the true "light" of the Masonic Order, cannot be fully comprehended without unveiling the Illuminati influence.

The date was May 1, 1776, just as the American Declaration of Independence and Revolutionary War were being birthed. Adam Weishaupt, originally a Jesuit and then ecclesiastical Professor of Canon Law, founded the Order of Perfectibilists subsequently re-named the Illuminati. As Macky's *Encyclopedia of Freemasonry* makes clear, Weishaupt connected the Order of the Illuminati with the Masonic Institution, "after whose system of Degrees, of esoteric instruction, and of secret modes of recognition it was organized...." "The character [a point within a circle], now so much used by Freemasons to represent a Lodge, was invested and first used by the Illuminati."[18]

Interestingly, May 1st, the day the Illuminati was founded, has become a universal warning to the world's citizens known as "May Day." May 1st was such a catastrophic day in the revolutionary history of the world, that it has since been woven into our societal conscience as "May-day! May-day!" when transmitted along radio waves as the international signal of distress. And one can hardly escape the world's current universal distress. The march of socialistic communism from the Soviet Union to this day marches under the red banner of the Illuminati's red colors, representing the blood to be shed in all future revolutions.[19] But that is just "the tip of the iceberg."

If the word *Illuminati* means the enlightenment of the "enlightened ones," a Latin plural noun, from where does the enlightenment come?

The Luciferian Enlightenment

The reality of what you are about to read should not be seen as either superficial or sensationalist, but should be seen as an unveiling of the Luciferian connection not only in Freemasonry but also woven through virtually all messianic hopes and themes exclusive of the Second Coming of Messiah Yeshua. This Luciferian thread is not to be taken lightly but gives greater import to the "mystery of the ages" that must be "unveiled."

Adam Weishaupt, as a professor of religion and former Jesuit, "used symbolism to conceal both the god and the assignment of the Illuminati." As we noted, the word *Illuminati* is a Latin plural noun meaning "enlightened ones." "In mystery religions, making a thorough examination of its etymology, we discover the disturbing truth that Illuminati means 'those who emulate Lucifer,' or 'followers of Lucifer'."[20] The word *Lucifer* is a Latin word that means "light bearer" and was originally the name for the planet Venus known as the "morning star."

In order to further connect the historical, spiritual and prophetic "dots," we go to the ancient books of Isaiah in the Bible, chapter 14, verses 12-14. Here the king of Babylon is likened unto Lucifer.

How art thou fallen from heaven, O Lucifer, son of the morning! How art thou cut to the ground, which did weaken the nations!

For thou hast said in thine heart, I will ascend into heaven, I will exalt my throne above the stars of God: I will sit also upon the mount of the congregation [the Temple Mount] in the sides of the north;

I will ascend above the heights of the clouds; I will be like the most High....

While this passage speaks by analogy to the then king of Babylon, it is generally also understood as a prophetic reference to Lucifer or Satan's role in the ultimate spiritual contest between the God of Creation and His envious, most exalted created being Lucifer who lusted to "be like the most High." Yet confusion remains and has been perpetuated throughout Freemasonry as to the identity of Lucifer by the preeminent General Albert Pike.

Albert Pike was a revered 33rd degree Mason. He was an adamant Luciferian yet opposed Satanic rituals in the inner shrines of Freemasonry. As a Luciferian, however, he refused to believe Satan and Lucifer were the same personality. "Satan," he said, "is the figment of the imagination of Christians. Lucifer is God, and unfortunately Adonay [the God of the Bible] is also God." "...the absolute can only exist as two Gods...Thus...the true and pure philosophic religion is the belief in Lucifer, the equal of Adonay; but Lucifer, God of Light and God of Good, is struggling with humanity against Adonay, the God of Darkness and Evil."[21]

Three decades later, Pike rewrote the Scottish Rite rituals in his 1871 book, *Morals and Dogma*, given to every 3rd degree Mason. In that book he states that "the true light of the world is Lucifer." Pike, and those who followed him, "rebuilt American Freemasonry on the principle doctrine that Freemasonry's Great Architect of the Universe is actually the Fallen Angel," Lucifer.[22]

The Luciferian Messiah

In 1959, Freemasonry published in its *New Age Magazine* its victory over parents declaring:

Every Mason becomes a teacher of Masonic philosophy to the community, and the Craft is the missionary of the new order, a liberal order, in which Masons become high priests. We proclaim that this Masonic philosophy which has brought forth a New Order has become a reality by the establishment of the public school system, financed by the State.

The February 1959 issue of the Scottish Rite *New Age Magazine* announced an "Evolution of American Education" and "mandated that members of the Fraternity disseminate Masonic materials in public schools." From 1959 to 1964, the Scottish Rite began selecting textbooks for the consolidated school systems.[23]

In 1968 Freemasonry declared the Bible obsolete in its *New Age Magazine* declaring…

The keynote of Masonic religious thinking is naturalism which sees all life and thought as ever developing and evolutionary…

The Bible is not today what it once was. Current higher criticism has made obsolete the idea that the Bible is a unique revelation of supernatural truth.[24]

It was the Luciferian Albert Pike who, in October 1885, envisioned the ultimate trajectory of Freemason "truth" in virtual combat with Evangelical Christianity. And so he presented his plan for Freemasonry's triumph over the precepts of the Christian faith and its vision of a common Messiah as both Prince of Peace and Righteous Judge. The plan was presented on the floor of an international Masonic convention in Paris, France, for all the 33rd degree Supreme Councils of Scottish Rites worldwide. His speech follows.

Supernaturalism [meaning Christianity], authority [meaning European monarchies], and anti-Masonic activity [in the U.S.A] must be destroyed. [Freemasonry shall accomplish this by] materialism of conscience, of education, and of state.

This must be imposed upon the family, the nation, and on humanity. By every means, whatever they may be, one must impose first on the Family, then on the Nation in order to achieve the aim of Imposing on Humanity.[25]

In January, 1926, the Scottish Rite *New Age Magazine* told Masons to join Christian churches. It was an order directly from the Supreme Council at Charleston, South Carolina, the headquarters of Universal Freemasonry, in an article titled "Let There Be Light." Every Mason was ordered to so do to infiltrate Protestant churches in particular, since the Vatican was in absolute opposition to the messianic movement of Freemasonry. Those who failed to heed the order were labelled treasonous.[26] Masons throughout the U.S. then flocked to join local Protestant churches, working their way into leadership, even into pastoral positions throughout the conservative Southern Baptist Convention.

The Masonic Messiah Unveiled

The Divine identity is in a Luciferian crisis. If, as Masonry holds. Lucifer is the God of Light and of Good and Adonay, the God of Israel—of Abraham, Isaac and Jacob—is the God of Evil, then by Freemasonry doctrine, one must necessarily pursue Lucifer as the ultimate savior and messianic figure. But how is that accomplished? By what human means is that identification confirmed? It involves a descriptive spiritual sleight-of-hand. The Mason, through his own mouth, declares his identification with Lucifer's envious declaration… "I will be like the most High."

In the Bible's book of Exodus, God chooses Moses to lead His people Israel out of Egyptian bondage. Moses considered himself to be inadequate for the task, ultimately asking, "…when I come unto the children of Israel [the descendants of Abraham, Isaac and Jacob], and shall say unto them, The God of your fathers hath sent me unto you; and they shall say unto me, What is his name? What shall I say unto them?

And God said unto Moses,
I AM THAT I AM:

> Thus shall thou say unto the
> Children of Israel, I AM
> Hath sent me unto you.

Moreover, God said to Moses "…this is my name for ever, and this is my memorial unto all generations" (Ex. 3:14-15).

Comes now the Royal Arch Mason to be confirmed as a candidate. When asked if he is a Royal Arch Mason, he is required to affirm with these words: "I am that I am," the very words with which the God of the Bible identifies himself as ultimate Deity. Thus, early on in pursuing the ever-exalting and deceptive degrees of Masonry, the Royal Arch Mason identifies himself as one with God…but which God? It is Lucifer who had declared: "I will be like the most High."[27]

The Mason therefore, whether wittingly or unwittingly, has not only declared his allegiance to the Luciferian dogma of the ever-increasing and demonically-directed degrees of the Craft but has actually declared himself as God—his own messiah—I AM THAT I AM.

Thus, the messianic "dots" of Freemasonry are connected. The Masonic messiah has been unveiled. As with all New Age spirituality, YOU are, and are increasingly becoming, a messiah made in your own image superimposed upon you by Satan in whom you have chosen to put your trust. The Bible calls this "blasphemy." What do you call it? The Royal Arch candidate is then called to take his shoes from off his feet, as God instructed Moses at the burning bush (Ex. 3:1-5) as the Masonic Master declares "The place on which you stand is holy ground."

Chapter 19

NOAHIDE LAWS AND "OLAM HABA"

"Will Noahidism Unite the World?"

PREPARE TO BE SURPRISED. Your entrance, as a Gentile, to *Olam Haba*, the world to come, is totally dependent upon your allegiance to and observance of the Seven *NOAHIDE Laws*, according to Orthodox Jewish beliefs. This may be both confusing and of great consternation to many, particularly those who proclaim Jesus as Messiah, for the penalty of such alleged "blasphemy" is death by decapitation under a Noahide court system. It should then be obvious that this belief, deemed to be the final and ultimate world system, must be surgically explored if, as Orthodox Jews are deeply convinced, we are already deeply enmeshed in the messianic age.

What Are Noahide Laws?

Small Noahide groups are multiplying worldwide, increasingly convinced that adhering to the 7 Noahide Laws is incumbent upon all Gentiles (in other words the whole world except Jews) if they have any hope of "the world to come" known in Hebrew as *Olam Haba*. Thus, their hope of "salvation" is exclusively predicated on their religiously faithful adherence to these laws. But what are they? And from where are these "laws" derived? Do they truly have the alleged significance so strongly declared? We must explore these questions and their implications for our world now in immeasurable chaos.

Rabbis agree that the seven laws were given to the sons of Noah after the Flood as derived from rabbinic interpretation of Genesis 9. These are described and derived in and by the Talmud, distilled for simplicity and clarity as follows:

1. Do not deny God.
2. Do not blaspheme God.
3. Do not murder.
4. Do not engage in sexual immorality.
5. Do not steal.
6. Do not eat the flesh of a living animal.
7. Establish courts and a legal system to enforce these laws.

In order to properly discern the implications of these 7 Noahide Laws, we must first define the Talmud and distinguish it from the Torah.

~ The *TORAH*, is the Hebrew word for "instruction." It is the first five books of Moses or the Bible, usually referred to by Christians as the Pentateuch (from the Greek for 5-fold book). The Torah is an actual part of the Bible (both Hebrew and Christian) collectively referred to as the Tanach (the Old Covenant/Testament).

The Torah contains 613 commandments, statutes, judgments and ordinances defining the whole of the law given by HaShem (God) to Moses at Mt. Sinai, confirming Israel's betrothal to the God of Abraham, Isaac and Jacob; the God of Israel. The Ten Commandments or Law of Exodus 20 was ordered placed by God inside the Ark of the Covenant under God's Mercy Seat. The balance of the commandments known as ordinances were NOT placed inside the ARK but "in the side of the ark," "that it might be a witness AGAINST" Israel if they failed to perform the marital covenant (Deut. 31:24-27; Col. 2:11-14).

~ The TALMUD is the Hebrew word for "learning." It does not contain the Torah but is rather an extensive rabbinic commentary on the Torah, comprising the Jewish religion, Judaism's history, laws and beliefs, referred to as Halakah laws—laws upon laws defined applicationally by rabbis. "The Talmud is the most vital manuscript of the conventional Judaism religion."[1] It is referred to as "the oral law."

> NOTE: All of this detail may, at the moment, seem irrelevant or disinteresting, but it has profound relevance as we proceed exploring the implications of the Noahide Law.

The Talmud was written by many rabbis over a very long period of time. Now we must introduce yet two more Jewish documents. The first is the Mishnah, which is a collection of the mostly halachic (operational and applicational) Jewish traditions which were not compiled until about AD 200 by Rabbi Yehuda HaNasi, or 130 years after the destruction of the 2nd Temple. These form the first and basic part of the Talmud. Further rabbinic commentary and analysis was then subsequently added to the Mishnah in a collection called the Gemara.

Why is all of this distilled detail relevant to you and to the world? While as it is said "The devil is in the details," so too is discernment of the greater truth and implications necessary for honest intellectual and spiritual understanding.

The truth for discernment lies not only with whether ostensible Noahide Laws can be somehow gleaned from the Torah in Genesis 9. Of equal significance is by whom was this interpretation introduced, when was it finally "revealed" to rabbis, and how and for what ultimate purposes were the proposed implications determined for the Gentile world (virtually all nations on the planet except Israel)?

Can Rabbis Edit or Post-Script Scripture?

This is a serious question, both for Jew and Gentile. The same question applies to pastors, priests and all religious or quasi-religious leaders, theologians and pontificators. If the scriptures are true, who (if anyone) has delegated authority from HaShem—God—to add to, delete from, or create their own applicational determination, realizing that every man—and woman—has undisclosed personal whims, agendas and sinfully colored glasses through which we all look, whether or not we, through monumental chutzpah, refuse to admit it.

Here, then, is what Jew and Gentile need to know about the rabbinic origin, interpretation and application of God's instructions to Noah and his sons after the flood.

FIRST - The seven Noahide Laws are not explicitly listed in the Bible. Therefore they are, as expressed, "extra-biblical."

SECOND - The idea of a formed set of laws given to all humanity (the sons of Noah) comes from the Talmud.

THIRD - Rabbis somewhere between 200 AD and 500 AD defined and installed their concept of the Noahide Laws in the Talmud, which, in Jewish practice, is their operational "Bible," with equal authority for life, practice and belief.

This is what is called "Rabbinic Judaism" because it is a system devised and designed by rabbis. It is not the biblical Judaism understood by Moses, David, the prophets or even Jesus (Yeshua), who warned Jewish leaders at that time about such extra-biblical burdens greater than men can bear (Matt. 23:4; Lk. 11:46).

FOURTH - According to Rabbinic Judaism, a Gentile does not have to follow the Mosaic Law but is required to keep the Noahide Laws, which are unequivocally binding. In truth, some rabbis have concluded it is blasphemy for a Gentile to either attempt or claim to keep the Ten Commandments or the other Mosaic statutes, judgments and ordinances.

FIFTH - Gentiles who follow and observe the Noahide Laws are then said to be *righteous* Gentiles, "one of the pious," and "assured of a portion of the world to come."[2]

SIXTH - Nowhere in Genesis 9 is mentioned or alluded to a call for the establishment of a Noahide court and judicial system.

SEVENTH - The punishment to be meted out to a Gentile (Noahide) for transgression of nearly all of the seven laws is decapitation.[3] Because Christians believe Jesus to be "the Son of God," Christians are by Jewish definition "blasphemous" and "idolaters."

Judaism, Islam and Christianity
The Noahide Connection

It is implicit in the record of a universal, world-wide flood that destroyed all humankind except Noah and his sons and their wives (8 souls) that all current inhabitants of planet earth are the physical descendants of Noah (Gen. 6-9). It is not implicit, however, that all of Earth's population are of the same spirit, mind and heart as described between Noah and his Creator, God (Gen. 6:8, 9). In fact, the breakaway from Noah's redemptive spirit and character in relationship with God as Creator actually began with the iniquity in Noah's own sons (Gen. 9:18-26), which has echoed with gathering crescendo to this messianic age.

Over four thousand years and until the birth of Yeshua (Jesus) around 4 BC, various religious beliefs spanned the earth until Abram was called by God to leave Ur of the Chaldees (Babylon) to journey toward the "Land of Promise" now known as Israel. From the loins of Abraham came Ishmael (son of the Egyptian servant Hagar, a Hamite) and Isaac, the "heir according to the promise" (Gen. 17:15-21, vs. 21). From these two sons come history's most divisive sibling rivalry, increasingly dividing the world politically, defying any and all efforts to unite in harmony, until the Abraham Accords were seemingly miraculously achieved under then U.S. President Donald Trump.

Yet that embryonic unity is even now being tested. The descendants of Ishmael (the broader Arab world) are largely embraced by vastly larger, non-Arab, nations and peoples which are now precipitating Arab and non-Arab Muslims into deep division over who will usher in the Islamic messiah, the Mahdi, and reign over a Muslim "New World Order" to govern the world's peoples under Sharia law.

Between 29 and 33 AD Yeshua, identified in Roman-governed Palestine by the Jewish inhabitants (descendants of Isaac) as a rabbi (teacher) who also performed miracles, was crucified under Pontius Pilate at the insistence of ruling Jewish religious leaders. They claimed he deserved death for blasphemy, because he claimed to be the Son of God. History records Yeshua rose from the dead three days after his crucifixion and burial (a fact denied by the ruling religious leaders as placing them in an untenable position having called for his crucifixion). These rulers, in blasphemous cover-up, suborned perjury of the Roman guards by paying them off—most likely with Temple tithes and offerings—having the soldiers pledge that Yeshua's disciples had stolen away his body.

Whether or not you agree with aspects of this historical picture, it is necessary to refresh a basic understanding of the spiritual dilemma now faced by the world. While seemingly irreconcilably divided, yet Muslims and Jews vehemently deny the deity of Jesus, as Messiah. That Jesus was the Son of God, Redeemer and Messiah, has been persistently and vitriolically rejected by the vast majority of followers of Rabbinic Judaism, claiming that to accept Jesus as deity is both idolatry and polytheism (believing in more than one God) since God is "One." Similarly, Muslims also reject Jesus as deity, since Allah alone is "God," and that Jesus never died on a cross or rose again, and that to claim otherwise is worthy of death as a consummate, blasphemous infidel.

Perhaps you are now becoming aware as to what might facilitate the uniting of these two spiritually-warring sibling factions. It has been oft said that, "The enemy of my enemy is my friend." So consider, what global messianic view is despised and rejected by both Rabbinic Judaism and Mohammedan Islam? Will their mutual antipathy toward Yeshua as Messsiah be sufficient to unite them in the growing struggle for world governance against the Christian proclamation that Jesus (a Jewish rabbi) was actually the Anointed One of God and will soon return to judge the world in righteousness?

Will Noahidism Unite the World?

Since we, whether Jew, Muslim or Christian…or of any faith—or not—are all descendants of Noah, it is perceived that to achieve unity we must return to find the resolution of our divisions in Noah. All then are "Children of Noah," but only those who truly openly embrace and pledge their allegiance to the Seven Noahide Laws are deemed the true "B'nai Noach." We must therefore follow the late historical development of the recognition of the Noahide Laws both among Jew and Gentile. The nations most representative are Israel and the United States of America.

In 1987 President Ronald Reagan signed a proclamation speaking of "the historical tradition of ethical values and principles, which have been the bedrock of society from the dawn of civilization when they were known as the Seven Noahide Laws, transmitted through God to Moses on Mt. Sinai."[4]

The Jewish scholar Maimonides (12th century) declared that God commanded Moses to **compel the world** to accept these seven commandments. He stated: "Anyone who accepts upon himself and carefully observes the Seven Commandments is of the Righteous of the Nations of the World and has a portion in the World to Come."[5] The same Maimonides declared that anyone who does not accept the seven laws is to be executed.[6]

On March 26, 1991, just six months before the infamous Islamic attack of September 11, "The U.S. Congress officially recognized the Noahide Laws in Public Law 102-14, referenced as *Education Day*. Congress and U.S. President George W. Bush declared by that law "that the United States of America was founded upon the Seven Universal Laws of Noah, and that these Laws have been the bedrock of society from the dawn of civilization." Therefore, this law was justified to promulgate the Noahide Laws as part of Education Day for the strengthening of civilized society.[7] What then happened to the Ten Commandments set forth in plaques, engravings and bas relief throughout America and on the walls of the Supreme Court?

As stated in a Chabad opinion, a boy of 13 and a girl of 12 become liable to conform to and embrace the Seven Noahide Laws, and similarly to be subject to their enforcement. Any court that does not administer and follow the Noahide Laws is considered to be "an instrument for driving G-d's blessings out of the world." Failure to establish a Noahide court is punishable by death, as is the establishment of a court other than one based on the "Seven Universal Laws."

In regard to this apparent goal of world domination, revered Lubavitch Rabbi Schneerson (seen by many to be the Messiah) made clear:

> Consequently, it is obvious and self-evident that in modern times we must carry out the Divine Command we received through Moshe [Moses]: 'To compel all human beings to accept the commandments enjoined upon the descendants of Noach.'[8]

> We must therefore deduce that this is an auspicious time to conquer the world with Torah....[9]

Another Lubavitcher article, "The Final War for Jerusalem," proclaims: "Judaism has always been a conquering religion, not for the purpose of converting gentiles to become Jews, but rather with the mission of returning the world to the universal covenant between G-d and Noah." "And as the Lubavitcher Rebbe [Schneerson] has explained, by transforming the gentiles we can quickly create a vast army of supporters who will help us reveal Moshiach [Messiah] and bring all Jews back to the Torah."

> Our most pressing task, to put it simply, is to launch an international Noahide revolution without delay. The process has already begun, with dozens of Noahide communities having appeared throughout the United States, generally composed of former Christians who have abandoned that religion....

> ...the growing Noahide movement will seize political power—using only peaceful, lawful means—in the capitals of

the Western nations...the United States, as a fairly religious, conservative nation, certainly tops the list of prospects."[10]

The Sanhedrin and Global Salvation

On October 13, 2004, the Sanhedrin, which is the highest tribunal of the Jewish state and religion, was re-inaugurated after 1600 years by 71 leading rabbis in Tiberias. In an unpublicized move, members of the newly established Sanhedrin ascended to the Temple Mount as a symbolic declaration of their primary intent and purpose to rebuild the Temple, considered crucial in preparation for the messianic age.[11]

Then on June 9, 2006, "A group of non-Jewish delegates have come to Jerusalem to pledge their loyalty to the Laws of Noah," reported *Israel National News*. "They appeared before the nascent [newly restored] Sanhedrin, which established a High Council for B'nai Noach [Gentile "sons" or followers of the Noahide Laws]."[12]

Here, then, was Judaism's highest religious authority, a collection of 71 of the most prominent and respected rabbis of Israel, revered among the followers of Rabbinic Judaism, officially setting the stage for urgently teaching and promoting to the gentile world the Seven Laws of Noah as the non-Jewish world's salvation, but also establishing a Tribunal (tantamount to a religious Supreme Court) to be the final arbiter and judge of whether a gentile would be entitled to "a portion in the World to Come," or would be subject to execution as proclaimed in the Talmud and reinforced by Maimonides.

In effect, failure of a gentile to fully embrace all seven on the Noahide Laws, including acceptance of the judicial jurisdiction of Rabbinic courts, would have committed the "unpardonable sin." Thus, the Noahide Laws become the immutable foundation governing the New World Order being even now established; already affirmed for the United States of America by proclamation of President Ronald Reagan in 1987 and by the U.S. Congress confirmed by President George W. Bush in 1991 under Public Law 102-14, as earlier cited, as "the bedrock of society.

While the Noahide Laws, as simply expressed (excluding the seventh mandating Jewish courts), are seemingly righteous and consistent with the Ten Commandments which (according to Jewish rabbis they replace for gentiles), the problem lies in the details of interpretation. Under the Talmud's Noahide Laws, for instance, the worship of Yeshua (Jesus) as Messiah is forbidden under penalty of death, since such worship of Christ is condemned by Judaism as both idolatry and blasphemy, the penalty for which is capital punishment by decapitation. Concerning Jesus Christ, Maimonides *Mishnah Torah*, in chapter 10 of the English Translation, makes unmistakably clear the vituperous view of Christians necessitated by Rabbinic Judaism.

> It is a mitzvah [religious duty] however, to eradicate Jewish
> traitors, minim, and apikorsim, and to cause them to descend
> into the pit of destruction, since they cause difficulty to the
> Jews and sway the people away from God.[13]

It is indeed fascinating, even troubling, that the book of Revelation, Chapter 20, verse 4, seems to state clearly that Christians in the Great Tribulation concluding the messianic age before the unveiling of Messiah will be beheaded—decapitated precisely as proscribed by the *Talmud*. Perhaps, in reflection, this is why Jesus is not to be mentioned in Freemason gatherings, having either wittingly or unwittingly embraced the Rabbinic Judaistic viewpoint, thus seeking to suit their world.

Uniting...or Dividing?

If one embraces the seven Noahide Laws, that person becomes "united" with the proposed new global order by virtue of the mutual allegiance pledged. Those who refuse to so pledge are dismissed from the earth through decapitation, thus increasing and enforcing "unity." This thinking is congruent with the New Age "theology," calling for those who refuse to become as One with the cosmic Christ to be "selected out" by the process of "selection," thus removed from the planet to increase and preserve unity. Therefore, a person is "free" to choose to embrace such promise of global unity, or be dismissed from the living as the enemy of world peace or shalom.

Since Rabbinic Judaism almost violently rejects the possibility of a divine Messiah, decrying such a thought as blasphemy, only two alternatives remain—either the expected "messiah" is a mere charismatic man, or there will be no actual messiah but merely a "messianic age" of peace and justice.

If indeed the "messiah" is a mere man, humanity is then mandated to pledge allegiance for future hope to such a man and his global system, resting his life and destiny upon the good graces of a mortal who gains dominion by flattery rather than divine favor as declared in the Tanakh, the book of Daniel, chapter 11, verse 21. Herein lies the test of truth. In whom…or what can a person place his or her ultimate trust when destiny is in the balance?

A Whole New World

It matters not whether the radical reconstructing of our world, its systems, its government, economy or its purported faith is called the New World Order, the new global community, the Great Reset or the Ark of Noah for, as Shakespeare observed, "A rose by any other name would smell as sweet." But are we facing global sweetness and harmony, or are we being thrust into a tyrannical reordering of our world promising peace and safety on the front-end culminating in massive disappointment rather than messianic hope? We will all be making a choice.

Rabbi Tzvi Freeman, senior editor at *Chabad.org*, promised an "age of wisdom and peace." He stated: "…today we stand at the doorstep of a whole new world," and that is "Why these seven principles become so crucial today." Everything—technology, science and social justice— "all drive us up a steady trench towards an age promised by the prophets and described by the sages…." "The common ground we need must be the ground from which we were formed, at the essence of humanity's purpose and the meaning of reality. And that lies only in the hand of the Infinite Light that found us. The voice that Noah heard."[14]

These sound, on the surface, like gracious words of legitimate hope. But what actual "voice" did Noah hear? And what was the intended meaning of the words themselves, but more importantly of the interpretation and application of those words as infinitely multiplied and even manipulated by rabbis who wrote the *Talmud* and *Mishnah* fifteen hundred years later, thus forming a new religion called Rabbinic Judaism?

Both Jew and Gentile are facing monumental choices in this glob-ally-recognized messianic moment? Who or what can you—will you—trust? If the world is destined to be dominated by a simple religion, which one will it be? Will it be a blend of many or all, predominated by the Noahide Laws? Who will be IN…or OUT? And who will reign over this new eclectic theocracy?

That decision was made by a group of Gentiles who came to Israel on January 10, 2006, and in front of the resurrected Israeli Sanhedrin made this pledge.

> I pledge my allegiance to HaShem, G-d of Israel, Creator and King of the Universe, to His Torah and its representa-tives, the developing Sanhedrin. I hereby pledge to uphold the Seven Laws of Noah in all their details, according to Oral Law of Moses under the guidance of the developing San-hedrin. May HaShem bless and aid me, my fellow council members and all B'nai Noah in all our endeavors for the sake of His name. Blessed are you G-d, King of the universe who has caused me to live, sustained me, and brought me to this day.[15]

Is this the Anatomy of a One World Religion? Is righteousness for Gentiles then achieved by absolute obedience to the Law of Noah? Is this, in reality, the "Anti-Gospel," a total repudiation of the Christian faith? David, as a prophet, wrote of the raging nations in Psalm 2. God spoke in response to their raging against His will that He would have them in derision. He then declared, "Yet I have set my king upon my holy hill," calling the leaders of the Gentile and Jewish world to "kiss the Son." "Blessed are all they that put their trust in him."

Who is that "Son"? Have either Jew or Gentile seen him yet? Would either Jew or Gentile recognize him if he showed up in person today? Why…or why not? Would you?

The Valley of Decision

The ancient prophet Joel spoke soberingly of these times and of a distinct time at the end of the age called "The Day of the LORD."

Are we rapidly approaching that "Day" when the true Messiah will be manifested? How would you know? How can we know?

One thing is certain. The prophet gave great warning of "that Day," declaring:

> Multitudes, multitudes in the valley of decision: for the day of the LORD is near in the valley of decision (Joel 3:14).

PART 5

THE CORRUPTION OF CERTAINTY

THE CORRUPTION OF CERTAINTY is *certainty* itself. Human experience tells us that it is a nearly universal characteristic woven into our psychological "DNA" to desire—even demand—certainty. Uncertainty leads to disillusionment and even despair. And there is no area tending more to hope than the expectation of a Messiah…or a delivering charismatic leader or just a "messianic" era promising relief from our uncertainties and a sense of peace.

The unfortunate competing desire, however, is that we tend to only want or accept certainty if it agrees with our own personal or group historic viewpoints or does not purport to interfere with other strongly-held desires, wants, or perceptions of personal control and freedom.

For these reasons, we become entangled in a kind of frustrating complexity of mind and heart that perpetuates a kind of shroud over our ability to see actual truth and to embrace genuine certainty. Thus, the peace we yearn for eludes us, actually setting the stage for a more acceptable promise of emotional relief while remaining open to the deceptive allure of an earthly "savior" whose glorious and global promise seems "certain enough" for the immediate future, allowing us to "breathe easy" for the moment. Does any of this resonate with you?

In the chapters that follow, we will delve more deeply into this conundrum of confusing complexity. We will see the dangerous unintended consequences of our persistent resistance to revealed certainty, as we also begin to pull back the veil preventing us from resolving "the mystery of the ages." Please follow patiently. You will be eternally rewarded.

WARNING!

THERE MAY BE SOME, PERHAPS MANY, WHO WILL FEEL DISCOMFORT IN READING THE FOLLOWING CHAPTER. HOWEVER, FAILURE TO PATIENTLY PROCESS AND PONDER UPON THE PROBING OF OUR BELIEFS MAY WELL FRUSTRATE, IF NOT PREVENT, "THE UNVEILING OF THE MYSTERY OF THE AGES."

MYSTERIES REMAIN "MYSTERIES" OFTEN BECAUSE, FOR A VARIETY OF REASONS, WE FAIL TO SEE THE OBVIOUS OR ACTUALLY RESIST "CONNECTING THE DOTS" FOR FEAR OF WHAT IT MAY DO TO—OR HOW IT MAY AFFECT—OUR LONG-ESTABLISHED BELIEFS.

ONLY THOSE SINCERELY DESIRING TO "UNVEIL THE MYSTERY OF THE AGES" WILL DEEPLY CONSIDER...THE MYSTIFICATION OF BELIEF.

Chapter 20

THE MYSTIFICATION OF BELIEF

"The very word Messiah should be sobering
to every sincere and serious-minded person."

THE WORD *BELIEVE* HAS BECOME A BUZZWORD in our post-modern world and culture. Plaques abound encouraging *belief* as do vague exhortations and promises from self-help, business and religious platforms.

Believe and you shall have…
    Believe and you shall succeed…
        Believe and be blessed…

Believe and become rich…
    Believe you are becoming…
        Just BELIEVE!

Believe what? Believe whom? What is the driving purpose of such belief, and what might be the consequences? Is the promised fruit of such belief CERTAIN? And upon what evidence is that alleged certainty dependent? In this rapidly advancing messianic age, these questions take on ever-greater significance and bear vast implications for our lives. Yet, in reality, what it means to BELIEVE is cloaked in largely unrecognized mystery that enshrouds our minds even when attempting to contemplate the truth, meaning or implications of the word *Messiah*.

What Does it Mean to "Believe"?

Whether or not we realize it, the word *believe* can be very slippery in definition, interpretation and implication. This is due to our human propensity—even intention—to superimpose upon words not just what they mean but also nuances of what we want or prefer them to mean to satisfy our rationalizations of truth, facts and behaviors. Yet if to "believe" has no unified accepted meaning, we are eternally at loss to resolve the meaning of Messiah and messianic age, leaving it behind an impenetrable veil that defies definition and consequential conviction of mind and heart.

Is belief absolute, variable, or dependent upon a variety of outlooks, experiences and opinions? Is an opinion that I state as a "belief" an actual belief? At first you may respond that such talk is mere toying with words. But on the contrary it is necessary if we are to honestly and with integrity seek to "unveil the mystery of the ages." That "mystery" of Messiah persists precisely because of our mystifying use of the word *believe*, the lack of known or accepted evidence upon which to base genuine belief, and our resistance to revelation of the implications of such evidence.

The dictionary itself reveals our perplexing dilemma with what it means "to believe." Here is a sample of various ways we use the word.

- To accept as true;
- To accept as real;
- A firmly held opinion;
- A firmly held conviction;
- A truth, faith or confidence in someone or something;
- To feel sure of;
- To think or suppose;
- To have confidence in a person or course of action;
- An opinion that something is right, proper or desirable.
  (Taken from the *Concise Oxford American Dictionary*, Oxford University Press, 2006).

Notice carefully! Every nuanced definition presupposes experience, information or evidence upon which a person's "belief" is based. Therefore, actual belief is totally dependent on whether a person has adequate evidence on which to base his/her belief (opinion) but even more importantly, the necessary condition of both mind and heart such that the person is willing to embrace the truth arising from that evidence, without ulterior motives leading to rejection, thereby choosing to "believe a lie."

Words are cheap and opinions even cheaper. Words matter. They must be chosen carefully, the definitions preserved persistently and the implications embraced without prevarication through mental and emotional—or political or religious—gymnastics. Therefore, the word *Messiah* must be approached with a seriously-seeking mind and heart or it will fall prey to fickle feelings, political power and religious pre-conceptions, as it has over the centuries. If we are, indeed, in the "messianic age," the very word *Messiah* should be sobering to every sincere and serious-minded person.

Barriers to Belief

If, indeed, there is an actual "Messiah" soon to be revealed, it might behoove us to understand the barriers we may have or to evade belief. If such Messiah's presence and purpose upon his appearance should carry the magnitude of import for life on earth or hereafter, the consequences of unbelief or disbelief could be catastrophic beyond belief. So let us briefly explore some of the common barriers to belief.

1. **The Barrier of Culture**—Cultures are vastly varied. Even within a broader culture are usually many subcultures. Thus, nations alone do not define outlooks, viewpoints and group ideas accepted within each such subculture as their operative "truths." Such "truths" are not actually *truths* but accepted group opinions and values. These group-defined "truths" present almost impenetrable barriers to a contrary belief absent a deeply-serious seeking mind and heart for a greater *truth* upon which to establish a believable *belief* that will stand the test of countermanding evidence.

2. **The Barrier of Relational Acceptance**—The family is the ordained foundation of society and therefore carries powerful persuasion in the formation and enforcement of beliefs. The family is, in effect, a miniature culture, including not only the immediate family but also the extended family. A family's collective and historical viewpoint concerning matters of politics and religion brings clear pressure upon family members to conform…or else. Few are willing to buck the family cultural belief system for fear of ostracization…or even death.

Fear of rejection or possible death for embracing a belief or conviction contrary to the family or culturally-accepted norm is one of the greatest barriers to belief based not on opinion but on a deeply sincere pursuit and love of truth. For one born into a Muslim family, to reject Islam is deemed blasphemy worthy of death. For one born into a Jewish family, to embrace Christianity is also deemed a form of blasphemy on the grounds of idolatry, thereby mandating severance from the family. Hinduism operates similarly, with family expulsion—very painful to the one being treated as an outcast.

This family and cultural barrier to belief has profound significance when considering if we are in "the messianic age" and whether or not we can…or will…identify and embrace a coming MESSIAH, which implies an absolute truth as to the existence and identity of such messiah.

A classic case involved a beautiful young lady in the United States whose family still lived in India as dedicated Hindus. She had become a Christian, embracing Jesus as Christ or Messiah, and was fellowshipping seemingly joyfully among other Christian believers. However, the heart tug of family rejection became overwhelming to her yearning to be accepted. She then knowingly forsook and abandoned her Christian beliefs and returned to India, re-embracing her family's Hindu belief system.

Many today, in our multiculturalistic world belief system, believing that all cultures and all religions are equally true and valid, would conclude nothing of negative significance from the young lady's decision, since political-correctness, religious pluralism and multiculturalism demand that all beliefs be accepted as true. Yet if there is, indeed, genuine truth to be believed, such believe-all-beliefs would be a horrific barrier of self-deception, perhaps depriving such a one of a desired eternal destiny.

True professing Christians well understand this defining dilemma, realizing that genuine truth always and inevitably causes division, culturally and even within families. Jesus himself spoke of this in a passage to which few today are willing to pay attention…yet must.

> Suppose ye that I am come to give peace on earth? I tell you, Nay; but rather division:
>
> For from henceforth there shall be five in one house divided, three against two, and two against three.
>
> The father shall be divided against the son, and the son against the father; the mother against the daughter, and the daughter against the mother; the mother in law against her daughter in law, and the daughter in law against her mother in law (Lk. 12:51-31).

Yeshua spoke these words, not for the purposes of creating division, but rather warning of the inevitable consequences flowing from genuine belief in the MESSIAH and accompanying truth, because *absolute truth divides absolutely.* The very context of the warning was in discussing the nature of belief barriers in these end times.

3. **The Barrier of "Truth"**—Truth itself is now portrayed as a veritable mystery. While the pursuit of truth has historically been embraced as needful, regardless of barriers, such genuine pursuit is now actually denigrated—even deemed undesirable.

Instead, the pursuit of absolute truth has been gradually replaced by the pursuit of a self-defined "truth" …my own "truth," hence the phrase "What's truth for you may not be truth for me," or "We are all entitled to our own truth." It should be obvious that massive confusion now reigns supreme, having done a mental sleight-of-hand now redefining what I *believe* as truth itself. What should be equally obvious is that such personally re-defined "truth" is not truth at all but merely a present opinion I choose to embrace.

Are all beliefs actually true? The world of science and its ever-advancing theories throughout history verifies that what was once embraced as true—even scientifically—was not at all true but a mere temporary belief or theory portrayed as true. Similarly, supposed political, economic, historical and even religious "truths" have proven to be false, yet were embraced as absolutes. This is one of the greatest barriers to genuine belief in TRUTH.

So…" What is truth?" That was the cynical—even sarcastic—question posed by a crusty Roman governor to Yeshua at his trial (Jn. 18:38). That question came as a result of Jesus' response to an earlier question posing political ramifications when Pilate enquired "Art thou the king of the Jews?" (Jn. 18:33). To which Jesus, proclaimed by many Jews as "the Anointed One" or MESSIAH, responded, "My kingdom is not of this world" (Jn. 18:36). Yeshua then went on to clarify his identity and purpose. His declaration is of consummate significance for anyone truly seeking to comprehend the meaning of truth when it comes to "unveiling the mystery of the ages."

> Thou sayest that I am a king. To this end was I born, and for this cause came I into the world, that I should bear witness unto the truth. Every one that is of the truth heareth my voice. (Jn. 18:37).

In vehement response, the Jewish High Priest and members of the Sanhedrin, having choreographed a mob, cried "Crucify him, crucify him" to which Pilate, having found Jesus innocent of their treasonous charges against Rome, asked "Shall I crucify your King?" But "the chief priests answered, We have no king but Caesar," choosing a thief and a murderer, Barabbas, to be released instead. Yet they hated Rome and Pilate as oppressors. Genuine truth was to be sacrificed on the altar of political correctness and the protection of power, perks and position upon which secular beliefs and motivations (masquerading as religious) the leaders relied (Jn. 19: 6-22).

So, again, what does it mean to believe? Ultimately, the real issue is not on *belief* but on *truth*. It is interesting that there are so many definitions and ideas about the word *belief*, yet there is really only one definition, as drawn from the dictionary, of the word *truth*. And here it is in profound simplicity.

> TRUTH: "The quality or state of being true; and also, *the truth* is that which is true or in accordance with fact or reality."

As we seek to "unveil the mystery of the ages," our pursuit must be to discover and embrace, therefore truly believe, that which is true and "that which is in accordance with fact or reality." Other opinions and beliefs, however strongly held or emotionally embraced, must be released and discarded. Destiny may well ride in the balance. Once again, VIEWPOINT DETERMINES DESTINY.

4. **The Barrier of Unbelief**—There are many who, when faced with seemingly obvious—even incontrovertible—facts, still refuse to believe that which is true. And there are a plethora of reasons we can concoct in our purportedly "rational" minds to justify such disbelief. Those reasons may be emotional, political, religious or cultural. Perhaps the classic example of such unbelief was demonstrated in the infamous quote coming from U.S. President Joseph Biden when he

unabashedly declared, "We believe in truth—not facts." He made clear to all, that facts are irrelevant if they contravene what I want to believe. Therefore, what I WANT to believe I deem and will declare to be "truth."

Willingness to believe facts is foundational to genuine human rationale. Anything contrary we call *rationalization*. Yet there is a more profound "fact" than that which is observable to the eye which must be understood if the mystery of MESSIAH is to become clearly visible or be unveiled. When God speaks, His very words are implicit truth, regardless of what I think or choose to believe. And this was Israel's persistent problem as the "chosen people." They consistently and persistently refused to agree with and conform to what HaShem had said, while ritualistically kissing the Torah.

So God periodically raised up a prophet to woo and warn His people of their unbelief and its profound consequences. Yet they continued to dis what God decreed for their good, turning their passive *unbelief* into affirmative *dis-belief*. And gentile Christians have become progressively guilty of the same pattern of unbelief leading to disbelief. So, what is God to do if His messianic hope is to be revealed. He chose to give a sign and direct words of prophetic significance. Listen carefully with your mind's ear as you read His exasperated words as spoken by the Hebrew prophet Isaiah to a perpetually disbelieving people.

> Hear ye now, O house of David; Is it a small thing for you to weary men, but will ye weary my God also?

> Therefore the Lord himself shall give you a sign; Behold, a virgin shall conceive, and bear a son, and you shall call his name Immanuel [meaning "God with us"] (Isa. 7:13-14).

But unbelief and disbelief are not easily broken notwithstanding progressive prophetic revelation. So HaShem persists in declaring prophetic hope amid persistent blindness as Isaiah again reveals.

> For unto us a child is born, unto us a son is
> given: and the government shall be upon his
> shoulder: and his name shall be called…

> Wonderful,
> Counsellor,
> The mighty God,
> The everlasting Father,
> The Prince of Peace (Isa. 9:6).

Notice carefully—each of these titles is capitalized, indicating descriptive titles for God himself. Furthermore, this child to be born was specifically referred to not as a mere man, as was Moses, but as God manifested in the flesh…

> The mighty God,
> The everlasting Father,
> The Prince of Peace.

And His messianic authority was to rest "upon the throne of David" as previously revealed by the God of Israel through the prophets from Samuel through Zechariah.

> To David by Nathan the prophet…
> And thine house and thy kingdom shall be
> established for ever before thee: thy throne shall
> be established for ever (II Sam. 7:16).

Isaiah made clear that the Messiah would sit on the throne of David as HaShem's final Anointed One.

> Of the increase of his government and peace
> there shall be no end, upon the throne of
> David, and upon his kingdom, to order it, and
> to establish it with justice from henceforth even
> for ever (Isa. 9:7).

Even the place of Messiah's birth was made manifest— the city of David—Bethlehem.

> But thou, Bethlehem Ephratah, though thou
> be little among the thousands of Judah, yet out
> of thee shall he come forth unto me that is to
> be ruler in Israel; whose goings forth have been
> from of old, from everlasting (Micah 5:2).

Not only would this ultimate ruler be born in Bethlehem, but Micah made clear that the One who would be so born had already existed as one with HaShem (God)

> "from of old," and
> "from everlasting."

In other words, this prophesied ruler and redeemer would be "God in the flesh," made after the likeness of men, just as the first Adam had been made (Gen. 1:26, 5:1), yet untainted by Adam's genealogical sin, therefore to be "born of a virgin" so as to give hope of salvation to the Jew first, and then to the Gentile (Isa. 42:1-7; Matt. 12:14-21).

Interestingly, it is a conundrum of the human condition, whether Jew or Gentile, to choose to refuse to believe the increasingly obvious and to disbelieve overwhelming evidence, however authoritative. For we all have our reasons… or create self-imposed barriers to belief. Belief becomes even more held at arms-length when our revered leaders, be they resistant Rabbis or Rt. Reverend Gentile pastors, priests, choose to ignore biblical authority in favor of their own.

It should be increasingly clear that the task of "unveiling the mystery of the ages" is held hostage to either ignorance or willful blindness. Each person, therefore, becomes somewhat complicit in perpetuating the shroud of mystery, but the greater burden is upon those to whom greater understanding has been revealed but rejected, whether Jew or Gentile.

5. **The Barrier of Majority Opinion**—The perception is prominent that a significant number or majority of people or of a large group or even race or culture maintains a particular belief is profoundly persuasive to color or determine

a person's personal belief. While this is understandable and can provide at least a threshold test in one's effort to ascertain truth, majority opinion is never dependable to establish actual truth because it is colored by many hidden factors often disconnected from actual facts. It is for that reason America's founders not only distrusted pure democracy but actually were terrified of it as potentially the most dangerous and tyrannical form of government. Hence Americans were given a democratic (representative) republic with multiple checks and balances.

As human beings we must always and intentionally probe our own minds and hearts as to the reasons we may be persuaded by the fickle feelings of the masses. Why is it I am prone to believe or accept what so many others seem to embrace? Are their opinions and beliefs authoritative, and on what basis? These are not merely idle or philosophical questions but actually are capable of setting a course for a destiny of unintended consequences.

6. **The Barrier of Fatalism**—The most common expression of *fatalism* is the famous French phrase *Que sera sera* expressed in the Doris Day song lyrics "whatever will be will be—the future's not ours to see, que sera sera." That view has been culturally distilled to a mere "Whatever." Thus, fate itself becomes the ultimate "fact" of my life beliefs.

So why is fatalism actually a fatal attack on true and genuine beliefs? It is because fatalism in effect removes any real consequences to what I believe or don't believe. And such a *whatever* outlook has implications for my ability or will to even see or embrace a messianic hope. We reason that what I believe matters not, therefore genuine hope disintegrates in increasing despair and an "Oh well…" response to life and the trajectory of history and prophecy. Facts became irrelevant, revelation is passively disregarded, and I relieve myself of the necessity to choose.

If a true Messiah is coming, such cavalier thinking is both dangerous and likely devastating when confronted with the reality of Messiah's appearance. It will be shocking to the core. And for that reason alone, the majority of humankind will be prone to passively embrace an imposter or counterfeit messiah.

7. **The Barrier of Fear**—Fear is immensely powerful. It can protect but it can also paralyze. One of the greatest and most pernicious barriers to "unveiling the mystery of the ages" is fear.

Fear frustrates genuine belief in the face of forces such as perceived majority thinking, family or cultural traditions and governmental mandates that can have potentially profound effects on our desire to be accepted or to carry on our lives as has become normative. It is here that truth and faith collide but must become congruent. The alternative is the paralysis of fear that will perpetually frustrate *unveiling* the mystery of Messiah. It is rapidly becoming time to choose, and genuine choice will demand we be unfettered by the paralysis of multiplied and self-justified fears.

De-Mystifying Belief

Genuine belief must be de-mystified. It must be seen and embraced for what it is, not for what we might wish it were or what we want to construe it to be, governed not by facts and truth but by the multiplied predilections of our ever-vacillating feelings.

Willingness to simply believe, unfettered by all of the distracting and distorting barriers that assault our wills, will determine whether you will benefit from the final "unveiling the mystery of the ages." The painful truth is that most will choose to perpetually enshroud their minds and hearts with perceived comforting barriers. They will be fully receptive to a coming fake-real messiah.

Chapter 21

THE CONFUSION OF COMPLEXITY

"Certainty alone brings peace, both Individually and collectively."

CHAOS REIGNS OVER OUR UNRULY GLOBAL REALM on the cusp of this messianic moment of history. In truth, history, prophecy and hopelessness have collided and are becoming glaringly congruent as the world sways precariously and seemingly uncontrollably amid a terrifying sense of uncertainty.

Uncertainty Breeds Chaos

Uncertainty is the breeding ground for chaos. And chaos, in return, supercharges growing uncertainty, which in turn deepens and accelerates chaos. In reality, uncertainty is the foundation and lifeblood of chaos, whether cultural, political, economic, or spiritual. And alleged complexity is the mothering womb of confusion creating uncertainty. The only remedy for dispelling the uncertainty is *certainty* itself, which demands the recognition and embrace of unadulterated TRUTH that wavers not amid a pressurized environment of ever-advancing uncertainty and chaos.

While on the surface, the unveiling and recognition of such *truth* may seem eternally elusive and hopeless, it is our only hope to escape the confusion of complexity. Such hope demands extraordinary desire coupled with decision. Your destiny, and that of the peoples and nations of our planet, depends upon your diligence in pursuing that desire and pressing undeterred into the requisite decision that will enable the "unveiling of the mystery of the ages," bathing all who will in unprecedented hope even amid global horror.

The curtain of complexity obscuring Messiah is now to be drawn back across the stage of history, revealing for many a life-changing "aha" moment sweeping away the frustrating cloud of confusion. A choice will be made for overwhelming hope or ever-advancing hopelessness and despair. So let us together begin pulling back the curtain for the *Unveiling*.

Certainty Breeds Peace

Peace—that is "personal peace"—seems frustratingly and persistently elusive. Peace defies national and global pursuit precisely because the inhabitants of nations and our world lack personal peace. And peace—perfect peace—is the product of certainty of mind, heart and conviction within the gates of our families first, that then echoes on throughout our respective spheres of influence, eventually washing over the world.

Why, therefore, is such personal and global peace defying our seeming disability to achieve it, whether individually or collectively? It is precisely because every man and woman pursues a self-defined peace on his or her own terms. In other words, as with ancient Israel, "…every man did that which was right **in his own eyes**" (Judg. 17:6) (Emphasis added). When humankind persists in doing that which appears right *in their own eyes*, the complexity of never-ending viewpoints necessarily results in confusion which inevitably breeds chaos—thus peace becomes little more than a figment of the imagination—a false hope.

Certainty alone brings peace, both individually and collectively. So, the question then becomes whether or not such certainty is obtainable and, perhaps ever more serious, how can such certainty be obtained when it has defied human DNA throughout history? That becomes the defining question as we pull back the curtain of *The Mystery of the*

Ages on the global stage as the world reels in chaos. What will we as human persons do in hot pursuit of this elusive peace in an effort to free us from the mushrooming tyranny of uncertainty and the chaos enveloping our planet? What will *you* do…think…or be willing to believe?

Pursuing the Unity of Certainty

The peace that dispels personal and global anxiety and chaos has, throughout history, resulted either in some human leader rising to power or seizing power. That power is attained either democratically or dictatorially, purporting to provide cessation from the confusion and chaos arising out of an environment of complexity and social break-down, every person does what he or she deems to be "right in their own eyes." The inevitable result, as proven throughout the collective experience of mankind, is that personal peace is ultimately assaulted as the strongman—or government—seeks to impose control as a sub-stitute for peace. And because human power corrupts, and absolute power corrupts absolutely, tyranny eventually reigns supreme, depriv-ing us of both freedom and peace.

What then can produce peaceful unity without externally-imposed power and tyranny? The actual answer resides in our hearts, hence the global desire for, or recognition of, a messianic age or moment growing exponentially. Many expect a Messiah to deliver on our hope for peace. Others anticipate an evolution of human consciousness to usher in world peace and personal tranquility.

Is there a trustworthy answer or solution to this dilemma now paralyzing our planet? To answer that question will require profound humility of mind and heart. Choices must be—and will be—made. Whether hope or horror lies ahead will depend on your choices, and mine, for as the poet John Donne once penned, "No man is an island."

The Historically-Preferred Option

It is no mystery that mankind prefers and virtually insists upon human rulership rather than divine rulership. When given the chance, even ancient Israel preferred, in fact insisted, upon a human king as opposed to Jehovah God, who delivered them from the bondage of Egypt. The elders collectively came to the prophet Samuel and demanded a king "like all the nations." Even when warned of the consequences of a strong-man savior, they nevertheless chose a human ruler such as themselves, with the same untrustworthy, selfish and power-hungry character, to take dominion over them to deliver from the chaos and confusion of uncertainty. And the Lord responded to give them a king, "for they have not rejected thee [Samuel], but they have rejected me" (I Sam. 8).

Israel, the Jewish people chosen of God, still chose a man rather than the Creator God to be their ruler and king, just like the goyim or gentile nations. And so they will do again, with immeasurably greater consequences (Isa. 29:14-22), joining the Gentiles in a "covenant with death" with the temporal promise of peace and salvation from chaos and confusion, having twice rejected God's "Prince of Peace" who would rule "with judgment and with justice," not for a few years but "even for ever" (Isa. 9:6-7). They vehemently rejected Jehovah's proffered divine Savior, declaring, "We will not have this man to reign over us" (Lk. 19:14).

Having submitted God's preferred and proffered "King of kings" to the authority of Rome for crucifixion, they enviously submitted to the global authority of Rome for crucifixion. They enviously submitted to the global authority of the Pax Romana (earthly Roman enforced peace) which they hated to protect their own power, perks and position; for even Pontius Pilate perceived that it was "for envy they had delivered him" (Matt. 27:18). But before they violently dispensed with the One promised as Jehovah's King Messiah, Yeshua—the Anointed One—Jesus foretold in whom they would choose to trust in their existential moment of chaos, confusion and complexity. "I am come in my Father's name, and ye receive me not: if another shall come in his own name, him ye will receive" (Jn. 5:43).

The warning of Israel's great prophet Daniel was thus confirmed. In "the last end" and "in the latter time," a king of fierce countenance… shall stand up" in whom Israel will, through craftiness and flattery through the promise of peace, put their trust. This king also will stand up arrogantly against "the Prince of princes," the promised Prince of Peace of Isaiah 9:6-7 (Dan. 8:19-27, 11:21-24). And the resurrected

Roman Empire of the West will again rule with an iron fist over both Jew and Gentile, just as it did when the Father first sent forth his Son as a babe in Bethlehem, of the house of David (Lk. 2:1-35; Dan. 7).

So great will be the consequences of a third rejection of God's decreed and proffered King over Israel, as Israel joins with the Gentile world embracing a counterfeit, that the great prophet Daniel declared: I "fainted, and was sick certain days" and "I was astonished at the vision" (Dan. 8:27).

Astonished…But Not Yet

Indeed, both Israel—the Jewish people, and the Gentile world— the goyim—will be astonished at that which is to come, but not quite yet. The unveiling of the mystery of the ages has not yet taken place. Messiah and the *messianic age* remain mysterious as covered by a veil. Of course, a bride always wears a veil before the moment of revelation before her promised husband. Israel's and the Gentile's astonishment will soon shake the planet with the unveiling.

PART 6

THE FAKE-REAL MESSIAH

"IMITATION IS FLATTERY" we are told. And wherever there is something of great perceived value, someone will always conceive of a way to copy it at much lesser cost. The purpose is to give one or many the feeling that they have obtained something of great worth at minimal expense, thus requiring little or no personal commitment.

Amazingly, such imitation has actually become a business norm, called one of the "Ten Ideas That Are Changing the World" by *TIME* as its cover story March 24, 2008. As Harvard business gurus explained, "Synthetic Authenticity" has become the preeminent path to success—promote the fake as real because "Jaded buyers love 'real' products—or at least ones that fake it well." And that is not only true of products but of principles, and even religious faith. Should we then be surprised that a fake-real messiah should be presented to the world requiring only that you receive his mark of allegiance to secure his promise of global salvation?

In the following chapters this "synthetic authentic" messiah will be unveiled. Such unveiling is essential to identifying the true Messiah, who will only then be unveiled, resolving the mystery of the ages.

Chapter 22

THE IMPOSTER

"When the manipulation of feelings becomes the machination of demonically cunning men, hell follows closely."

THE IMPOSTER IS someone who pretends to be someone else in order to deceive others. Since Satan, the Deceiver, ordains or commissions his counterfeit christ to sit in his satanic seat and to stand in his stead, it should come as no surprise that this IMPOSTER messiah will appear to the masses as God's "anointed one." The degree of deception will almost defy description. Hence Jesus' warning: "Take heed that no man deceive you" (Matt. 24:4). But the prophet Daniel also warned in the Tanakh of the flattery and deceptive chicanery of the Imposter.

Imitation and Flattery

It is frequently said that "Imitation is the greatest form of flattery." Yet when deception is the foundation of flattery, it is no more flattery but rather fraud.

The IMPOSTER'S introduction to our world will be relatively brief...seemingly meteoric. Just as Jesus, at thirty years of age, seemed to "come out of nowhere," even so will Satan's counterfeit messiah make his debut, catching the globe in a growing, almost gleeful, state of surprise. Many will initially harbor suspicion, but most will, in effect, "roll out the red carpet" in hope-filled welcome. As we have already seen, he will be led in as a lamb, but will soon roar as a lion. But his power and authority will have been secured beyond resistance, ultimately declaring himself "God" (II Thess. 2:4).

Just as Robespierre was flattered as "messiah" before he was deposed as the deepening deception of the French Revolution took its course, so the IMPOSTER will be deposed by the true Messiah at the seeming culmination of his demonic career (Rev. 19:11-21; II Thess. 2:8). Just as Yeshua fulfilled the Father's calling through His ministry of God's kingdom for a period of approximately 3½ years, even so will the false messiah carry out his satanic mission to convert the world to worship of Satan for "a time, times, and a half," a period of 3½ years, until "he shall have accomplished to scatter the power of the holy people..." (Dan. 12:7).

Thus, the counterfeit's purported "flattery" of imitation will culminate in global carnage, a testimony to the temporal consequences of radical rebellion against the Creator, to be followed by eternal damnation as the "son of perdition" (II Thess. 2:3; Rev. 19:19-21).

Just as Jesus was the "Son of God" born to "save his people from their sins" (Matt. 1:21), even so the IMPOSTER will be the son of Satan, consigning those who follow him to the eternal consequences of their sins (II Thess. 2:8-12). Even as Jesus was called "Emmanuel," **God with us**, the Deceiver presents his demonic representative to be that WICKED with us (Matt. 1:23; II Thess. 2:8).

Messiah brings righteousness, peace and joy with hope (Rom 14:17; Eph. 2:12). The IMPOSTER deviously promises great things such as peace and prosperity through unrighteousness leading to unprecedented horror (Dan. 7:8, 10; Dan. 8:9, 25; II Thess. 2:8-12).

Was Yeshua "The Messiah?"

What should be one of the most troubling historical concerns is the question: *Why did the Jews not receive or recognize Jesus as the Messiah?* This is also a most telling conundrum facing both Jew and Gentile in these latter days of the end times. If the Jewish people, who were looking for and anticipating the promised Messiah, failed miserably to recognize Him, even as Jesus performed unprecedented miracles in their midst, why should either Jew or Gentile believe we will recognize Him when He comes...especially since our Jewish brethren deny He has already come?

This is not an idle question! And, in reality, few of us (whether Jew or Gentile) would readily receive or contemplate the consequences of the true answers, because they have profound implications for us today, if indeed we are on the near edge of the Second Coming of the Savior, or as our Jewish brethren would say "the appearance of the Messiah." Let us, then, attempt to honestly open our own hearts to consider the unfolding drama that will soon define the destiny of untold millions.

Why the Jews "Received Him Not"

We are told by John, a Jewish disciple of Jesus: "He came unto his own (the Jewish people) and his own received him not. But as many as received him (a very small remnant), to them he gave power [authority] to become the sons of God, even to them that believed on his name" (John 1:11-12).

If Jesus, proclaimed and promised by the Father God to be His Anointed One, the long-expected Messiah, was not recognized or received even by his own kin and people, perhaps we can see a bit of ourselves in the mirror image of their rejection, if we have eyes to see and hearts to humbly contemplate the devastating consequences. We must then review and probe some of the principle causes of their rejection of Yeshua as the promised Messiah.

1. **"He came unto his own."** It is said that familiarity breeds contempt. The closer one comes to physical or group relationship, the less likely will be his or her receptivity to unique giftedness or authority. Jesus replies poignantly to this problem, declaring that the people in closest proximity to His life, who knew His family, became offended in Him, because "A prophet is not without honor, save in his own country, and in his own house" (Matt. 13:53-58). Thus, virtually all of the Old Testament (Tanakh) prophets were rejected by their own people, Israel.

2. **He spoke with authority–not as the religious leaders.** When a prophetic voice speaks with perceived authority

unlike the usual religious "truth" and traditional patterns to which people have become accustomed, it creates an inner necessity to choose between uncomfortable truth and comfortable tradition. Since the leaders, referred to more commonly as "the Jews," had their power, perks and position secured in the people's trust in their traditions, conflict was inevitable...and can be seen throughout the Gentile church even today. Most default in favor of comfortable tradition, therefore blinding them to the very truth they so desperately need for revived faith, instruction and correction in righteousness.

3. **He confronted leadership hypocrisy.** Jesus was gentle, compassionate and merciful to the outcast, the simple and the rank-and-file. But Jesus spared no words railing upon the deceptive hypocrisy of the revered religious leaders–the scribes, Pharisees, Sadducees and Sanhedrin–who preserved their religious power over the people by pretense and pride, casting them out of the synagogues if they deigned to believe Jesus as Messiah (Matt. 23; John 9:1-39; John 12:10-11).

4. **He threatened the place of Jewish religious leaders in Roman culture.** Unbeknownst to many, the High Priest was appointed by the secular imperial Rome that the Jews purported to hate. Therefore, the powerful religious and revered leaders of the Jewish people actually played religious politics with Rome and the Roman governor, including King Herod, in order to secure and preserve their ongoing power, perks and position. When wealth and power are at stake, any purported "Messiah" must be dealt with, even to the death. And so, the chief priest and Pharisees called a council after Lazarus was raised from the dead, declaring: "What do we? for this man [Jesus] doeth many miracles." Now listen carefully to their reasoning!

> If we let him thus alone, all men will believe on him: and the Romans shall come and take away both our place and nation (John 11:47-48).

This identical pattern is clearly visible today, not only in Israel, but in the manner in which vast numbers of purported Gentile Christian leaders deal with secular political and cultural powers. Rome still maintains dominion.

5. **"We have no king but Caesar"** (John 19:15). "Give us Barabbas" they cried! Give us a murderer, even a deified emperor, but don't threaten our religious and traditional power...or our denominational retirements.

What Will The Imposter Emulate?

To *emulate* means to imitate, to match or even to surpass. What would be needed for the Deceiver's IMPOSTER to so emulate the Messiah, the Anointed One as to convince people throughout the world to embrace him as a global savior in whom they should trust for meeting their deepest felt needs of the moment while providing their hope for the foreseeable future and beyond? The answer to that haunting question is both scary and somewhat speculative.

The first and most obvious problem in framing a broad answer is to establish...

1. Who the Messiah was to be.
2. For what purpose was He to come?
3. What would He be expected to do?
4. In what fashion would He be presented?
5. With what attitudes and behaviors will he conduct himself?
6. Who would be most expected to gravitate to Him...and why?
7. Does the proffered Messiah match biblical expectations?

Yet, in attempting to answer these threshold questions, we are faced with further difficulty due to the filters of our individual or group viewpoints, some of which are rooted in history, or in tradition, or in religious dogma or in agnosticism and atheism. Furthermore, the 22,000 denominational distinctions among Christians globally, coupled with the various distinctions and emphases among even Jewish peoples, complicate our ability to discern the identity... or even expectation...of a coming Messiah. Added to this confusion, while the majority of Jews (at least in Israel) now believe we are in "The Messianic Age," many who believe in the *Messianic Age* do not expect a physical messiah but rather look for a time of redemptive peace enveloping the world through a kind of global consciousness that unites humankind through *tikkun olam*–a world-wide "redemption" brought about by increasing good works.

The exact nature and extent of the counterfeit messiah's emulations remains unknown and largely speculative, except insofar as clearly revealed in both Old and New Testaments. The following questions may be of varying degrees of interest, yet because there is no defined biblical mandate, the answers remain speculative and non-determinative.

1. **Will the Anti-Messiah be born in Bethlehem?** While the prophet Micah declared that out of Bethlehem "shall he come forth unto me that is to be ruler in Israel," i.e., the Messiah (Micah 5:2), which was confirmed by the chief priest and scribes to Herod in Matt. 2:1-6, no mention is otherwise made in the Bible of the birthplace of Christ's counterfeit. If a proffered counterfeit were confirmed to be born in Bethlehem, would that be conclusive as to his identity? Would Jews be likely or willing to embrace an imposter whose birth could not be verified in Bethlehem, even though Jesus WAS born in Bethlehem?

2. **Will the IMPOSTER have a virgin birth?** This is a fascinating consideration. Most professing Christians consider the virgin birth of Christ to be essential to verify His identity. Yet many Jewish leaders and theologically liberal professing Christians deny a virgin birth, claiming rather that the Messiah was to be born merely to "a young woman" rather than to a virgin.

   Might a "virgin birth" be synthesized or made to appear as if it were true? There seems now to be no end to the plausible extent of digital deception or holographic simulation.

   Yet consider further the global confusion generated by the seeming sudden thrust of Barack Obama into both national and global politics. Who can forget the "birth" issue questioning his birthplace and origin as it related to eligibility for the U.S. presidency that constitutionally mandated a candidate be a "natural born citizen." He claimed to be born in Hawaii, yet Hawaii refused to provide the original birth certificate.

Obama's father was a Kenyan, his kin lived in Kenya as did his grandmother, who claimed he was born in Kenya. Moreover, Michelle Obama, his wife, once spoke of her husband born in Kenya, and the Kenyan nation celebrated that a "son of Kenya" should become president of the most powerful nation on earth. In addition, no social security number issued in Hawaii could identify him, yet he had at least one, if not two, social security numbers issued to him in the East Coast where he never lived. Without arguing the verity of any or all claims regarding Mr. Obama's origin, it should at least reveal how the true origin and birth circumstance of the Anti-Christ could be so camouflaged or even deceptively constructed as to satisfy the masses who will be drawn to other more dramatic and seemingly compelling characteristics.

3. **Will the IMPOSTER experience a resurrection?** This question is a bit more problematic. Since the resurrection of Jesus was and is the centerpiece confirming the Christian faith, his counterfeit may, at least for reasonable speculation or even expectation, appear to experience such a miraculous event.

Only one biblical passage seems to perhaps corroborate such an event, at least insofar as the planet perceives it to take place. That passage is found in Rev. 13:1-9, leaving us wondering as to what explicit occurrence might precipitate such a seemingly miraculous resurrection.

> And I stood...and saw a beast rise up out of
> the sea, having seven heads and ten horns, and
> upon his horns ten crowns, and upon his heads
> the name of blasphemy.

And...the dragon gave him his power, and his
seat, and great authority

And I saw one of his heads as it were wounded
to death; and his deadly wound was healed:
and all the world wondered after the beast.

And they worshipped the dragon which gave
power unto the beast: and they worshipped the
beast, saying, Who is like unto the beast? Who
is able to make war with him?

And he opened his mouth in blasphemy against
God...

If any man have an ear, let him hear.

Is the "beast" a man or is it a political power? Viewpoints
differ. Was, or is, the "deadly wound" a real wound or a
feigned wound? Is it a man who is wounded to the head, or
is it a world power? Has it already occurred as some contend
when Napoleon arrested the Pope, or is it yet to occur? It
would seem to this writer that there is a beast empire, and
there is also a "beast" person who rules or leads that power,
and that the event remains yet to occur.

We are also told that a false prophet will mastermind the
miraculous deceptions that appear to validate the authenticity of the IMPOSTER as the real Messiah (Rev. 13:11-18).

And he doeth great wonders, so that he maketh
fire come down from heaven on the earth in
the sight of men,

And deceiveth them that dwell on the earth by
the means of those miracles...saying...that they
should make an image to the beast, which had
the wound by a sword, and did live.

We are then told that the false prophet, advancing the
dominion and receptivity of the Anti-Christ "beast," will

devise an economic system compelling every person on the planet to receive a mark, thus identifying and confirming allegiance to and trust in the counterfeit christ. That number is said to be "the number of a man" designated as "Six hundred three-score and six" (666) commonly known as *the mark of the beast*, to be avoided at all costs (Rev. 13:16-18).

We will not discuss the issue of "the number," but to identify the "beast," be it a person or an empire–or both– is our present challenge. The seeming miracles will move the masses to belief in a divine origin and character, not considering the serious demonic deception being perpetrated. The world will be won by the "wow factor." Only when favor and authority have been democratically bestowed upon the beast will the demonically-devised economic trap be sprung, ensnaring the unbelieving world together with vast numbers of those who purport to embrace the Christ of God. The testing of true believers will be intense!

Many of the great dictators of history, from Nero and Caligula of Rome, who reigned after Jesus' ministry and resurrection, to Hitler and Stalin of more recent vintage, all of whom viciously persecuted both Jews and Christians, have been labeled with the beast mark, yet none presented the "mark of the beast." From the centuries before the Protestant Reformation, a pervasive conviction began to present the Roman Catholic Church, ensconced in a geopolitical state called the Vatican, as a major player in the final beast empire, claiming the pope to be the counterfeit christ, ruling "the great whore" of "Mystery Babylon" "The Mother of Harlots" (Rev. 17). Indeed, history records the untold millions killed under papal rule, both through ghoulish inquisitions, crusades and other pursuits against those who resisted the diabolical and shockingly dissolute behavior perpetrated by those claiming to be "The Vicar of Christ," turning the Roman See into a veritable brothel.

Suffice it to say, the warning words "He that hath an ear to hear, let him hear" could not have greater significance than in identifying the IMPOSTER at such time as the beast power begins to present itself. If we do not truly trust God revealed in our loving obedience now, how then shall we master such faith when all of the "chips are down"? Truth must always triumph over tradition...beginning today.

4. **Will he be a Jew or Gentile?** Since Yeshua and His disciples were all Jews, it would not be unreasonable to conclude the IMPOSTER will be a Jew. Judas, who betrayed Jesus, was also a Jew, giving even further credence to the possibility the Anti-Christ would likewise be a betraying Jew. But lest such a thought should appear *anti-Semitic*, Jewish people are not alone in either rejecting or betraying Jesus daily. Pastor, priests and popes, as well as most professing followers of Christ, have at some time or other betrayed their alleged trust in the Savior. Yet Judas alone was labeled the "Son of Perdition."

   The prophet Daniel makes an eyebrow-lifting statement regarding the IMPOSTER. "Neither shall he regard the God of his fathers...nor regard any god..." (Dan. 11:37). Some have concluded this to mean this counterfeit is Jewish but refuses to identify with Judaism. It could just as easily be construed, however, that his heritage was profoundly Christian, yet he rejects the Christian faith. In reality, we do not know but can only speculate.

5. **Will he be European or Muslim?** Historically, until very recently, the prevailing view has been that the counterfeit Messiah would emerge out of Europe. Recently, however, a growing minority have theorized that the beast empire and the representative counterfeit "christ" may well be Islamic. Looking at recent Muslim immigration overtaking Europe... even America...perhaps he could be both European and Muslim. But would Jews, under any circumstances, embrace a Muslim "messiah?"

Yet such identification is relatively insignificant in light of all other more definitive characteristics of which we are informed by the Scriptures.

6. **Will his message be one of love?** Absolutely! If not, it would be nearly impossible to deceive most people, especially professing Christians. Yet how could a devious counterfeit messiah preach or present a message of love? The answer may be surprising.

   Love is being "progressively" redefined. The agapè or self-less love of Scripture, as taught and displayed by Yeshua and His disciples, has been radically reformed into an ostensible love defined solely by temporal feelings rather than eternal, biblically-defined faith. Feelings have finally become the recognized final arbiter of truth. And feelings are easily manipulated to achieve intended agendas, even in ministry. But when the manipulation of feelings becomes the chosen machination of demonically cunning men, hell follows closely.

   Beware the advancing lordship of feelings over biblical truth as declared from the lips of Yeshua, His apostles and prophets. When our feelings are choreographed to embrace as an expression of "love" what God says He hates or is an abomination, it will be an amazingly short step to embrace an imposter, redefining the "Anointed One" to appear as a culturally-mandated counterfeit. Thus, the false becomes "real," authenticated by fickle feelings.

   In truth, that step was already taken December 19, 2019, when the new Archbishop of York, appointed by the Church of England and approved by the Queen, blasphemously, yet boldly, stated: "The Bible must yield to the cultural beliefs of contemporary society on matters of sexual behavior." In asserting his spiritual authority as "Father in God" to all of you, he demanded ecclesiastical obedience for a "radical new Christian inclusion." All to which there was much celebration as reported broadly throughout the UK and by wnd. com on December 29, 2019. Should we be shocked when the *Church Times* in the UK described the new blessing of homosexuality in the church as "the beauty of holiness?" (churchtimes.co.uk, Dec. 20, 2019).

Beware the lordship of feelings that betrays biblical truth. "Study to shew thyself approved unto God, a workman that needeth not to be ashamed, **rightly dividing** [discerning and applying] the word of truth" (II Tim. 2:15). When what our Creator has defined as love is culturally renamed "hate speech," and when that which God declares to hate or opposeth is labeled "loving," the IMPOSTER is knocking at the door...perhaps even your door.

Chapter 23

THE "LITTLE HORN"

*"The prophet Daniel was distressed beyond
measure at the revelation of the 'little horn'."*

"BEHOLD, THERE CAME UP...A LITTLE HORN," declared the
prophet Daniel. This "little horn" arose to prominence out of a beast
of ten horns that was "dreadful and terrible," having "great iron teeth"
which devoured and crushed all other powers, and was substantially
different from the three identified world powers or beasts that preceded it, identified respectively as a **lion** (Babylon), a **bear** (Medo-Persia) and a **leopard** (Greece) (Dan. 7:7-8).

The Great Beasts

The prophet Daniel, a captive in Babylon, had a grievous vision
that profoundly troubled him. When the meaning of that vision was
revealed, the "great beasts" he had seen were identified as "four kings
which shall arise" with the fourth beast being "exceeding dreadful" and
"diverse from all the others" having teeth of iron, nails of brass, and
stomping all before it to pieces (Dan. 7:16-19).

That fourth beast has been well-understood to be Rome or the
Roman Empire which ruled the world through its legions with an iron
fist for many centuries, producing what is known as the *Pax Romana*
or world peace under Roman rule. It was that version of "peace"

that prevailed over the then-known world when Yeshua, the "Prince of Peace" was born in Bethlehem, the "City of David," upon whose throne the Messiah was prophesied and destined to reign (Isa. 9:6-7; Luke 2:1-5). While the Roman Empire purportedly "fell" around the fifth century AD, it never disappeared but rather produced replicating progeny throughout what is now known as the West or western world. These Roman "children" became the nations of Europe, the British Empire, the German, French and Spanish Empires and their colonies, culminating in the Americas and the United States of America over which the foundations of Roman law and even architecture rule, including Roman numerals.

It is this Roman "beast" out of which Daniel describes a *little horn* emerging out of ten horns, powers or authorities. While there seems little dispute that the little horn represents the Imposter messiah, much dispute—even radically different viewpoints—exist as to the identity of the ten horns, which seem to correspond to the ten toes, part of iron and part of clay, described by Daniel into which the final beast kingdom will be (or has been) broken (Dan. 2:40-43).

With reference to the ten horns or ten toes, timing seems to be at the root of their identity. Some contend that these ten horns existed before Rome–the fourth beast–emerged as a world power. In that event, one might conclude that Daniel speaks of the ten barbarian tribes which troubled Rome known historically as: Ostrogoths, Visigoths, Franks, Vandals, Suevi, Alamani, Anglo-Saxons, Heruli, Lombardi and Burdundians.

Alternatively, if the ten horns or powers come into existence or authority toward the time of the end, the barbarian tribes of millennia past become, at best, precursors to or triggers of the actual powers referred by Daniel. Looking, then, at the times more immediately preceding the Coming of Messiah, attention was drawn by prophetic voices to the emerging European Union which began as ten nations within the European Common Market. As the EU expanded to 27 nations, now reduced by Brexit to 26, further conjuncture arose as to the identity of these ten toes or horns.

Interestingly, over the seventy years that passed since the earliest advent of the nascent EU, many other such unions have formed throughout the world. These unions have joined, or have been in the birth pangs of forming, such that they collectively encompass most of the nations of earth. As of this writing, there have been at least 15 such unions either formed or in the process of forming, with some seeming to edge toward merging, perhaps thus leaving a total of ten.

On issues such as this, no one (however sure they may purport to be) knows with certainty the actual identity of these ten powers out of which the little horn emerges. We can exercise historical and prophetic conjecture. We can reason with our best spiritual speculation. But in the end, we dare not propose to "die on that hill," but rather agree to form our viewpoints and hold them somewhat loosely in humility of heart.

What, Then, Is The "Little Horn?"

The "little horn" is not *little*, either in history or prophecy. Rather, just as Yeshua HaMashiach, Jesus Christ, was said to be "the express image" of God in the earth (Heb. 1:3), even so the *little horn* will be Satan, the Deceiver's, express image in the earth to draw all human-kind unto himself. The little horn, "speaking great things" (Dan. 7:8), will masquerade as the Master, "having eyes like the eyes of man," as if Satan himself were incarnated in him. Even as Jesus Christ was lifted up by the Father, drawing all men unto Himself through crucifixion on the cross (John 12:32), so the IMPOSTER savior will be "lifted up" among men by powers not his own, drawing the world to himself by "his power [that] shall be mighty" (Dan. 8:24).

This *little horn* emulation of the Messiah does not stop there. Just as Jesus was not married, so Satan's counterfeit will not regard "the desire of women." As Jesus, to the Pharisaical viewpoint, seemed to not "regard the God of his fathers," so the counterfeit messiah will not "regard the God of his fathers," but rather "shall magnify himself above all" (Dan. 11:37). Through his initial appearance as world peacemaker, the IMPOSTER will emulate the "Just One," the Prince of Peace, convincing the multitudes (who then clamor for someone to bring unity to global chaos) that he, if not the promised peacemaker, will fulfill their desperate desires (Dan. 8:25; 11:21) and should be trusted.

It should thus be obvious that even as Jesus Christ was born, lived, died and was resurrected, declared to be the Father's sole hope for and

251

"savior of the world," (John 4:42; Luke 1:47, 2:11; II Tim. 1:9-10), so the Deceiver's counterfeit will be perceived and received as the world's savior and hope.

Just as God the Father ordained and "put all things in subjection under his [Messiah's] feet (Heb. 2:5-9), Satan will claim global dominion through his masquerading messiah, placing virtually "all things" under his feet. Even as the Son, who "made the worlds" as "the brightness of God's glory," "upholds all things by the word of his power" (Heb. 1:1-3), likewise Lucifer will invest the best of his brightness (Ezek. 28:17) in his Son of Perdition, who will deign to dominate the world by the mighty, yet dark and devious words of his delegated power (Dan. 8:23-24).

Darkness for Light

The prophet Daniel was distressed beyond measure at the revelation of the *little horn*. How could that which emerges so "little" fill the entire earth with unprecedented destruction and damnation? After the vision of Satan's little horn emulation of himself, Daniel declared, "I was astonished" and "fainted and was sick certain days," "but none understood it" (Dan. 8:27). The vision was "shut up" or hidden because it was not intended to be revealed or comprehended until "the last end of the indignation: for at the time appointed the end shall be" (Dan. 8:26, 19).

This is that time, friends! And the Father, in His mercy and through His grace, is making manifest the gravity of that which was foretold over 2400 years ago. As it is well said, "To be forewarned is to be forearmed."

We have been forewarned that in these latter days, "...darkness shall cover the earth, and gross darkness the people" (Isa. 60:2). Yeshua made clear the reason, "...men loved darkness rather than light, because their deeds were evil" (John 3:19). Having rejected God's Anointed One sent to be "the light of the world" (John 8:12; John 9:5), both unbelieving Jew and Gentile remain in damning darkness (John 9:39-41; John 3:17-21), and will embrace Lucifer's counterfeit light-bearer.

Yet professing Christians have a profound problem living in an ever-darkening world. And it is we who are warned, since the non-believing world is "condemned already" (John 3:18). For this reason, we must be reminded...again...that ALL of the warnings of Scripture as to deception are directed to purported believers—both Jew and Gentile—not to pagans. Obviously, this recognition does not bring rejoicing to many whose theological notions reject the implications that professing Christians and Orthodox Jews might become damnably deceived. Yet if that were not the case, neither the Prophets, nor Jesus' warnings nor those of Paul, Peter, James and John...nor Jude would have meaning or merit.

Consider soberly Yeshua's words to those who purported to be His true followers...by implication the church today. Are we also subject to be potentially enveloped by and embrace the spirit of darkness that will be revealed through the Deceiver's emissary after his grand global entrance? Here are Jesus' words recorded in Matthew 6:23:

> If therefore the light that is in thee be darkness, how great is that darkness!

These are not idle words to be lightly dismissed. Rather, they imply that notwithstanding our once profession of faith as "children of light," we nevertheless can yield to encroaching darkness, perhaps unsuspectingly, because the drift not only of humanity but of Jews and of the church itself progressively embraces the Hellenizing spirit and values of the world, thus rendering us susceptible to receiving the counterfeit messiah. In spiritual reality, it is precisely this dangerous susceptibility that ultimately determines only a small remnant will be saved, or "enter the strait gate," the "narrow way," which leadeth unto life, and "few there be that find it," (Matt. 7:13-14).

The *little horn* will come in like a lamb, then roar like a lion. Even so Yeshua came in as "the Lamb of God" but shall "roar out of Zion" as the "lion of the Tribe of Judah" (John 1:29; Joel 3:16; Rev. 5:5). Jesus came as "the light of the world" while Lucifer (as purported light) sponsors the prince of darkness– "the prince of this world" (John 12:31). Jesus calls us to embrace Him as Truth by faith, but the little horn gains his global following by fraud and flattery (Dan. 11:21).

All humans are susceptible to respond favorably to flattery. Are you? We have been warned that Flattery lays a snare for our souls (Prov.

26:28; 29:5). Most will be snared or seduced by the IMPOSTER'S flattery. Will you? Genuine faith will be our only victory to overcome the world proffered by the Son of Perdition (I John 5:4).

Chapter 24

DANIEL'S UNVEILING DRAMA

"At that time...there shall be a time of trouble, such as never was since there was a nation" (Dan. 12:1).

NO DESCRIPTION OF THE IMPOSTER is more detailed, nor more dramatic, than that revealed to and through the prophet Daniel's various and disturbing visions of our future. But why Daniel? Did he have some special favor with God such that the God of the universe could entrust him with the most profound revelation of the Son of Perdition who, through a majestic beast empire, would rule the world as a counterfeit messiah, a consummate betrayer of the Messiah himself? The answer is a resounding "Yes," but why?

Daniel's Unique Favor

Daniel, from God's viewpoint, was unique among the sons of men. In a generic sense, we are all unique before God, having special purpose and calling. Yet Daniel was a man set apart from others in the mind and heart of God. He was a man whom HaShem was convinced could be trusted with one of the greatest, most solemn and serious revelations that would have profound impact on humanity, particularly in the season of prophetic history leading to the End of the Age and the Coming of Messiah.

While God is no respecter of persons in a broad sense, we all having joyful access to the Father by His Spirit through forgiveness of sins and a walk of righteousness (Acts 10:34-35), there are nevertheless those whom God has identified throughout history who enjoyed unusual favor, apparently due to their greater sacrificial devotion to His Kingdom and to their greater willingness to surrender to the Word and Will of the Father – to hear His voice and to obey despite the cost.

We find, then, that Daniel, a Hebrew young man having been taken captive to pagan Babylon, a godless and sinful culture, nevertheless remained wisely true to his deeply-rooted convictions, revealing an unusual means of applied faith (to which we are all called, but from which most fall short). While deeply righteous in his own ways, he purposed to identify himself with the devastating sin of his own nation (Judah) that was bringing the Father's judgment upon them. And so, he prayed perhaps the greatest identificational prayer of Scripture which is found in Daniel 9, declaring...

> We have sinned, and have committed iniquity, and have
> done wickedly, and have rebelled, even by departing from thy
> precepts and from thy judgments.
>
> Neither have we hearkened unto thy servants the prophets...
> O Lord, to us belongeth confusion of face, to our kings,
> to our princes, and to our fathers, because we have sinned
> against thee.
>
> Neither have we obeyed the voice of the LORD our God to
> walk in his laws....
>
> Yea, all Israel have transgressed thy law, even by departing,
> that they might not obey thy voice; therefore the curse is
> poured upon us....
>
> As it is written...all this evil is come upon us (Deut. 28), yet
> made we not our prayer before the LORD our God, that we
> might turn from our iniquities, and understand thy truth.

It is instructive that while Daniel was humbly speaking this profound prayer, the angel Gabriel touched him and informed him saying, "I am now come forth to give thee skill and understanding" concerning the earlier vision, "for thou art greatly beloved: therefore understand the matter, and consider the vision" (Dan. 9:21-23).

Perhaps we should consider well the faithful foundation upon which the Father declared Daniel "greatly beloved." It could well change our own lives as we delve more deeply into the devious deception and destruction coming upon we denizens of earth. Yet the full tale of Daniel's status with God, the revealer of secrets, has not been told.

God warned Israel by the mouth of the prophet Ezekiel what was required for them to recover favor with the Father. Three times God declared Daniel to be one of the three most righteous men in history. Yet He warned, "Though Noah, Daniel and Job were in it, as I live, saith the Lord GOD, they shall deliver neither son nor daughter; they shall but deliver their own souls by their righteousness" (Ezek. 14:12-20).

Favor is born of profound faith revealed in righteous obedience to the Word, Will and Ways of the Father. It is here that we receive grace to both endure and find victory amid the vast betrayal ahead. We must, in the simple words of a song deeply ingrained in my childhood memory:

DARE to be a Daniel;
DARE to stand alone;
DARE to have a purpose firm, and
DARE to make it known.

Daniel's Disclosure Dilemma

Imagine for a moment having been given by God a detailed glimpse into the world's future up to the very time of history's final hour, yet being frustrated by the failure to have the exact timing and full implications disclosed. Consider Daniel's final words, revealing that he was to be left without full comprehension of the shocking visions committed in trust to him by HaShem, the Lord of Creation and history.

> And I heard, but understood not: then said I, O my Lord, what shall be the end of these things (Dan 12:8)?

God responded, not with further revelation but by declaring there would be no further disclosure, either for Daniel's understanding or for him to deliver to those who would read his written words of prophetic warning.

> And he [God] said, Go thy way, Daniel: for the words are closed up and sealed till the time of the end.

> But go thou thy way till the end be: for thou shalt rest, and stand in thy lot at the end of the days (Dan. 12:9, 13).

If the words from the Father were "closed up and sealed till the time of the end," what more are we then to glean from what was given? Although much has already been unveiled in earlier chapters, here we take a further look, seeking to digest that which has been disclosed, following the trajectory of prophetic history culminating in our times...the latter days of the last days...progressing inexorably toward the soon-coming Day of the Lord.

Further information alone, differently packaged, may be ever so interesting, yet surely the heart of the Father was and is more importantly for our transformation in the advancing trials and tribulations accompanying the appearance of the IMPOSTER. To this end, we revisit Daniel on his visionary journey, seeking to apply the dramatic revelations to this decisive moment when you and I must make decisions for destiny.

The Drama That Demands Decision

We must now explore the decisive themes that arise from Daniel's various visions and their prophetic implications for each of us and for a collective people who call themselves by the name of the Lord.

DOMINION WILL BE DOMINANT

Make no mistake! Satan's goal is to take dominion over the entire earth...beginning with you. That has been his declared intention from the time of his rebellion in the heavenlies and will be his final move to become *KING of the Mountain* of God, i.e., the Temple Mount, and to be ruler of the "mount" of your heart, your body being "the temple of the Holy Spirit" (I Cor. 6:19; I Pet. 2:5; Isa. 14:12-14; Ezek. 28:14-17). (Note: For deeper understanding of Satan's amazing end-time battle to become *KING of the Mountain*, see this author's book of that title published by Elijah Books, ©2013).

This prophesied dominion drama began in the Garden of Eden with Adam forfeiting earth's dominion to the Deceiver by equivocating, through human reason, with God's simple command by means of Satan's fleshly seduction (Gen. 3:1-13). The Deceiver's desperate attempt to seize final world power as a pseudo-religious authority will arise with the false enlightenment of the IMPOSTER who will ultimately claim the throne of Messiah in the temple of God (II Thess. 2:3-4).

This prophesied trajectory of world dominion was first revealed to Daniel by means of the great colossal statue (Dan. 2). Babylon, being the head of gold, descended to the Medo-Persian empire, followed by the Grecian empire, and culminated in the iron fist of the never-fully-disappeared Roman empire. This battle for dominion is ultimately for the souls of men, culminating in the "everlasting dominion" of Messiah Yeshua "which shall not pass away" (Dan. 7:13-14). Those embraced in Messiah Yeshua's dominion will be only those who have not submitted to the IMPOSTER's deceptive dominion. Such as do wickedly in "forsaking the holy covenant" shall the counterfeit christ "corrupt by flatteries" but, praise God, "the people who do know their God shall be strong, and do exploits" (Dan. 11:30-32).

DIVERSITY CAN BE DREADFUL

The fourth great beast of Daniel's colossal vision was described as "diverse from all others, exceeding dreadful..." (Dan. 7:19). This beast – the final great world power manifested in the vision – is most commonly identified as Rome. And it is further described as "dreadful and terrible, and strong exceedingly...." It had...and has... "great iron teeth," "devouring and breaking in pieces" and again "diverse from all beasts that were before it," having "ten horns" (Dan. 7:7). It is then out of this unprecedented *diversity* that the little horn or counterfeit messiah begins to come forth to rule as Satan's ultimate emissary over planet earth.

The word *diverse* means "showing a great deal of variety or difference." Never in history has the word *diverse* or *diversity* had greater prominence or popularity. In truth, the word *diversity* has become the central pillar of political correctness, multiculturalism and religious pluralism. It is a new cultural moniker purporting to describe the ideal and ultimate social and cultural milieu for global unity and peace. It is the perceived and promoted roadmap for utopian government that conveniently disregards the biblically-described sinful human nature that defies unity in diversity and renders the final historical representation of Rome so "dreadful," "terrible" and "devouring?" Its governmental foundation and popular presentation is neither monarchy nor dictatorship. Rather, it is the final expression of man's best effort to rule or govern – not by a single individual, whether king or self-exalted revolutionary dictator – but by the people, in their diversity, commonly known as *democracy*.

The very nature of unfettered democracy is the profound danger that the so-called diversity of people, when banded together without restraint, will ultimately manifest in a horrific dictatorship destroying all others not aligned with the purported majority. So dangerous was such pure democracy deemed to be by America's founding fathers that it was feared and warned to be potentially the most dangerous of all forms of government.

What form of government was America then given at its Constitutional Convention? In the words of Benjamin Franklin – "A republic, madam, if you can keep it." A republic is a democratic form of government protected insofar as possible from majority and godless tyranny by a series of checks and balances that would maximize the security of life, liberty and happiness for all. Yet even under such secular precautionary protections, they were still deemed to be inadequate due to the understood deeply-rooted sinful nature of mankind. For that reason, John Adams, America's second president, well stated: "Our government was made for a moral and religious [understood to mean Christian] people, and is wholly inadequate to the government of any other." Robert Winthrop warned: "We will either be governed by a power within or by a power without; either by the Bible or by the bayonet."

Perhaps shockingly to our sensibilities, since the early 1960s America's peoples have been gradually and insidiously rejecting the protections of the republic, instead progressively embracing pure democracy, casting all caution to the wind in pursuit of absolute, unfettered power. Having rejected "the God who made and preserved us a nation," we have rejected the fundamental notion of the innate sinfulness that troubles us all, resorting to a politically-correct conviction that humankind is fundamentally good – hence no longer needing the checks and balances provided by a republic of God-fearing people.

Interestingly, Rome **WAS** a republic that shed its republican protections in favor of a man exalted democratically to the status of emperor who ultimately clothed himself in deity, assuming public worship as the *Pontifex Maximus*, the complete merger of civil government and religious authority. This title and identical authority was then transferred, as the Roman Empire declined, to the Bishop of the Roman Catholic Church, which under the precepture of the Vatican, the world's smallest city-state, now claims to rule over all governments of the world as Pontifex Maximus, more commonly known as the Pontiff. Yet it all began as a democratic republic.

It should not then take undue brilliance to discern the immense danger lurking in the unfettered power of a godless democracy of globally diverse peoples to impose their will on the planet by democratically elevating a counterfeit savior to global power through political flattery and glorious promises. When the world's democratically established ten powers or "horns" then repose their ultimate authority in a charismatic leader, the "little horn," for global peace and security, all protection will have been forfeited on the wings of a false faith.

Daniel describes that "little horn" as, again, being *diverse* from the ten powers that delegate their authority to him for world redemption (Dan. 7:24). When this IMPOSTER'S power is secured, he begins to reveal his identity through his modus operandi. "He shall speak great words against the most High, and shall wear out the saints of the most high..." (Dan. 7:25). All of this shall be done under the progressively established authority of democratic diversity...without God.

The progressive and unremitting call for diversity throughout the western world, in the name of democracy, is a prescription for end-time destruction. Beware its bitter betrayal!

DELEGATION DETERMINES AUTHORITY

The IMPOSTER will not gain dominion authority in the earth by his own power (Dan. 8:24). Rather, his ultimately dictatorial power will be the end result of progressive democracy that empowers ten regional powers which divest themselves of real power and delegate their power and authority, by faith, with the desperate expectation that the charismatic counterfeit messiah will bring peace on earth and temporal salvation. In reality, it is Satan who facilitates this delegation which will determine planetary destiny.

DELEGATION OF POWER IS DEMONIC

The progressive delegation of world power, first to "ten horns," by demonically-informed democracy, will then culminate by demonically-inspired delegation to Satan's personal representative who will rule the planet and its peoples dictatorially "for a time and times and the dividing of time" (Dan. 7:24-25). The apostle Paul (Rabbi Sha'ul) refers to him as "that Wicked," "...whose coming is after the work of Satan with all power and signs and lying wonders" (II Thess. 2:8-9). Many...no most...will believe and will be betrayed by his unholy inspiration, but why? The answer is clear, but greatly troubling.

DEVIOUS ACTIONS–DECEITFUL ATTITUDES

Actions proceed from attitudes and beliefs. As it is written, as a man "thinketh in his heart, so is he" (Prov. 23:7). Even so, Daniel describes the coming IMPOSTER as "working deceitfully" (Dan. 11:23). He will gain power and dominion through pretense and false promises, coming in ostensibly as a purveyor of peace (Dan. 11:21-24). He will enter into the world's most infamous league or covenant, only with intent to ultimately break it as soon as his intended purpose is achieved, giving him unprecedented dominion over "the glorious land" deeded as an eternal leasehold by God to the physical descendants of Abraham, Isaac and Jacob (Gen. 15:18, 17:7-8). And having secured the land, he "shall divide the land for gain," and in his final act of demonic dominion, fulfill Satan's declared goal of establishing his own worship on the Temple Mount, declaring himself "God." As it is written, "And he shall plant the tabernacles of his palace between the seas in the glorious holy mountain" (Dan. 11:39, 45). "...he shall exalt himself... above every god, and shall speak marvelous things against the God of gods..." (Dan. 11:36).

> Who opposeth and exalteth himself above all that is called
> God, or that is worshipped; so that he as God sitteth in the
> temple of God, shewing himself that he is God (II Thess. 2:4).

DELUSION YIELDS DAMNATION

This wholly attractive and compelling incarnation of Satan's rebellious heart seduces the planet, its peoples, and its governmental and religious authorities "with all deceivableness of unrighteousness... because they receive not the love of the truth...."

> And for this cause God shall send them strong delusion [a
> reprobate mind as in Rom. 1] that they should believe a lie:

> That they all might be damned who believed not the truth,
> but had pleasure in unrighteousness (II Thess. 2:9-12).

DEPARTING AND DESTRUCTION

Departing and consequential destruction; both temporal and eternal, are key elements of all Last Days' wooings and warnings. Yet they are seldom addressed by rabbi, pastor or priest. Why might this be? Perhaps we are just not prepared to receive or respond to this infinitely loving, yet sobering, message. It is, however, an integral part of Daniel's' prophetic message, both as to Jew and Gentile professing "believers" and as to the Son of Perdition.

As to the Son of Perdition, we are told "...and he shall do that which his fathers have not done, nor his father's fathers..." (Dan. 11:24). "Neither shall he regard the God of his fathers, nor the desire of women, nor regard any god: for he shall magnify himself above all" (Dan. 11:37). Somehow, despite all of this dramatic departing, he shall "increase with glory" (Dan. 11:39). This increase in glory would seem to reflect the pervasive receptivity of the planet's people to his rebellious departing demeanor and decisions.

Some educated speculation may be required in an attempt to comprehend these generalized descriptions of *departing*.

1. How shall the IMPOSTER depart from the God of his fathers? The answer requires understanding as to who his "fathers" are, followed by understanding who the "God" of his fathers is normally identified to be. The answers to these questions are not clearly given, either by Daniel or by the writers in the Old and New Testaments. The most likely educated conjecture is that the IMPOSTER will be either Jew, or Gentile Christian...or perhaps both, thus placing him by heritage within the ambit of Jesus Christ and His followers. Some now even suggest he may be Muslim, but such heritage would be profoundly difficult for any Jew or Christian to identify as counterfeiting the messiah. So great will be the IMPOSTER's departure that "he shall do that which his fathers have not done, nor [even] his father's fathers. That is a glaring defection which should be clearly evident to any sincere spiritual observer who is rooted in Scripture.
2. The IMPOSTER shall not regard "the desire of women." The clear implication here is that the counterfeit messiah is a man. It would also seem clear that this man is either homosexual, transsexual or simply has no active desire for relationship with the opposite sex...either because of no internal drawing or attraction or because of a religious prohibition, i.e., a celibate priest or pope under vow, as supposedly married to Christ.

The dramatic departure of the IMPOSTER as disclosed by Daniel reveals that this deceiver is either seriously opened to demonic influence or has already given sway to such controlling influence. In either case, he becomes dangerous to the point of unholy desperation to grasp his destiny, taking all living with him.

DEVOURING WITH DETERMINATION

Daniel aptly describes the IMPOSTER as "a vile person" (Dan. 11:21). The word *vile* is a horrific characterization implying moral debasement, pure wickedness and unadulterated despicableness. Only such a person, the veritable incarnation of Satan himself, could wreak such destruction and havoc in the earth as will soon come and is already becoming manifest.

After appearing peaceable, he will work deceitfully, and gradually then "stir up his power and courage" against resisting powers, even the "king of the south" – perhaps aggregated Muslim forces (Dan. 11:23-25). Finally, he shall "have indignation against the holy covenant" and shall conspire "with them that forsake the holy covenant," thus enabling him to "enter into the glorious land [Israel]," causing "many countries to be overthrown" (Dan. 11:30, 41). (Note: Some believe such is a description of Antiochus Epiphanes who died in 165 BC, whose name meant "God Manifest" and who, in a rage, desecrated the Jewish Temple. It is the conviction of this writer, however, and many others, that Antiochus was only a type of the coming Anti-Christ or counterfeit messiah).

So great will be the determination of this deceiving "prince of peace" that nothing will seem to deter him in his frenetic pursuit of absolute world dominion on behalf of his "boss," Satan–the Deceiver. As Daniel earlier foretold, the fourth beast (Rome) out of which the "little horn" counterfeit messiah emerges, will be "exceeding dreadful" and will "devour, break in pieces, and stamp the residue with his feet" (Dan. 7:19). In fact, it "shall devour the whole earth, and shall tread it down, and break it in pieces" (Dan. 7:23).

This terrifying, devouring destruction will be unprecedented on this planet. "And at that time...there shall be a time of trouble such as never was since there was a nation" warned Daniel (Dan. 12:1). Jesus reiterated this warning just two days before His crucifixion.

When ye therefore shall see the abomination of desolation, spoken of by Daniel the prophet, stand in the holy place...

Then shall be great tribulation, such as was not since the beginning of the world to this time, no, nor ever shall be (Matt. 24:15-21).

OUR DESOLATIONS AND DELIVERANCE

In the midst of Daniel's dire prophetic drama, he breaks to lament the spiritual condition of God's own people. It is one of the greatest prayers to be found in all of Scripture, in which he declares "We have sinned...and have rebelled, even by departing from thy precepts and from thy judgments: Neither have we hearkened unto thy servants the prophets...." "Neither have we obeyed the voice of the LORD our God...." (Dan. 9:3-10).

Daniel laments that Israel, God's chosen people, were experiencing seventy years of "desolations" due to their rebellion. And he cried out to the Lord, "...because for our sins, and for the iniquities of our fathers, Jerusalem and thy people are become a reproach to all that are about us" (Dan. 9:16). In the same way, America, the professing church in America and throughout the so-called "Christian West" or "Christian Europe" have sorely departed, rebelled and disobeyed the Father's Word. And as if that were not enough, we have refused to hearken [listen to and respond] to the wooings and warnings that God, in His mercy, has sent over the last generation to call us to repentance.

Both Jew and Gentile now face the moment of truth, both individually and collectively, as families, congregations, denominations and nations. Time is truly short! Our only hope is in our heart-broken repentance and in the Father's mercy (Dan. 9:17-18). It is not only Daniel but the spirit of Elijah that now implores us to "Prepare the Way of the Lord" (Isa. 40:3-4; Matt. 3:3; Mal. 4:5-6).

Our deliverance in these desperate times lies not now in Daniel's prayer, but in ours, for God has no grandchildren. Even while massive persecution arises in the raging scourge of the Imposter to "destroy the mighty and the holy people" (Dan. 8:24), even so the humbly repentant people who are walking in righteousness and holiness......

266

"people that do know their God [as did Daniel] shall be strong and do exploits" (Dan. 11:32).

Even in the "time of trouble, such as never was since there was a nation," "thy people [true and faithful believers in Messiah Yeshua, both Jew and Gentile] shall be delivered, every one that is found written in the book."

> Many of them that sleep in the dust of the earth shall awake, some to everlasting life, and some to shame and everlasting contempt.
>
> And they that be wise shall shine as the brightness of the firmament; and they that turn many to righteousness as the stars for ever and ever (Dan. 12:1-3).

PART 7

THE UNVEILING
OF MESSIAH

A VEIL PARTIALLY OBSCURES, conceals or disguises that which is under the veil. While in various religions and cultural practices, veils have been expected to be worn as a sign of respect or reverence, veils have also been used to cover unusual or very special items not yet ready to be introduced for public identification or recognition. Such products or artistic creations initially veiled before being introduced include paintings, sculptures and even new models of automobiles. Even serious announcements are veiled in advance.

The purpose of such preliminary veiling is twofold:

1. To garner attention before the official unveiling; and
2. To preserve and protect the specific identity of the item before the appropriate time of its revelation by unveiling.

For these same reasons, the clear identity of Messiah has remained a relative mystery over the ages, waiting for the propitious moment of the unveiling. The Bible itself, throughout its pages, whether in the Torah, Prophets, or even the Wisdom literature, as well as in the

Gospels and Epistles, speaks repeatedly of the existence of such messianic veiling. The Torah makes clear HaShem's (God's) demand that the Holy of Holies in the Tabernacle (later in the Temple by implication) be obscured, shrouded and divided by a veil or (vail) so as to make clear the difference between the holy and the profane—between man's realm and the holiness of God and His mercy. Thus, the Holy of Holies remained profoundly mysterious to Israel.

The Gospels maintain that "the veil of the temple was rent in twain from the top to the bottom" amid a great earthquake at the time of Yeshua's death, thus removing the veil and opening the way more clearly in access to God as Father through the veil of the crucified flesh of Christ, anointed by HaShem for that precise purpose (Matt. 27:51; II Cor. 3:14). In the same passage, Rabbi Shaul (Paul) explains of Israel that "remaineth the same vail untaken away in the reading of the old testament; which vail is done away in Christ. Nevertheless when it [Israel] shall turn to the Lord, the vail shall be taken away" (II Cor. 3:13-16).

Yet it is not Israel only that remains in a veiled position, but Gentile believers in Christ also, for the same Rabbi Shaul proclaimed: "For now we see through a glass, darkly…" (I Cor. 13:12).

Prophetic Veiling

The expectation and identity of a future Messiah was periodically revealed by and through veiled revelations of Israel and Judah's ancient prophets. Such ancient prophetic foretellings, however, seemingly vague, do not resonate with significant historical manifestations through the religious heritage of other religions, but only for those of Jewish or Christian faith. While Muslims claim a coming Mahdi, a type of messiah as the "twelfth Imam," their expectation is radically inconsistent with and diverse from virtually all descriptions of or biblical reference to the nature, character and purpose of a coming Messiah.

The first such veiled prophecy is found in Genesis 3:15, where HaShem declares to the serpent, a type of Satan:

And I will put enmity between thee and the woman, and between thy seed and her seed; it shall bruise thy head, and thou shalt bruise his heel.

This veiled prophecy was followed perhaps a millennium later by a covenantal promise by God to Noah through whom He had saved humanity from total destruction.

> And God spake unto Noah, and to his sons with him, saying,
> And I, behold, I establish my covenant with you, and with
> your seed after you (Gen. 9:8-9).

Interestingly, Noah was not a Hebrew but a descendant of Adam, of whom both Jew and Gentile are descendants. Therefore, the covenant was generic to all of Adam's descendants—all who have inherited Adam's sin nature of rebellion against HaShem's authority. How and when, then, do the Hebrew people, later called Jews and Israel, embrace and claim the flow of messianic prophecy and expectation through their own heritage? The answer is found in Abram, whom God re-named Abraham.

The foundation of "Jewish" messianic faith began with the Lord's prophetic call to Abram in Genesis 12:1-7, calling Abram to leave his father's house, originally in Ur of the Chaldees, and to go "unto a land that I will show thee." Then came the prophetic promise.

> And I will make of thee a great nation, and I will bless thee…
> and thou shalt be a blessing: And I will bless them that bless
> thee, and curse them that curse thee: and in thee shall all
> families of the earth be blessed (Gen. 12:2-3).

That promise was reiterated in part in Genesis 15, including now a covenant of land, the metes and bounds of which are defined broadly in Genesis 15:18, a land now referred to as *Eretz Yisrael* or "the land of Israel," and ultimately after the time of Moses as "the Promised Land."

God then revealed more explicitly that this Abrahamic covenant was to be actually two-fold—a covenant of land as "an everlasting possession" (Gen. 17:8) but also a greater spiritual covenant.

> As for me, behold, my covenant *is* with thee, and thou shalt
> be a father of many nations.

Neither shall thy name any more be called Abram, but thy name shall be Abraham; for a father of many nations have I made thee (Gen. 17:4-5).

Although God reiterated His covenant running with the land (v. 8), He made clear that the greater and more eternal covenant was a spiritual covenant "between me and thee and thy seed after thee in their generations **for an everlasting covenant, to be a God unto thee, and to thy seed after thee**" (emphasis added) (Gen. 17:7). That covenant was ultimately to be confirmed in the birth of Isaac as "an everlasting covenant" (Gen. 17:19-21).

Yet again the Lord made clear the extent of this Abrahamic covenant to not only make of Abraham a great nation but "all nations of the earth shall be blessed in him" (Gen. 18:18). Three times that greater spiritual theme is repeated to extend beyond Abraham's physical descendants to "many nations" and "all families of the earth."

Thus the prophetic veil is opened sufficiently to reveal God's plan and purpose that, while now for a time invested in physical descendants, the greater purpose will be manifested throughout the nations. It is here that the seed of the messianic vision and hope is sown through prophetic expectation.

The looming question then hovers over our human discernment of the spiritual covenant. Surely for a time it resides in and through Abraham, Isaac and his son Jacob, whose name was changed to Israel (Gen. 32:28). Indeed, the covenant of land and the spiritual covenant of blessing was affirmed by HaShem both to Isaac (Gen. 26:24) and to Jacob (Gen. 28:3-4; Gen. 35:10-12).

Truly the entire Torah and Tanakh present the ongoing call of God to Israel, then Ephraim and Judah, to trust and obey Him as the ongoing foundation for the fulfillment of the promised blessing to the physical descendants of Abraham. But what of the nations? What of the gentile families of the earth?

With limited human vision and discernment, rabbis have concluded that gentiles can only claim Abrahamic "blessing" by blessing Israel and keeping the "Noahide Laws." Yet there are many further prophetic references throughout the Jewish Prophets implying, if not outright declaring, a further and greater unveiling of the messianic mystery. These present such unique challenges to rabbinic thinking that unusual interpretive gymnastics have been employed as well as outright exclusion from public reading to avoid dealing with obviously messianic passages and prophecies in the Tanakh or Old Testament.

The Messianic Age

If indeed, as both rapidly exploding expectations of Jew and Gentile reveal, we have entered the Messianic Age, it would seem to behoove all peoples to seriously re-consider the evidence of a coming Messiah as well as the identity and purpose of His coming. Obviously, all cannot be right, yet maintain radically divergent viewpoints. Perhaps we have now encountered our global moment of truth in the "valley of decision." As declared the prophet Joel…

Multitudes, multitudes in the valley of decision: for the day of the LORD *is* near in the valley of decision (Joel 3:14).

Chapter 25

IF GOD IS DEAD...?

"...mankind is preemptively taking His place..."

"IS GOD DEAD? Asked *TIME* magazine on the cover of its historically provocative issue of April 8, 1966. The public response of 3,500 letters to the editor became the largest response to any one story in the magazine's history. So...to reiterate the question a half century later, is God dead? If so, did He ever live? Similarly, if He is dead or dying, with what or whom will He be replaced, since it is a truism that "Nature abhors a vacuum."

The Test of Time

It is often said that "time heals all wounds," but it is also said that "time answers all things." In other words, if we are patient and wait long enough, answers to plaguing, paralyzing or provocative questions will eventually be answered. The obvious problem with our actual acceptance of this time test is that our lives are clearly finite, and individually we may not live to see the ultimate answer.

This conundrum was implicit in the final album of the British Beatles who once declared "We are more popular than God." Obviously, popularity itself does not provide the answers to the deep issues of life, yet often reflects them. And so, the Beatles announced...or reiterated in their 50th anniversary celebration a claim they asserted fifty years earlier in their career-capping album "Let It Be." The lyrics and tune were somewhat haunting and even prophetic. "There will be an answer, Let it be." And if God is dead, will there be a messiah?

As the Beatles "prophesied," "When broken-hearted people, Living in the world agree, There will be an answer, Let it be." But how broken-hearted and yearning must the planet's people be before the elusive answer becomes a reality. And will people embrace a counterfeit in haste to bring a temporarily satisfying "answer"?

The writer of Ecclesiastes declared that "time and chance happeneth to all" (Eccl. 9:11), but it also is true that *time* and *choice* are available to all as well. And time is very telling! Where we fail to seize the choices that time affords, they pass us by, and we wonder, as sang the Pozo-Seco Singers with the classic lyrics penned by Don Williams:

Time, oh time, where did you go?
Time, oh good, good time where did you go?

The popular tunes of the West from the early 1960s to the mid-1970s passionately expressed the pathos of an era that revealed the abandonment of hope in God and the expectation of a messiah. Life began to look bleak, as the Kingston Trio lamented, "Where have all the flowers gone?" "When will they ever learn" (Lyrics penned in 1955 by Pete Seeger).

It should be increasingly obvious that a people and generation that lose their hope in God will incur a vast array of unintended consequences. Again, the songs of the era revealed the resort to drugs as a counterfeit savior from the pain of increasing hopelessness, a pattern that now pervades the entire Western world in the children and grandchildren of God-forsaking darkness.

The lyrics do not lie! The Beatles released "Nowhere Man" December 3, 1965. The shear hopelessness pervading a vacuum of messianic hope is painfully unmistakable.

He's a real nowhere man
Sitting in his nowhere land
Making all his nowhere plans for nobody.

Doesn't have a point of view
Knows now where he's going to
Isn't he a bit like you and me?

Perhaps the famed Simon and Garfunkel of the same broad era were more prophetic than they even realized when they sang...

The words of the prophets
Are written on the subway walls
And tenement halls
And whispered in the sounds of silence

Time Marches On

The *New York Times* was not to be left out of the God-abandoning cry of the times. "God is dead, and religion is dying" the paper proclaimed.[1] The test of time marches on unabated.

The *Times* referenced Malachi Martin, the former Jesuit priest and professor at the Pontifical Biblical Institute in Rome, who wrote *The Encounter*. He asserted that "Modern man is deciding...he can rely upon his scientific outlook, that he can best provide for his earthly salvation by...accepting differences without making the binary moral judgments of former times."

Therefore, our modern—now post-modern—times have shifted dramatically from a view toward eternal salvation to a temporal salvation "coordinated by the efforts of mathematicians, economists, engineering managers, social scientists, sociologists and public administrators." Martin warns, "something is shaking the human race."[2]

Clearly, if God is dead or dying, mankind is preemptively taking His place, building his case for self-salvation from Darwin's *Origin of Species* and *Descent of Man* to a soon-to-be-revealed New World Order. The march of time seems to be inevitably leading to a progressive and accelerating abandonment of genuine spiritual messianic pursuit to the wholesale embrace of scientific materialism counterbalanced by a corresponding messianic search, however vague or passionate it may be. A great chasm or vacuum of hope now widens in a world increasingly desperate for answers in which we believe.

Filling the Vacuum

It is no mystery that "Nature abhors a vacuum." What remains a "mystery" is what will be deemed in the human mind and heart to fill the obvious void. And the yearning to fill that void is growing exponentially, resulting in massive pressures on all earthly pursuits that will, if one accepts the biblical trajectory of history, result in a time of unprecedented global pressure both on man's spirit and on his social environment increasingly defined by the lordship of scientism. That time of pressure will, as with all unrelieved pressure, result in global explosion of which the French Revolution is but a minor harbinger. The English translation of that time (*thlipsis* in the Greek) is preceded by increasing "tribulation" for a period of years. Are you feeling or sensing it yet?

The spiritual vacuum will be, and is now being, filled. To the extent that God is, for all meaningful or practical purposes, "dead" or "dying" in your life, whether or not you perceive it, that void is being willfully filled with alternative hopes and "messianic" expectations. Those expectations are, whether or not we want to admit it, inbred in the very nature of man, and are inevitably defining destiny, whether for Jew or Gentile.

Our times are demanding resolution. The real test of time will be determined by how and if each person resolves the issue of Messiah— the mystery of the ages. It is the ultimate time to choose.

As again made clear by the ancient Hebrew prophet, Joel:

Multitudes, multitudes in the valley of decision: for the day of the LORD is near in the valley of decision (Joel 3:14).

Chapter 26

THE VALLEY OF DECISION

*"The ultimate moment of testing and
trial is rapidly approaching. It is at the door."*

DECISIONS DETERMINE DESTINY! And decisions are the product of our viewpoints, which inevitably set the course for further decisions which, if unchanged, lead either to a desirable or grossly undesirable end.

Our human dilemma is that we are either ignorant of or blinded to the consequential nature of our decisions in the moment. And those decisions in the progressive moments of our lives, over time, set a trajectory that propels us toward a destiny that, without serious course corrections, cannot be altered. For that reason, it behooves us to review the varied messianic viewpoints that are defining that destiny for the masses of humanity.

As the Trial Draws Near…

It may seem strange that a former veteran trial attorney should plead such a case as this. Yet in reality, in the context of the fulness of time which we are rapidly approaching, this "unveiling of the mystery of the ages" becomes the case of a lifetime before a jury of human peers, regardless of nationality, race or cultural heritage.

The stakes are high, beyond most human comprehension, because the choices we make regarding Messiah are consequential beyond mere human imagination limited to earth, chance and time. Those choices and decisions are actually defining a spiritual destiny that endures, whether or not admitted, beyond earth, time and space that, for now, commands our attention. The time for consideration and weighing of evidence is wrapping up and the time for trial is rapidly approaching.

The trial attorney takes a case with a preliminary consideration of the facts as then understood, together with an initial evaluation of the likelihood of prevailing, before the jury. But there are always at least two sides that must be considered. That is true in both civil and criminal cases. It is also true of the case regarding Messiah. In fact, as we have seen, the viewpoints are many and varied. Yet is there evidence that demands a verdict? Or, can we comfort ourselves persisting in our individual or collective divergent "beliefs"?

Enter, then, the looming date of trial before the judge in an eternal courtroom, where time and eternity collide. As cases, whether civil or criminal, proceed over time through the process of evidentiary discovery, the parties increasingly solidify their positions as to what the evidence will prove. A kind of positional hubris grows as their lawyers jockey for position to best present their cases. But as the time of trial grows near, the parties and their attorneys are compelled of necessity to re-evaluate the strength of their respective beliefs and positions.

The parties must increasingly consider that the real issue is not just what I believe but what the judge or jury believes based upon the evidence. Does the evidence upon which I rely actually DEMAND a favorable verdict? Or is the evidence weak, suggesting a serious re-evaluation of my position, considering the risks of being wrong and losing the case?

Consider then the consequences. Perhaps you have devoted years to a particular position and have framed a lifetime of expectations based upon supposed "evidence" that, when truly considered, is neither fully persuasive nor capable of fulfilling developed expectations. And the risks attendant to trial are looming, resulting in a growing uncertainty. Will I persist in promoting my viewpoint as persuasive, or will I seek to settle or resolve the matter based upon a more realistic or persuasive position in consideration of the mounting evidence?

In light of potential eternal consequences, this is the dilemma faced by our planet and its peoples with regard to the mystery of Messiah, because the ultimate moment of testing and trial is rapidly approaching. It is at the door to the valley of decision. And, at least from a biblical perspective, there is a judge who will decide the case. The decisive question then hovers over our lives as time and eternity move inevitably toward congruency. Will my viewpoint regarding Messiah prevail, and if not, what will be the consequences?

Perhaps it would be well, under such looming "trial" pressure to review the evidence or beliefs upon which I rely, or upon which my religious or cultural group relies. Where do they lead? If there be a final judge, without resort to appeal, what would such a judge be likely to conclude notwithstanding all protestations of "sincere" belief to the contrary?

Pre-Trial Evidentiary Review

The following are many of the issues to be tried before the ultimate tribunal of history. From a biblical perspective, the presiding judge is called the "only Potentate, the King of kings, and Lord of lords" (I Tim. 6:15) who will "judge the world with righteousness, and the people with his truth" (Psa. 96:13). The questions for judicial determination are:

1. On what basis do you claim "standing" to appear and plead before a righteous court?
2. Do you, without hypocrisy, have clean hands and a pure heart so as to stand before a court of equity?
3. Do you have hope, both now and for life after death? On what basis?
4. On what or whom do you believe is your source for ultimate truth?
5. On what evidence do you rely for your beliefs, opinions or convictions? Would you hang your very life and destiny on that evidence?
6. Is the evidence or testimony upon which you rely limited primarily to your culture, your tradition and your personal ideas...or is it universally applicable to all peoples?

7. Are your feelings the ultimate arbiter of "truth," and if so, will the varied feelings of billions of people be persuasive before an ultimate judge who will pass judgment solely based upon truth?
8. Upon what or whom do you place your absolute truth for the future…even a future that may extend beyond time as we know it?
9. On what basis should the court extend mercy if the evidence of your life fails to meet the judge's standard of truth and righteousness?
10. To whom or what do you consider yourself ultimately accountable?

These are all fundamental probative questions as we now seek to summarize the range of messianic beliefs that we have already considered at length. What are the themes that unite or differentiate these ideas about a messiah. Do they pass muster against a standard of truth, or do they bow at the altar of a boundless diversity that celebrates a boutique faith such that, in reality, each person becomes his or her own "messiah"?

The Burden of Proof

The proof of a matter is its ability to withstand contrary evidence. Argument is not proof but rather the weighing of evidence. Proof demands a link of evidence sufficient to persuade a reasonable, unbiased person of the likely truth of the issue presented before a court. The jury is called the "trier of fact," trusted in a law-abiding, truth-seeking society to weigh the evidence so as to render a verdict.

You, the reader, are the ultimate jury in unravelling and then weighing the evidence that will "unveil the mystery of the ages"— the nature and identity of Messiah. You are, of necessity, a jury of ONE, because your verdict carries weight ultimately only for yourself, even though your verdict may seem to be persuasive to others. In this unique instance, your determination is of such enduring magnitude as to mandate—at least from a biblical perspective—the imprimatur of God as ultimate authority, divining ultimate truth outside the cultural,

THE VALLEY OF DECISION

religious, historical or personal biases endemic to human nature. In other words, will my verdict in weighing of the messianic evidence be in total agreement with God's eternal and divine discernment?

Since the *burden of proof* is on each of us in weighing the evidence, thus validating our freedom to choose, we must then consider the weight of evidence deemed sufficient to form and declare our verdict. The law of men assists us in evaluating the needed weight of the evidence. The weight of evidence is directly related to the destiny-determining consequences of the verdict. In civil cases involving money or property, the evidentiary standard of proof is generally a *preponderance of the evidence* (just over 50 percent).

In criminal matters, because life and freedom are at stake, the evidentiary standard is generally *beyond a reasonable doubt* (meaning the evidence is so persuasive as to cause a reasonable-minded, unbiased person to declare a verdict) even though there still may remain some unresolved question or doubt). In other words, this high standard of proof does not require absolute certainty. A further, lesser known to the public, standard of proof is *clear and convincing evidence*. The evidence must be "clear" and it must be "convincing" but is not necessarily "beyond a reasonable doubt."

Weighing the Evidence of Messiah

Whether or not you, as a juror, are conscious of it, you have been "weighing the evidence" as you have been reading. You are presumed, as a juror, to be *reasonable-minded*. You will soon, therefore, render your verdict as to whether the "mystery of the ages" has been unveiled, revealing the truth, identity and significance not only of a "messianic age" but of Messiah.

On what basis and through what process must the evidence be weighed in order for you, as a juror, to render a verdict with intellectual and personal integrity as a seeker of truth? That will depend upon the level of significance and seriousness you attribute to the need to ultimately resolve this "mystery of the ages," both for yourself and for the multitudes of the world's peoples. Consider, then, these questions in *weighing the evidence* and in establishing the requisite *burden of proof.*

1. Is this a meaningless pursuit of no consequence?
2. Is this merely a matter of intellectual curiosity, without significant consequence?
3. Is the evidence, in whole or in part, challenging my pre-conceived notions of truth and history?
4. If evidence is persuasive but, in whole or in part, seems to contravene my culture, tradition, or previous beliefs, should I render verdict in favor of overwhelming proof or in favor of feelings that frustrate my willingness or desire to render a verdict in favor of truth?
5. How serious are the consequences, both now and in the future, if I fail to render an honest verdict?
6. If I knew, or was at least deeply concerned, that my verdict would ultimately determine not only the course of my life but also my eternal destiny, would it make a difference?

The Valley of Decision

It is now time for a brief review of much of the evidence regarding the matter of a messiah, because *the moment of truth lies in the valley of decision.* Our viewpoint, in such a review, will determine destiny, since there are never any neutral viewpoints. All viewpoints, of necessity, set a trajectory of mind and heart either for or against what may be ultimate truth.

THE NEW AGE MYSTICAL "MESSIAH"

You are becoming God! According to New Age religion in the *Age of Aquarius*, godhood is evolving in you as you progressively, in the spirit of this "New Age," develop or evolve into increasing global "Christ consciousness."

As mankind universally embraces this undefined global consciousness, Global Unity will be achieved through universal harmony, economic unity and a one-world religion supporting political oneness in a One World Order or government.

Every human who embraces this universal, non-dogmatic, spiritual consciousness becomes his or her *Messiah.* Those who reject or refuse to embrace this mystical, esoteric system are not only outliers but must be eliminated as enemies of world harmony and peace.

To those who have embraced this mystical mindset, it becomes the glorious hope of salvation of the world, needing no actual Messiah to come, to deliver, to save or to judge. Such thinking is anathema, except for those who refuse to embrace the New Age dogma of absolute relativism that promises a utopian "heaven on earth." Those who reject are banished, through force or threat of force, in the soon-coming "selection process."

SALVATION BY SYNCRETISM

"WE HAVE TO WAGE PEACE!" declared the New Age spirited leader Mariane Williamson on prime-time television. This is the only way we can "dismantle hatred" she insisted. In this ultimate moment of history, divine global oneness resulting in world-wide peace will be achieved through the New Age/New Gospel of "Salvation by Syncretism."

As Alice Bailey made clear, "The spirit has gone out of the old faiths and the true spiritual light is transforming…and will manifest on earth eventually as the new world religion." "Humanity in all lands await the Coming One – no matter by what name they call him. The Christ is sensed on his way." "Therefore," prophesied Bailey, "in the new world order, spirituality will supersede theology."

Syncretism is the blending of all beliefs to the extent that they serve to make us *feel* unified in order to achieve elusive peace on earth. It is "sexy" and profoundly alluring – seductive. Without recognizing the offensive idea that our species is inherently sinful needing salvation for sin, syncretism leads to a belief we need only a little more patience to experience our individual *divinity* in global unity and ONENESS, therefore needing no savior or Divine Messiah.

This new syncretistic and synthetic spirituality is in the process of forming the New World Order's one-world, unifying religion based upon trust in self-salvation. As Dr. Robert Muller, called the "Prophet of Hope," boldly stated as Assistant Secretary General of the United Nations, world unity cannot be achieved through political unions and alliances. According to Muller, such unity "requires a one-world religion."

"SINCERE" SEDUCTION

SINCERITY IS NO SUBSTITUTE for truth. We know that in theory, but in experiential reality our self-justifying spiritual nature clamors for and claims "sincerity" as a legitimate substitute for embracing and being accountable to truth.

Seduction reveals the fallen state of human nature which, on the one hand demands a divine messiah for deliverance (salvation), yet on the other hand seeks to absolve ourselves of such need by claiming sincerity as an acceptable alternative. The result is that each, through the claim of sincerity of belief, becomes a self-defining and self-fulfilling "messiah."

The self-defense of "sincere belief" becomes a seriously seductive enterprise in an age of multiculturalism, religious pluralism and political "correctness." All of the various and multiplied "ISMs" of the world can be synchronized for acceptance through the claim of sincere belief, thus, in effect, denying any demand for absolute or even persuasive truth.

Consider by way of illustration the following prominent ISMs.

Mohammedanism (Islam)
While believing in Isa (Jesus son of Mary), Islam actually denies Jesus' divinity or that he was crucified and rose again, claiming rather that Jesus, upon his return, will embrace and promote the Islamic Mahdi (the 12th Imam) as the true messianic redeemer, restoring global peace by eliminating all religions except Islam.

Judaism
Traditional Judaism expected a future Jewish king from the line of King David, who would be "anointed" and rule Israel as "Melech HaMashiach." Rabbis and Orthodox Jews see a messiah as a non-divine charismatic human who will gather Jews back to Eretz Yisrael (the homeland) and usher in an era of world peace. Reformed or "liberal" Judaism believes in a messianic AGE of world peace, but not in an actual messiah.

Buddhism
Messianic Buddhism is the liberation and "salvation" theology of a Buddhist *messiah*, who discovered the Four Noble

Truths believed to relieve or free the mind from suffering leading to Nirvana. Buddhism acknowledges several "messiahs," the best known being the 14th century Dalai Lama and Wirathu, the terrorist monk of Myanmar. Buddhism offers personal "salvation" attained by the SELF through pursuit of Nirvana.

Confucianism

Confucianism is not a religion with its own gods. Rather, like vast and growing numbers of Americans and Western Europeans, Confucianism believes that all people are basically good and capable of self-salvation by leading a good and noble life—yet to no defined eternal end. It became the foundation of Chinese life and government for 2000 years.

Hinduism

Hinduism is a mystical and polytheistic religion embracing untold numbers of gods. Hinduism believes in the unity of everything and is therefore foundational to much New Age thinking, spreading prominently to the western world in the early 1960s. The top three deities are Brahma, Vishnu and Shiva, with Vishnu worshipped as savior.

Hindus claim Jesus' proclamation "The Father and I are one" confirms Hindu belief that everyone, through rigorous spiritual practice, can realize his own universal "god consciousness." Deepak Chopra therefore declared: "Christ-consciousness, God-consciousness, Krishna-consciousness, Buddha-consciousness—it's all the same thing." Which means, we are all gods, needing no personal savior. Our only need is for a world-wide Kalki Avatar or New Age "messiah," bringing universal peace.

Bahá'i ism

The Bahá'i faith teaches the essential worth of all religions and the unity of all people. Bahá'i believes the world, as we know it, is at the "end of the age" revealed in maximum moral and spiritual decline, therefore awaiting the coming Hindu Kalki Avatar. Bahá'i therefore believes in the synthesis of all religions, merging their desirable aspects toward the utopian fulfillment of the "messianic age."

Moralistic Therapeutic Deism

The pursuit of a global "morality" has taken on a powerfully persuasive messianic tone over the past century, now reaching a crescendo. The concept of what is "moral" or immoral has evolved dramatically, reaching the level of *dogma* driven by the unholy trinity of political correctness, multiculturalism and religious pluralism.

The very words *moral* and *morality* are wrapped in a mystical cloud of ever-vacillating feelings and perceived cultural standards of acceptable human behavior and attitudes enforced by the high priests of cancel culture and globalism.

This is a profound and destiny-defining shift from a morality defined by the never-changing sovereignty of God to the absolute sovereignty of man in establishing the ultimate authority of SELF and purported self-government. Thus, man becomes the ultimate arbiter of truth and morality and the "divine" dispenser of consequences for violation or failure to conform. Thus, man has defied himself, becoming his own messiah.

This is called Moralistic, Therapeutic Deism because it makes us *feel* moral, in feeling *moral* we protect ourselves from the guilt of our own immorality, and therefore begin to believe in ourselves as the final determiner of our own *spirituality* that will present no barrier to the unwashed masses to unify in collective good feelings.

Here, then, is a god-defying A-Morality embraced as a virtue, setting the stage for a counterfeit virtue of immorality able to destroy divisions and thus enable global citizens to unite in purported peace under a New World Order. We will each have become our own "messiah," gods made in our own image.

This, then, is the theological underpinning of Universalism. Since I, and collectively We, determine what constitutes good, both I and We, on our own self-declared sinless merit, declare our certain eligibility for Heaven as "the ultimate participation trophy." I now am my own "I AM," both judge and jury of my own destiny. By the conclusive testimony of my ever-changing but unassailable feelings, I have become *messiah*.

The "Spiritual Democracy"

Democracy is a government and attitude of the heart giving man supreme power and authority over himself, thus justifying every man to do that which is right in his own eyes. For that reason, America's founders cringed at the concept of pure democracy where man becomes an absolute sovereign—a virtual "god" or self-ordained messiah. Thus, America was given a republic, where absolute democratic authority was counter-balanced by numerous checks and balances.

Both Israel and America have become the ultimate testing ground in this messianic age over our response to the words of Genesis 3:1, "Hath God said…?" The issue is *authority*. Will man or his Creator be deemed the absolute sovereign, the determiner of destiny?

The choice of messiah, therefore, becomes the hinge of spiritual history, both for Jew and Gentile. America itself stands as the ultimate gentile testing ground, increasingly drifting from a God-fearing and exalting nation into a man-fearing country, thus setting her course for a god-defying destiny. America, in effect, is the consummate spiritual surrogate for the entire western world and beyond. Yet Israel has historically, and to this messianic age, followed the same pattern for millennia, even as he purportedly awaits the Messiah.

Challenge of the "Cafeteria" Christ

The ultimate choice of history, both for individuals and nations, now looms ominously before us. Is there a true Messiah? If so, who is he? And on what basis or evidence will I, individually, form such a destiny-determining decision? And furthermore, what may well be the consequences of my choice at the spiritual buffet table offered by the various messianic or spiritualistic religions and viewpoints we have presented here at length?

Where does the conclusive evidence lay? Upon what actual facts can such a momentous determination be decided? Or must all caution be cast away upon a free-floating bed of feelings or cultural predilections?

In review of the offerings of the spiritual cafeteria, is there any choice that overwhelms all others, demanding a conclusive verdict? Or have none of these spiritual alternatives of identifying a messiah been persuasive upon which I would rest my life and eternal future? Has any option been persuasive by…

-A preponderance of the evidence?
-By clear and convincing evidence?
-By evidence beyond a reasonable doubt?

Is it possible there may be an alternative far more convincing that might actual grip my soul? Perhaps "the unveiling of the mystery of the ages" has not yet occurred due to spiritual blindness, whether cultural, experiential, or willful.

But Bahá'i offers a compromise—if indeed compromise will satisfy your soul and be sufficient upon which to rest your eternal destiny. Bahá'i presents the ultimate spiritual democracy to unifying the world in a pseudo peace. Here is the offering of "unrestricted individual belief." It is "the new way of looking at faith—as the free exercise of each person's conscience and consciousness…." "There are no insiders or outsiders, no saved or damned, no clean or unclean, no believer or apostate, no righteous and infidel, no Other." You are the sole diviner of "truth"—a democratically-ordained and self-anointed messiah.

Welcome to the New World Order—a worldwide spiritual democracy—the dispensation of the Cafeteria "Christ."

The mystery of the ages may-will-soon be revealed, unless compromise is your eternal crutch. Multitudes remain in the "Valley of Decision."

Chapter 27

WHO IS THIS?

"Traditions have become the shroud that continues
to envelop the very idea of a Messiah and His identity…"

MESSIAH'S IDENTITY DEMANDS reconciling of **Truth** and **Tradition**. Truth and Tradition must become congruent in order for tradition to be true and for truth to verify tradition.

To become congruent requires that tradition and truth must be indistinguishable from each other, and for truth to be "truth" demands that tradition be wrapped completely without any observable difference, by the truth that must support it. This is perhaps the greatest challenge to both Jew and Gentile in "unveiling the mystery of the ages," because we humans inevitably create and embrace traditions that supersede the truth upon which we claim our traditions rest.

Torah, Tanakh and Truth

Undoubtedly, the deepest-rooted traditions regarding Messiah are found in both the Torah and Tanakh, the five books of Moses and the Law, Wisdom Literature and Prophets. Historic biblical Judaism embraces these sources as the ultimate, consummate expressions of *truth* upon which Jewish *tradition* has been established. The same may be arguably claimed by Conservative Bible-believing Christians, the difference being an interpretation of various passages, particularly those pertaining to a coming Messiah. It is indeed a fascinating fact of spiritual history that substantially differing views related to Messiah are maintained within what is commonly referred to as a "Judeo-Christian" heritage, particularly in America.

It should be patently obvious that the differing views and viewpoints of Orthodox Jews and Bible-believing Christians as pertaining to Messiah cannot both be true in their totality, since they are ostensibly predicated upon the same "truth" of Scripture. The claimed views of Jew and Gentile "believers" in HaShem, the God of Creation, and His revealed Word must therefore, through some means of profound humility, be reconciled for truth to prevail. Until then, the "mystery of the ages" will remain a mystery.

This reconciling is made supremely difficult since truth itself is significantly superseded by our traditions which, in effect, become a new and culturally-embraced level of purported "truth." But this reconciling is made much more difficult by the ever-evolving traditions and re-defining of truth within both the Jewish and Christian worlds. Few, therefore, are either willing or able to truly recognize why the world remains shrouded in messianic mystery even as it careens like a drunken man toward the very end of the age.

Traditions themselves have become the shroud that continues to envelop the very idea of a Messiah and his identity, and those traditions are not coalescing but rather multiplying, thus defying reconciliation with anything resembling actual truth. Is it possible, even conceivable, that such differing views regarding Messiah can be reconciled and brought to congruency, thus uniting Jew and Gentile in glorious expectation of the unveiling? It is to that end we proceed, daring to explore areas of difference where perhaps even "angels fear to tread."

The Evolution of Judaism and the Christian Church

There are foundational cultures and proliferating subcultures within Judaism and the broader "Christian" Church. For the Jew, the foundation is in Moses and Abraham. And the Torah (first five books of the Bible) are ascribed to the pen of Moses. Therefore, historical Jewish tradition developed from embracing the truth of the Torah (or

Mosaic teachings). The Torah is therefore unadulterated and unquestioned "truth" for biblical Judaism.

Interestingly, conservative (more orthodox) Christians also believe that not only is the Torah God's truth but likewise the entire Tanakh – the Law and the Prophets, collectively referred to by Christians as the "Old Testament" or "Old Covenant." The obvious seemingly separating problem or hurdle for the Jew with the Christian is the introduction of the word *old*. For the true Christian, Yeshua is the fulfillment of the promises and prophecies of the "Old" Covenant, therefore ushering in a "New" Covenant to complete that which was prophesied in ages past. For that reason, Christians believe Yeshua was and is that Messiah or "Anointed One" that has been anticipated by Israel since the days of Moses 3500 years ago.

What then becomes a seeming impenetrable barrier between Orthodox Jew and "orthodox" Christian? Is the barrier one of truth, or tradition, or both? If this barrier, hurdle or impasse is not resolved by embracing of actual truth rather than by reluctant compromise of tradition, the "mystery of the ages" will remain shrouded in mystery even as our world collapses before our eyes. And for many, the promise of redemption will remain an illusion facilitated by delusion.

The evolution of the "fundamentals" of Judaism and Christianity has served to divide further than unite. In fact, Judaism and the Christian church have followed the same degenerating, compromising pattern, just on parallel tracks, over the past 150 years. As Arutz Sheva (israelnationalnews.com) clearly explained by Rabbi Prof. Dov Fischer:

1. What is called "Conservative Judaism" today is "Reform Judaism." It no longer has any anchor to the Torah or to Tradition. It has almost no followers in the USA.
2. Reform "Judaism" today is akin to Unitarian Christianity *without a Messiah* (emphasis added).
3. The Reform Movement began in 1800's Germany. [Note: Germany was also the source of Protestant liberalism]. They fantasized that, if they "reformed" Judaism to be like the surrounding liberal Protestantism, then the German non-Jews

would come to accept Jews in their society. [Note: This pattern has followed in the Christian Church through the Church Growth movement, the Seeker Sensitive movement and the Emerging Church movement since the early 1970s, while mainline churches degenerated into culture emulators].

4. Among the Reformed Movement's key "reforms," its founders abandoned all belief in the coming of Moshiach (Messiah) and in revival of the dead.

Thus arose the Jewish Conservative Movement, wrote Rabbi Fischer, the early version of which was actually not that different from what we now call "Modern Orthodox" Judaism. Yet from the 1950s, the Conservative Movement migrated toward Reformed Judaism, "onto a descending cycle of increasingly extreme liberalizations that ultimately have resulted in it becoming the new Reform, while today's Reform 'Judaism' has descended into Unitarianism without a Messiah." "The Conservative Movement had become indistinguishable from the radical extremes of the Reform Movement…." Yet in a word, true "Judaism is absolutely incompatible with the abandonment of the Torah."[1]

"Mashiach: Man or Movement?"

Judaistic viewpoints regarding Messiah are rooted not only in Torah but in progressively-formed traditions derived in and from rabbinical, interpretive works such as the Talmud and Mishnah. These voluminous works of Jewish sages are revered and embraced within the Orthodox world as co-extensions and expanded reiterations of the written Torah itself, coupling the interpretations and applications of the Torah.

In effect for most, the Torah, Talmud and Mishnah have become HaShem's foundation of "truth" for the Jewish people even though, in reality, the extra-biblical works are rabbinical opinions superimposed upon the Torah or biblical text provided by HaShem's revelation to and through Moses. They are, then, traditions embraced as "truth" over time.

But are these interpretations actually "true" in their entirety as defining Mashiach from the Creator's viewpoint? Could it be that, through the Jewish rabbis' best efforts, a virtual veil may have, through the law of unintended consequences, frustrated a clearer revelation and understanding of the promised Messiah? VIEWPOINT ALWAYS DETERMINES DESTINY, either revealing or camouflaging "truth." No viewpoints, either Jewish or Gentile, are neutral. All such viewpoints, opinions and traditions derived therefrom lead inevitably toward some ultimate destiny. All must therefore reassess long-held ideas regarding Messiah if indeed we are in "the messianic age," for

> The day of the LORD is near in the valley of decision (Joel 3:14).

Yshai Amichai penned a fascinating piece published through israelnationalnews.com titled "Moshiach: Man or Movement?" He states that the Rambam (the revered rabbi Maimonides) clarifies what is to be expected of the Mashiach. "In the future, the Messianic king will arise and renew the Davidic dynasty… He will build the Temple and gather the dispersed of Israel." Such king, he writes, "will not be required to 'work miracles and wonders'" or "resurrect the dead…." Rather, declared the Rambam, "If a king will arise from the House of David who diligently contemplates the Torah and observes its commandments… and rectify the breaches in its observance, and fight the wars of God, we may with assurance, consider him Mashiach." "If he succeeds in the above, builds the Temple in its place, and gathers the dispersed of Israel, he is definitely the Mashiach."

Yet Amichai rightly observes, the exiles or dispersion of Israel are already being regathered without the appearance of the Mashiach. Furthermore, he notes that "Israel has been fighting wars and winning them, without the Mashiach, so… we seem to be fulfilling the prophecies without a Davidic king." The only thing missing is to reinforce the Torah and rabbinically-devised halakhic laws and to rebuild the Temple. The conclusion, then, is that the Mashiach is not merely a "man" but a "movement," yet he writes, "theoretically, a Davidic king could claim to have been chosen by God based upon his accomplishments."[2]

All of this conceptualizing of identifying the Mashiach, based upon the best rabbinic viewpoints, leads one to conclude that:

1. If a man claims, to the satisfaction of trusted rabbis, to be the descendant of king David; and
2. If such a man assists in the regathering of Jewish exiles; and
3. If such a man facilitates the rebuilding of the Temple, ostensibly to make possible the restoration of the sacrificial system required by the Torah,
4. Then – Israel and the Jewish people should recognize the man as the long-desired Messiah.

Yet the question must be asked, can any or all of these claimed prerequisites be seemingly confirmed, yet with undisclosed devious intent, so as to ultimately destroy rather than to restore? As Rabbi Berel Wein so aptly noted, again in israelnationalnews.com under the title "Heaven's perfect timing":

> There is a famous statement that reverberates throughout Jewish society over the ages that states: "…what cannot be solved by wisdom, will eventually be solved by the passage of time."

Rabbi Wein wisely notes: "The timing of heaven and God's guidance in human affairs is always mysterious, inexplicable, and irrational to us ordinary mortals," but "in retrospect, one sees the perfect involved, and the exquisite nature of the timing that governs human events."[3]

Perhaps, then, the lens through which revered Jewish rabbis view both the coming and identity of Mashiach is clouded or veiled such that the actual "truth" remains shrouded in traditional views so profoundly limited as to render revelation of Messiah through both Torah and Tanakh undiscoverable, only to be made devastatingly clear over the divine passage of time. What, then, might the consequences be?

A brief review of rabbinic history reveals that the revered Sanhedrin composed of 71 noted rabbis, openly and violently rejected a man who fulfilled all of the stated rabbinic requirements for Messiah, except for rebuilding the Temple which then actually existed. A brief summary may be instructive in our pursuit of truth unveiling the persistent "mystery" of the ages.

1. He was born in Bethlehem of Judea as prophesied by Micah (Micah 5:2).
2. He was of the Davidic line, both through his mother and through his surrogate father.
3. He was a Jew.
4. He was a man "like Moses."
5. His ministry was to the Jewish nation.
6. He revered the Torah and Tanakh, applying them righteously rather than exclusively by rabbinic tradition.

Why, then, did Israel's trusted spiritual leaders not recognize him as likely the long-awaited Mashiach? Why did they only test him according to their traditional expectations rather than trust him as conforming to the simply-defined qualifications of both the Law and the Prophets? Might the reasons be that they simply superimposed their own traditional expectations of a Maccabean-type king/warrior to deliver from the Roman domination and further feared loss of their own power, perks and position among the people?

Culture and tradition present perhaps the most difficult challenge when seeking to ascertain actual truth. That challenge becomes insurmountable if the mind and heart are not truly desiring truth or have purported reasons for rejecting truth even when dramatically confronted with it. In order to assist in unveiling the persistent "mystery of the ages," perhaps the best, non-confrontive way is to ask probing questions that, by themselves, provoke righteous response.

Who Is This?

In reality there is no mystery of whom we must speak. Two thousand years ago, a man named Yeshua was born in Bethlehem, of the house of David. After thirty years, as it was with Joseph centuries earlier, he began his ministry, both teaching as a priest and speaking as a prophet. He performed miracles unprecedented in Israel, but for Elijah and Elisha. The common people increasingly saw in him the character and message of the long-promised Messiah. Even a few of the Sanhedrin came to agree, mostly in private for they feared retribution from the High Priest who was, for political purposes, under the thumb of the despised Romans, so as to retain his power and position.

While *Messiah* meant "anointed One," Gentiles using a Greek interpretation, referred to him as "Christ," also meaning "anointed One." It should then be clear to any truth-seeking Jew or Gentile that the greater question before us is…

Was Yeshua the awaited Messiah?

Since Yeshua was not recognized then or now by Israel's religious leaders as Yeshua ha Maschiach – Jesus the Christ – the awaited "Anointed One" of God, such a Messiah is yet anticipated by Orthodox Jews to be revealed in the near future – for the FIRST time. For Christians or "followers of the Way" as they were first known, Yeshua was indeed the awaited Redeemer of Israel but was rejected, and now, in this "messianic age," will come again described as the "Second Coming." That presents yet a further question:

If Israel's respected religious leaders failed to recognize Yeshua as the promised Mashiach, on what basis can they be trusted to identify someone else now expected to appear as Israel's redeemer?

We must now let the Torah and Tanakh, the Law, Prophets and Wisdom writings, speak for themselves. As the famous Latin phrase known by every lawyer declares *res ipsa loquitur* – "the thing speaks for itself." You are the jury and must, with integrity, weigh the evidence. The verdict you render now will carry unintended consequences – perhaps eternal consequences. Let us all proceed with answering the question before us – "Who is this?"

1. **Would Messiah be a Man?**
   Declared Moses in Deuteronomy 18:15…

   "The LORD thy God will raise up unto thee a Prophet from the midst of thee, of thy brethren, like unto me; unto him ye shall hearken."

- Was Yeshua deemed a Prophet? Yes
- Was Yeshua an Israelite? Yes
- Was Yeshua "like unto Moses?" Yes. He was a man and a prophet.

2. **Would Messiah also be divine or deity?**

   Note: In order to understand this question, one must understand the rabbinic view based upon Deuteronomy 6:4 beginning the "Shema."

   Moses declared: "Hear, O Israel: The LORD our God is one LORD." That theme is repeated in Zechariah 14:9. The rabbinic view, understandably, is that because Yeshua admitted to being the "Son of God" and therefore deity, he was necessarily an idolatrous blasphemer claiming to be equal to God. Thus, no further consideration must be given him as Mashiach.

   Yet Yeshua did not deny the "oneness" of God but admitted and reinforce it by declaring "I and my Father are one" (John 10:30).

   Furthermore, the rabbinic view essentially ignores the clear admission of God in the Genesis creation account... "Let **us** make man in **our** image, after **our** likeness" (Gen. 1:26, emphasis added). God, as one entity, self identifies in the plural form, implying distinct roles or functional beings within the Godhead.

3. **Who is the "Son of Man?"**

   The Prophet Daniel spoke precisely regarding a vision in which "one like the Son of man came" (Dan. 7:13-14). When asked by a caller on his show on Arutz Sheva, israelnationalnews.com, Orthodox Rabbi Tovia Singer responded to the question as to the identity of this "Son of Man," declaring without hesitation that it is the Messiah.

   Here are the exact passages spoken of from Daniel:

> I saw in the night visions, and behold one
> like the Son of man came with the clouds of
> heaven, and came to the Ancient of days, and
> they brought him near before him.
>
> And there was given him dominion, and glory,
> and a kingdom, that all people, nations, and
> languages, should serve him: his dominion is
> an everlasting dominion, which shall not pass
> away, and his kingdom that which shall not be
> destroyed" (Dan. 7:13-14).

The popular rabbi, purportedly representing absolute biblical truth, then declared that even though this passage definitely referred to Messiah, it could not be Yeshua (Jesus) because, as he said, all nations did not bow down to Yeshua. Yet Daniel was speaking of the distant future. As historical fact, at least in cognitive belief, people now from virtually all nations and people, including many Jews, now proclaim Jesus as Messiah, now totaling arguably one-third of our planet's entire population.

But the seeming blindness of the rabbinic response goes much deeper. The prophet proclaims that in the distant future from his prophetic moment, this "Son of man" would be given "dominion, and glory, and a kingdom" and "his dominion is an everlasting dominion, which shall not pass away."

Would that not seem to imply that this "Son of man" is actually eternal, is himself deity, and directly connected personally to "the Ancient of days" – a reference to the one and only God eternal, maker of heaven and earth?

Is it not fascinating that Yeshua himself seemed to protect the "messianic mystery" of his priestly and prophetic presence by referring to himself as "Son of man," referring continually to the "mystery of the kingdom" that only those who had "eyes to see and ears to hear" would understand, quoting the warning to Israel by Isaiah the prophet (Isa. 6:10; Matt. 13:15)?

Perhaps shockingly to some, the Jewish High Priest and Sanhedrin had to force Yeshua to clearly divulge his identity and divine mission. They arrested Jesus clandestinely so as not to incur the wrath of the people who were convinced he was "that prophet" and then, while a prisoner, coerced him by asking "Art thou the Christ? Tell us." To which Yeshua responded, "If I tell you, ye will not believe."

Jesus then further identified himself as the "Son of man" to which the esteemed council demanded: "Art thou then the Son of God?" To which Yeshua responded: "Ye say that I am" (Luke 22:66-70).

The question therefore remains for every man, woman and child – "Who is this Son of man?"

4. **Who is this King?**

Perhaps the most succinct prophecy concerning the end of the age and these messianic times is found, surprisingly, in the Psalms, as are an abundance of very specific prophecies of the coming Messiah, particularly descriptive of the precise details concerning his crucifixion.

We focus now exclusively on Psalm 2, which inquires why the heathen or gentile nations rage against the Lord and his anointed. In response to their ever-growing rage approaching the end of this age, the Lord "laughs" at their hubris, causes them to be in chaotic derision, and then boldly states:

> "Yet have I set my king upon my holy hill of Zion" (vs 6).

The Lord then reveals who this king actually is, stating:

> "Thou art my Son; this day have I begotten thee" (vs 7).

If God has no "Son," then the psalmist is a false prophet. But if God has a "Son," then the rabbinic understanding of "the LORD our God is one" is in error, and must be understood in accordance with the words of Genesis 1 – "Let **us** make man in **our** image…." Perhaps then "us" includes Father and Son and perhaps the Ruach HaKodesh (Holy Spirit), all collectively "God" with these distinct roles.

But a warning to the world, both Jew and Gentile, follows:

> Serve the LORD with fear, and rejoice with trembling.
>
> Kiss the Son, lest he be angry, and ye perish from the way… Blessed are all they that put their trust in him [the Son] (vs 11-12).

Who, then, do you trust? Why are we told to put our ultimate trust in the Son rather than the Father? Might it be because the Son is, in fact the Mashiach?

5. **Can God be born?**

This may well be the most troubling question of all. We get the clearest, most descriptive and unassailable insights from Isaiah the prophet. Of all the prophets other than the psalmists, Isaiah speaks most profoundly of the Messiah in ways and with such detail as to be virtually determinative of Mashiach's identity. We look now with eyes and hearts wide open at the words of Isaiah:

> For unto us [the Jews or Israel] a child is born,
>
> unto us a son is given:
>
> and the government shall be upon his shoulder:
>
> and his name shall be called
> Wonderful,
> Counsellor,
> The mighty God,
> The everlasting Father,
> The Prince of Peace.

Of the increase of his government and peace
there shall be no end,

upon the throne of David,

and upon his kingdom,

to order it, and to establish it with judgment
and with justice from henceforth even for ever.

The zeal of the LORD of hosts will perform
this (Isa. 9:6-7).

Time and space require the briefest possible review of these otherwise simple yet profoundly instructive verses.

FIRST — A child is born! Born to whom? How conceived? Where conceived or born? And how could such a child be recognized for his obviously-described messianic role and purpose? Who would be required to recognize him so as to effectuate that purpose for Israel and the world? What might inhibit such recognition?

SECOND — The child is called "a son." Is this the same "Son of man" prophesied by Daniel? Will he appear and be recognized as a prince or be unrecognizable until a propitious moment? And who must recognize him?

THIRD — "The government shall be upon his shoulder." Whose government? Is this man's government or God's government? On what basis and under whose authority will he govern? How would the government of this "Son" be distinguishable from a counterfeit who seems to fit much of the rabbinic objections and desires?

FOURTH — This "son" is given five names revealing his five distinct roles. These roles must be embraced and received by the Jew first and then by the Gentile.

- He must be seen as "Wonderful," fulfilling the heart's yearning.

~ He must be perceived and received as a Councilor, guiding the people in an accurate understanding and application of the Word of God, without multitudinous and complicated halachic rabbinic rules and regulations developed to build "a fence around the Torah," placing burdens upon the people greater than they can bear.

~ He must be recognized, received and embraced as "THE MIGHTY GOD." So if, as rabbinic Judaism maintains, Messiah is a man only and not God, the prophet Isaiah was a deceiver and false prophet, worthy of death for blasphemy.

~ He must also be recognized, received and embraced from the heart as "The EVERLASTING FATHER" and not a mere charismatic leader. In other words, this Son is "God with skin on" or incarnated in human flesh so that the Torah might be revealed "in Spirit and in Truth."

~ And finally, he is the ultimate Prince of Peace. And for that purpose was he born to bring consummate redemption – peace on earth and peace in the heart as proclaimed by the angelic host (Luke 2:14).

FIFTH — He will rule, both in time and for eternity (for ever) upon the foundational throne of David, a man after God's own heart.

If Messiah is a mere man as adamantly claimed by revered rabbinic authority, how then will he rule and reign for ever? Will a mere man never die?

6. **If God can be born, where will he be born?**
Obviously, the question is somewhat deceptive and certainly perplexing, depending upon one's presuppositions.

If it is meant that God was actually "born" or evolved into Godhood as claim the Mormons, we have a serious problem since such a thought defies the pre-existence of a Creator of all things and defies the very concept of "God."

If, on the other hand, we accept the reality of Isaiah's prophecy, the pre-existent and all-knowing, all-powerful God reveals himself in the flesh as a "Son" to whom the Father, in the fulness of time, reveals himself as "the Word made flesh," translating the truth of the Word into one that can be seen and touch the feelings of our infirmities, yet without the sinful contaminating spiritual DNA of Adam.

So, where would such a "Son" be born? The prophet Micah gives us the answer – the same answer recognized and embraced by the "chief priests and scribes" when demanded of by Herod "where Christ should be born." And they said unto him,

> In Bethlehem of Judea: for thus it is written by the prophet (Matt. 2:1-6).

What, then, did Micah prophecy?

> But thou, Bethlehem Ephratah, though thou be little among the thousands of Judah, yet out of thee shall he come forth unto me that is to be ruler in Israel; **whose goings forth have been from of old, from everlasting** (Micah 5:2, emphasis added).

Should it be surprising, despite rabbinic contradiction, that HaShem revealed to Micah that Mashiach was not only to be "born" in Bethlehem but that the one to be born as Israel's Messiah had existed "from of old" and "from everlasting?" Does this testify to a mere man, or to incarnate deity, God revealing Himself in the flesh?

The Messianic Jury

The jury is now out! You, as a juror, do not have authority or power to determine and declare the identity of Messiah for the world, but only for yourself, be you Jew or Gentile. Purported religious or spiritual leaders bear a profoundly greater burden due to their power of influence. Yet identifying and recognizing Messiah is only the thresh-old decision you must make. In the final chapter, your final verdict will be revealed and the "mystery of the ages" will be fully unveiled insofar as possible in these pages.

In this chapter we have explored six fulcrum questions for your determination. These questions, biblical passages and corresponding issues, distill the most decisive objections to Yeshua as Messiah. Yet the pattern and immense panoply of prophetic revelation from Genesis 3:15 through Malachi 4 is so vast as to be beyond our ability to present here.

There remains, however, two passages presenting profound and provocative prophecy that cannot be escaped without some reference.

FIRST—The prophet Isaiah, in chapters 52 and 53, called the "Suffering Servant" passages, lays out in shocking detail what the *servant*, the *Son* and promised Messiah would endure so as to offer himself as Israel's savior. One cannot, in good conscience and with integrity of heart, refuse either to read or to seriously ask of whom the prophet writes. Yet Israel's rabbis almost categorically refuse to read these verses publicly. If you are an honest-hearted juror you must ask "Why?" and not receive a blithe rabbinical slap and sleight-of-hand in response declaring "this must represent Israel as a whole rather than a person representing Israel."

SECOND— The prophet Zechariah speaks both troublingly and triumphantly of earth's final messianic moment. He foretells exactly how Yeshua would be betrayed and for what price. He further speaks of Israel's grief and mournings in profound bitterness as the veil is finally withdrawn and the "mystery of the ages" is suddenly made clear. The Lord declares that in that day, when all nations come against Jerusalem, the Jewish people:

> Shall look upon me whom they have pierced, and they shall mourn for him, as one mourneth for his only son, and shall be in bitterness for him, as one that is in bitterness for his firstborn (Zech. 12:10).

So great will be the mourning that they will be unable to mourn corporately as a people but will feel compelled to mourn "every family apart" and even husbands and wives apart.

Messiah, God in the flesh, will be revealed for Israel's ultimate deliverance in their existential hour as all nations come against Jerusalem. Only then will Israel see through the veil, Yeshua HaMashiach coming in great glory for their rescue (Zech. 12:8-14).

The Day of the Lord

"Behold," declared Zechariah, "the day of the LORD cometh." The *Apocalypse* meaning "Unveiling" declares the same:

"Behold, I come quickly."

Three times that message is repeated by the soon-coming King in his Revelation known as the "Unveiling" or Apocalypse (Rev. 22:7, 12, 20). And "the LORD [Messiah] shall be king over all the earth: in that day there shall be one LORD, and his name one" (Zech 14:9) — "The LORD our Righteousness" (Jer. 23:5-6).

Chapter 28

PIERCING THE VEIL

*"The Tanakh bears ever persuasive testimony
of the coming light-bearer, redeemer, King, and
Prince of Peace upon whose shoulder eternal
government shall rest on the throne of David."*

ACCURATE DISCERNMENT IS ESSENTIAL to identifying and
embracing that which is actually *true*. In this messianic age, the very
concept of actual truth that is genuinely *true* is increasingly dispensed
with, being defined not by facts but by feelings or traditions. Thus, the
very idea of "accurate discernment" is at best deemed illusive. But is
that actually TRUE? This is the profound conundrum that both Jew
and Gentile face if, indeed, this is history's messianic moment.

Discernment and Yeshua's Claims

How are we to respond to the claim of Yeshua (Jesus) when he
declared:

> "I am the good shepherd; the good shepherd giveth his
> life for the sheep." "I lay down my life for the sheep…no
> man taketh it from me, but I lay it down of myself" (John
> 10:11-18).

"I am the door: by me if any man enter in, he shall be saved…" (John 10:9).

"I am the resurrection, and the life: he that believeth in me, though he were dead, yet shall he live" (John 11:25).

"I am the light of the world: he that followeth me shall not walk in darkness, but shall have the light of life" (John 8:12).

"I am come in my Father's name, and ye receive me not: if another shall come in his own name, him ye will receive" (John 5:43).

"I am the way, the truth, and the life: no man cometh unto the Father, but by me" (John 14:6).

These claims reveal either an extreme narcissist, a deranged personality, a profoundly deceiving imposter, or one invested with spiritual wisdom, perception, knowledge and discernment far beyond those with whom he lived and ministered for a time. It was as if he was not bound by the traditional viewpoints, religious power structure and political proclivities of the age and those around him. He perceived things differently, but why?

Yeshua, addressing the Jewish leaders of his day, warned them…

…there is one that accuseth you, even Moses, in whom ye trust.

For had ye believed Moses, ye would have believed me: for he wrote of me.

But if ye believe not his writings, how shall ye believe my words (John 5:45-47).

If indeed Moses did speak of or allude to Yeshua as Messiah, why was this not perceived and embraced by revered rabbinical leaders for centuries, beginning with Jesus' three and a half years walking, ministering and performing unprecedented miracles among them? Apparently, Yeshua did not appear as they expected. Their perceptions, being the totality of their reality, seemingly paralyzed them from seeing the bigger or more accurate picture.

Isaiah had prophetically warned of this paralyzing problem of perception. He said, "I heard the voice of the LORD saying…

> Go, and tell this people, Hear ye indeed but understand not; and see ye indeed, but perceive not.

> Make the heart of this people fat, and make their ears heavy, and shut their eyes; lest they see with their eyes, and hear with their ears, and understand with their heart, and convert, and be healed (Isa. 6:8-10).

> If ye will not believe, surely ye shall not be established.

> Hear ye now, O house of David; Is it a small thing for you to weary men, but will ye weary my God also?

> Therefore the Lord himself shall give you a sign; Behold a virgin shall conceive, and bear a son, and shall call his name Immanuel [meaning God with us] (Isa. 7:9-14).

Resolving Paralyzing Perceptions

As human beings, regardless of our religious or spiritual orientations, beliefs or traditions, our perceptions dare us to disagree with them. Therefore, perceptions tend to "lord it over" us, demanding we conform to their dictates, until such time as something occurs that so shakes our confidence in their "lordship" that we are open to re-consider their truth that gives them power over our lives and thinking.

This problem that plagues us all is made glaringly apparent to the trial lawyer. Witnesses, when called to testify, vow to tell "the truth, the whole truth, and nothing but the truth." Yet assuming they are persons of integrity, valuing truth, the actual "truth" to which they testify is actually their perception or best recollection. It remains for the jury, after receiving evidence both documentary and testamentary, to discern the actual truth as best they perceive it. Often evidence is tested by cross-examination. How often a witness' testimony is found or discerned to be inaccurate in whole or in part after the jury sees the whole picture.

A further and fascinating revelation of our human perceptual problems is found in what is known as "Figure-Ground" perception. This problem of how we see things has been described by Gestalt psychology. The Gestalt theory of perception proposes that people make sense of the world around them by taking separate and distinct elements and combining them into a unified whole, which becomes their conclusion/viewpoint on what they think they are seeing.

There are dozens, if not hundreds, of visual "figure-ground" illustration, and you have most likely been fascinated by a few, being asked by the presenter — "What do you see?" Here are just a few by way of illustration.

DEAD…or ALIVE?

HATE… or LOVE?

OLD WOMAN… or YOUNG WOMAN?

Resolving the Spiritual Figure-Ground Problem

The lawyer learns in law school of a doctrine or principle called "Piercing the Corporate Veil." The meaning is that even though the formation of a corporation is intended, among other things, to protect from personal liability, there are conditions under which that "veil" may be pierced, when the purported veil was primarily a pretense rather than a sincere effort to operate corporately. This, then, becomes somewhat of a legal "figure-ground" problem.

This "figure-ground" problem concerning our human perception also has even more significant spiritual application and implications, for both Jew and Gentile. If a veil of some sort clouds our ability to discern or identify the Messiah or Mashiach, how is that veil to be "pierced?" How can pre-conceived ideas or perceptions be re-assessed in the pursuit of actual truth without contamination by personal feelings or compromise? Obviously, traditional perceptions may well be a casualty if we are truly sincere.

Comes Now the "Apocalypse"

It is now time to "think out loud" yet on paper. The very word *Apocalypse* is enshrouded by an air of mystery. In fact, the word is increasingly used in pop culture expressions describing movies, economic developments, the climate or virtually anything marketers believe might be described as "apocalyptic." The actual truth is that these marketing applications and descriptions actually mask and manipulate the actual meaning of *apocalypse*.

The word *apocalypse* is a Greek word meaning: "To Uncover, To Un-Veil, To Reveal." For this reason, the last book closing out the New Testament is called "The Revelation of Jesus Christ" or of Yeshua HaMashiach (Rev. 1:1). In other words, the Book of Revelation is actually the Book of the Unveiling—the Apocalypse. The Greek word *apocalyptic* occurs 18 times in the New Testament.

What must be understood, however, is that this "unveiling" has been taking place progressively from the very first messianic promise in Genesis 3:15, throughout the Torah (even by means of the seven "Appointed Times of the Lord" or moadim—Lev. 23). The Psalms then increase the "revelation" continually, unveiling Messiah as prophet, priest and king. Isaiah and Jeremiah expand the unveiling as do the prophets Joel, Micah, Amos, Zechariah and Malachi. Thus, the Tanakh bears ever persuasive testimony of the coming light-bearer, redeemer, King and Prince of Peace upon whose shoulder eternal government shall rest on the throne of David.

When the Gospels of Matthew, Mark, Luke and John are superimposed upon the progressive revelations of Messianic identity in the Torah and Tanakh, an unmistakable picture emerges, connecting all the dots of messianic prophecy and expectation.

The Jury Must Decide

The challenge now for you, as a juror, is to weigh the evidence presented. It requires, as with any honest juror with integrity, to set aside pre-conceived notions, personal feelings, paralyzing perceptions and even well-worn traditions in favor of a fulfilling good news that satisfies the soul and paves the way to a hope-filled eternal destiny at one with Messiah.

You, the jury, are now dismissed for heart-rending deliberation. Was Messiah a "suffering servant"? Will he be a reigning King? If he was a "suffering servant" as described in Isaiah 53, when did his suffering take place, for whom, and for what purpose? If he was once a suffering servant, how and when will he become a reigning king as prophesied from Psalm 2 and repeatedly through the Psalms and Prophets, culminating in Zechariah's pronouncement?

> And the LORD shall be king over all the earth: in that day shall there be one LORD, and his name one (Zech. 14:9).

If then Yeshua claimed truthfully: "I and my Father are one" (John 10:30) and that "he that hath seen me hath seen the Father" (John 14:9), that then confirms "oneness" and eliminates the rabbinical claims of blasphemy ostensibly contrary to the Torah's declaration that "The LORD our God is one LORD" (Deut. 6:4), and that Yeshua was a mere man claiming godhood. Perhaps "piercing the veil" is largely a matter of how the historical and prophetic declarations are perceived and received…or perhaps whether traditional viewpoints are elevated as persuasive over actual truth itself.

The jury is now out. And destiny rides in the balance of your verdict. Perhaps a revisiting of the Eternal Judge's written instructions regarding His Temple may provide further needed perspective before a final verdict is rendered. When, if as recorded, "the veil of the temple was rent in twin from the top to the bottom; and the earth did quake and the rocks rent" (Matt. 27:51), what, from HaShem's viewpoint, actually happened, and why?

Chapter 29

"THE THIRD DAY"

"Be ready against the third day" (Ex. 19:11).

MESSIAH IS COMING! And as the prophet Malachi penned before the 400 years of silence preceding the birth of Yeshua…

> The Lord, whom ye seek, shall suddenly come to his temple, even the messenger of the covenant, whom ye delight in: behold he shall come, saith the LORD of hosts.

> But who may abide [endure] the day of his coming? And who shall stand when he appeareth? For he is like a refiner's fire…and he shall purify the sons of Levi… (Mal. 3:1-3).

Has this "messenger of the covenant" already come and was unidentified as such? Is he being prepared to come for a first showing to Israel and the world? Or is he coming yet again to fulfill all prophecy and all righteousness, having given Israel and the world two thousand years of gracious patience to fully recognize whom both Jew and Gentile have pierced and to embrace him as King — King not only of a people but of our individual lives as living temples reconciled through repentance to joyous salvation?

The Symbol of Sinai

It should come as no surprise to knowledgeable Jews and rabbis that Israel's experience at Mt. Sinai was not only experiential substance for that moment in time but was also symbolically prophetic for a future fulfillment in the messianic age. Gentile Christians should likewise not find this connection mysterious if truly familiar with the Scriptures. It is necessary, then, that we observe closely the pattern portrayed at Sinai for the future unveiling of Messiah.

After the children of Israel had been delivered by God's mighty hand from Egyptian bondage under Pharaoh (a type of the coming IMPOSTER messiah), the Lord met with Moses as a proxy for the people and "called unto him out of the mountain," instructing him to carry to Israel a proffered marriage covenant conditioned on: "…if ye will obey my voice indeed, and keep my covenant, then ye shall be…"

"A peculiar treasure unto me,"
"A kingdom of priests," and
"A holy nation" (Ex. 19:3-6).

In response to this proffered marriage covenant with HaShem, "all the people answered together, and said, All that the LORD hath spoken we will do. And Moses told the words of the people unto the LORD" (Ex. 19:8). Thus, HaShem and Israel pledged their troth or betrothal, saying "I DO and I WILL." History reveals throughout the Torah and Tanakh that Israel never did keep his covenant and suffered greatly now over 3500 years unto this messianic moment. Yet the profound and prophetic symbolism of HaShem's confirmation of that covenant at Sinai remains and is grippingly instructive at this historic moment as history and prophecy converge to ultimate fulfillment.

The Third Day Demand

The symbolism of Sinai now portrays the pattern of eternal substance for both Jew and Gentile.

Be ready against the third day: for the third day the LORD will come down in the sight of all the people…" (Ex. 19:11).

Here was the most solemn and sobering warning for Israel's first "messianic moment," the actual manifestation of God on the planet before a people pledged as His betrothed.

BE READY!
Be ready for the THIRD DAY!

How were the people to get ready… and why? The otherwise unholy people were to present themselves as holy and unblameable before a perfect and immeasurably holy God. They were commanded in Exodus 19:10-15 to:

BE SANCTIFIED—set apart exclusively a bride for the bridegroom.

BE PURIFIED—wash their clothes as a symbol of being clothed in a white gown before their betrothed.

BE EXCLUSIVELY COMMITTED—to have no sexual relations for three days as a sign of being spiritually exclusive in betrothed commitment to God, without fleshly compromise.

The Third Day Drama

The drama that followed was unprecedented in human history and would, unsuspectingly to the people, become a prophetic declaration both terrifying and, for those truly ready on the third day, triumphant.

Three distinct manifestations of God's unprecedented presence to humanity then took place ON THE THIRD DAY. These signs or "messianic" manifestations were followed by the Lord delivering His Word, His covenantal Will defining His fundamental Ways to which He expected His bride to follow. To these signs and holy expectations Israel was to take holy heed. Here, then, are the three signs of HaShem's coming to His people.

1. The Lord will come in a "THICK CLOUD" (Ex. 19:9, 16),
2. The Lord will come with THUNDER and LIGHTNING (Ex. 19:16), and

3. The Lord will come with the VOICE of the TRUMPET.

Just in case the people had not taken the initial commands for covenantal purity seriously, the enveloping signs upon Sinai riveted them indelibly to the mind and memory such that as "the voice of the trumpet [grew] exceedingly loud," "all the people that were in the camp trembled" (Ex. 19:16). Thus, the people were taught with divine drama to tremble at the Word of the Lord, and so they did as the Ten Commandments were declared, which had been written by the finger of God in stone (Ex. 20:1-17; 31:18).

The Coming Third-Day Drama

The Scriptures (Bible) are written such as to foretell the future by giving a prophetic foretaste. The more intimately a person becomes acquainted with the Bible, the more clearly are its true meaning and implications revealed, progressively lifting the veil that has clouded the understanding. While previously perceived as pure information, increasing revelation gradually transforms seemingly irrelevant *information* into life-giving *transformation*. And even now it is high time for that veil-lifting revelation to take place through fulfilling *application*. This should be thrilling to both Jew and Gentile who have any semblance of messianic *expectation*.

We now leap forward perhaps 1000 years to the prophet Hosea, who pleads on behalf of HaShem to His betrothed, Israel, who have forsaken His marital covenant. Here are his words, foretelling a future confrontation with Messiah "in the third day." As it was at Sinai, so it will be with the coming Savior.

Come, and let us return unto the LORD: for he hath torn, and he will heal us; he hath smitten, and he will bind us up.

AFTER TWO DAYS will he revive us: in the **THIRD DAY** he will raise us up, and we shall live in his sight (Hos. 6:1-2 – Emphasis added).

Was this prophecy ever fulfilled, and if so, how and when? And is the fulfillment yet complete? Be prepared for THE THIRD DAY unveiling.

The Third-Day Dilemma

It was a "whale of a story," but Yeshua took it literally and applied it prophetically. If, or when, you believe it, the veil will be removed from your eyes and heart, and the mystery of the ages will become manifest. Please make every effort to set aside pre-conceived notions, traditional prejudices and personal doubting pride for our few remaining moments together. Your reward may exceed expectations and resolve the haunting mystery that has hovered continually over humankind, both Jew and Gentile.

The Jewish leaders, scribes and Pharisees, inquired of Yeshua, saying, "Master, we would see a sign from thee." Let us then pay particular attention to Yeshua's response to their professed desire to have the messianic mystery solved.

> An evil and adulterous generation seeketh after a sign; and there shall no sign be given to it, but the sign of the prophet Jonas [Jonah] (Matt. 12:39).

Yeshua is now about to reveal the first stage of the progressive unveiling for those who have eyes to see, ears to hear and hearts to understand. The Master now declares the sign that solves the mystery of the ages.

> For as Jonas [Jonah] was **three** days and **three** nights in the whale's belly; so shall the Son of man be **three** days and **three** nights in the heart of the earth (Matt. 12:40 – Emphasis added).

The dilemma now facing the scribes and Pharisees, the revered and trusted spiritual leaders of Israel, becomes decisively "clear"… *What is this man revered as a prophet talking about? What does he mean by declaring he will be "three days" in the earth?* But then the same leaders condemned Yeshua to death, declaring to the Roman Procurator Pilate: "Sir, we remember that that deceiver said, while he was yet alive, After **three** days I will rise again. Command, therefore, that the sepulchre be made sure until the **third** day…" (Matt. 27:63-66).

The record then resolves the "third day" mystery until its final and eternal revelation or unveiling. History reveals Yeshua's resurrection after three days in Aramathea's sealed tomb, buried before sundown as the Passover sabbath approached, arising again early on the first day of the week (Luke 23:52-56; 24:1-8). Early on the first day, "very early in the morning," women came bearing burial spices only to discover the sealed stone was rolled away, with angelic appearance present to testify of the fulfillment of the promised sign, saying to the bereaved:

Why seek ye the living among the dead?

He is not here, but is risen: remember how he spake unto you when he was yet in Galilee,

Saying, The Son of man must be delivered into the hands of sinful men, and be crucified, and the **third day** rise again.

And they remembered his words (Luke 24:5-8).

But the unveiling of the messianic mystery is not yet complete. This was but a preliminary foretaste… a prophetic preview… of the final unveiling or *apocalypse* as it is frequently known. To this point we have seen "the sign of Jonah" fulfilled in the life of Yeshua as the only truly obedient Israelite who ever lived, born not of man but of HaShem through a virgin, raised miraculously from the dead on the **third day**, defying death that human destiny might have the eternal hope of salvation for those who believe and receive His sacrifice for forgiveness of sin. Comes now the *Apocalypse…* the final unveiling.

The Apocalypse

It is time now to revisit the *Apocalypse*. As used in common parlance, whenever the word *apocalyptic* is used, it is used to imply or convey something catastrophic – impending doom. It is fascinating to realize that the word has been used with ever-increasing frequency since the 1970s to describe the growing perception of the dire nature of world events and has been applied broadly to issues of economics, climate, health, lawlessness, etc.

But what does the word *Apocalypse* really mean? From where does the word come, and why is the Book of Revelation called "The Apocalypse?" Has our pattern of common usage actually observed its true meaning and implications?

In actuality, the word *Apocalypse* is translated "Revelation," in the final book of the Christian Bible, therefore, it is actually the "Apocalypse of Jesus Christ" meaning "revelation." This is significant beyond mere information, because the Revelation calls for profound transformation in view of the eternal nature of that which is revealed. A true translation of Apocalypse is therefore "The Unveiling" of Messiah, Yeshua HaMashiach.

For historic and spiritual clarity, we must understand from what source the word *Apocalypse* is derived. The profound meaning and its implications then emerge from mere information to set the stage for ultimate personal and world transformation as we choose to embrace the awesome nature of what is actually made manifest, thus forever unveiling "the mystery of the ages."

The word *apocalyptic* occurs 18 times in the New Testament (the prophetic completion and fulfillment of the Torah and Tanakh). It comes from the Greek noun *apokalupsis* and also appears 26 times in the verb form *apokalupto*. The words derive from the combination of the Greek preposition *apos* and the verb *kalupto*, resulting in the definition "to uncover, to unveil, or reveal."[1] Thus, the Book of Revelation is the final unveiling of the mystery of the ages. Yet the "mystery" will only be solved by those who both now "see" the truth of what is unveiled and receive it as true to define the destiny of their lives.

Message of the Unveiled Messiah

What, then, is the distilled message of the unveiled Messiah – the long-awaited Yeshua HaMashiach from the Unveiling or Revelation?

1. The purpose was to "show unto his servants the things which must shortly come to pass (Rev. 1:1).
2. "The time is at hand" for the unveiling and its eternal consequences (Rev. 1:3).

3. Jesus Christ – Yeshua HaMashiach "is the first begotten of the dead [through resurrection] and is "the prince of the kings of the earth" as foretold by Isaiah (Rev. 1:5).
4. Yeshua HaMashiach is "Alpha and Omega, the beginning and the ending," "which is, and which was, and which is to come, the Almighty" (Rev. 1:8).
5. Yeshua is "he that liveth, and was dead" and "is alive for ever-more," and has "the keys of hell of death" (Rev. 1:18).
6. Yeshua HaMashiach "has created all things" and for "[his] thy pleasure they are and were created" (Rev. 4:11).
7. Yeshua is "the Lamb that was slain" for salvation from sin and to bring reconciliation to God without the blood of bulls and goats, therefore "every creature which is in heaven, and on the earth" shall cry "Blessing, and honour, and glory, and power, be unto him that sitteth upon the throne, and unto the Lamb for ever and ever" (Rev. 5:12-13).
8. Yeshua "wast slain, and hast redeemed us to God by [his] blood out of every kindred, and tongue, and people, and nation" (Rev. 5:9).
9. Yeshua's wrath will finally fall upon "the kings of the earth, and the great men… and every bondman, and every free man" which will "hid[e] themselves… from the face of him that sitteth upon the throne, and from the wrath of the Lamb: for the great day of his wrath is come; and who shall be able to stand?" (Rev. 6:15-17) (Note: See also Psa. 2; Joel 1:15; 2:1-2, 11-12; Amos 4:12; 5:15-24; Mal. 3:1-18).
10. True followers of Yeshua HaMashiach as the prophetic "Lamb of God" who took away the sins of those who would trust Him must continue through trying times, not pledging allegiance to and trust in a counterfeit messiah and his "beast" empire by receiving his mark. "Here is the patience [endurance] of the saints: here are they that…"

> "Keep the commandments of God," and
> Keep "the faith of Jesus" (Rev. 14:9-12).

11. "Whosoever will not be found written in the book of life" (having received by faith the substitutionary sacrifice of Yeshua as the prophesied "Lamb of God") will be "cast into the lake of fire (Rev. 20:15).

12. A "new heaven and a new earth" is prepared for the "Bride of Christ" who has figuratively washed their garments in his blood and "made themselves ready" (Rev. 21:1-2, 19:7-10) for the THIRD DAY.

13. Yeshua HaMashiach is "Alpha and Omega, the beginning and the end, the first and the last" (Rev. 22:13).

14. "Behold, I come quickly" (Rev. 22:7, 12, 20).

Behold – He Comes

Messiah came once as an inconspicuous babe, just as prophesied by Isaiah, saying, "For unto us a child is born, unto us a son is given…" confirmed by angels and shepherds one starry night at Bethlehem, the birthplace of King David, upon whose throne Mashiach was promised to reign (Isa. 9:6-7; Matt. 1:18-25; Luke 1:26-55). As foretold, this child and son would ultimately reign over both Israel and all nations, the government of which would be "upon his shoulders" out of which righteous government the redemption of the world would be effectuated, bringing "peace on earth, good will toward men" as "Prince of Peace" (Isa. 9:6-7; Luke 2:1-14).

Again, as foretold by Hebrew prophets, He must come again. Just as HaShem came to Israel on Mt. Sinai on "the THIRD DAY," even so will HaShem, manifested in His Son, return on "the THIRD DAY" of prophetic history, for it was written:

Come, and let us return unto the LORD…

After two days will he revive us: in the third day he will raise us up, and we shall live in his sight (Hos. 6:1-2).

Two thousand years ago the "child was born" and "the Son was given." He was crucified even as the Psalmist had prophesied in Psalm 22:1-18, and after **three days** in the grave, He was raised from the dead, much to the fear and consternation of the reigning religious leaders who suborned perjury to protect their reputations, so that the reality of the promised redeemer would not be recognized among the Jewish people.

Have We Entered "The Third Day?"

Since God does not inhabit time but rather eternity, "one day is with the Lord as a thousand years, and a thousand years as one day" (II Pet. 3:8). Dear reader, have we not entered, "THE THIRD DAY?" We are now in the third millennium following the birth, ministry, death and resurrection of the ONE born to rule on the throne of David as KING of kings and LORD of lords. His name, again, is "Wonderful, Counselor, The Mighty God, The Everlasting Father, The Prince of Peace." He is the incarnate expression of the "I AM," full of grace and truth (I John 1:10-13).

"Behold the Lamb of God, which taketh away the sins of the world" (John 1:29), crucified on Passover, yet a lamb without blemish (I Pet. 1:18-21) "Surely," declared Isaiah, "he hath borne our briefs and carried our sorrows...." "But he was wounded for our transgressions, he was bruised for our iniquities: the chastisement of our peace was upon him: and with his stripes we are healed." Yet, "we esteemed him not." Even so, "the LORD hath laid on him the iniquity of us all" (Isa. 53:3-6).

The world now awaits the manifestation of Mashiach...Messiah... in this "third day." Time and eternity are rapidly becoming congruent such that, with the trumpet sound of the seventh angel from heaven "there should be time no more" for "in the days of the voice of the seventh angel, when he shall begin to sound [as at Sinai], the mystery of God should be finished, as he hath declared to his servants the prophets" (Rev. 10:7).

"Today if you will hear his voice, harden not your hearts, as in the provocation, in the day of temptation in the wilderness" (Heb. 3:6-19), and as both Jew and Gentile have to this day. To whom did HaShem swear "that they [Israel] should not enter into his rest [the Promised Land], but to them that believed not [did not obey]? So we see that they could not enter in because of unbelief." "Let us therefore fear, lest, a promise being left us of entering into his rest [the eternal presence of Messiah], any of you should seem to come short of it" (Heb. 3:18-4:1).

> Now all these things happened unto them for ensamples: and they were written for our admonition, **upon whom the ends of the world are come.**

> Wherefore let him that thinketh he standeth [is ready] take heed lest he fall (I Cor. 10:1-12).

"See that ye refuse not him that speaketh. For if they escaped not who refused him that spake on earthat Sinai, much more shall not we escape, if we turn away from him that speaketh from heaven."

"Whose voice then shook the earth [at Sinai]: but now he hath promised, saying, Yet once more I shake not the earth only, but also heaven."

"Wherefore we receiving a kingdom which cannot be moved [the eternal Kingdom of Messiah for those who receive Him], let us have grace, whereby we may serve God acceptably [through Messiah] with reverence and godly fear."

"For our God is a consuming fire [just as at Sinai]" (Heb. 12:25-29).

Are You Ready for "The THIRD DAY"?

Are we nearing History's Final Hour? Have we entered "The THIRD DAY," or is it lurking unsuspectingly around the corner? Time will tell the tale, concluding the "mystery of the ages." But will it for you remain a *mystery*?

Consider soberly that we have seemingly entered the seventh millennium based upon biblical history. Since the time of Creation, approximately 6000 years have passed, affording humankind a "week" of work in preparation for a Millennium "sabbath rest," even as God created, as recorded, in six days, and the seventh day "blessed and sanctified," ceasing from His work (Gen. 2:1-3). All of the signs of our times and the rapid progression of prophetic fulfillment seem powerfully to indicate that our world now faces its ultimate messianic moment – a destiny-determining time to choose. The choice is relatively simple – HaShem's revealed Messiah... or a counterfeit. On whom will you place your eternal trust on THE THIRD DAY?

Before the first coming of messiah as a suffering servant to save us from our sin, the prophet foretold a forerunner who would "Prepare the Way of the LORD" (Isa. 40:3). It was, as it were, a voice "that crieth in the wilderness," implying that few would truly heed and respond by faith. That voice cried once for about six months to prepare for the coming messianic "Lamb of God" (John 1:23-34; Luke 3:3-22).

HaShem (God) is again raising up such a voice in a veritable "wilderness" of iniquitous unbelief to prepare the way for the mystery of God to be fulfilled in Yeshua HaMashiach. Again God, in His mercy and longsuffering, His *chesed* (lovingkindness) and divine patience, is sending forth the voice of "Elijah," just as He did with John the Baptist. As it is written:

> Behold, I will send my messenger, and he shall prepare the way before me...

> But who may abide [endure] the day of his coming? and who shall stand when he appeareth? for he is like a refiner's fire, and like fuller's soap (Mal. 3:1-3).

> Behold, I will send you Elijah the prophet before the coming of the great and dreadful day of the LORD: And he shall turn the heart of the fathers to the children, and the heart of the children to their fathers... (Mal. 4:5-6).

Chapter 30

BEHOLD!
HE COMES QUICKLY!

*"Suddenly, the unveiling explodes in unfathomable
and fearful glory before terrified eyes."*

TIME AND ETERNITY ARE RAPIDLY BECOMING CONGRUENT! While it is said that "Time marches on," there is soon coming a moment in which "time shall be no more" at the consummate merging of history and prophecy revealed in the glorious appearance of Messiah.

The ancient prophet Joel gave dramatic warning of that no-longer-mysterious expectation with words wooing and warning all humanity, Jew and Gentile, to be prepared. Consider soberly his pleas…

> Gird yourselves, and lament… Alas for the day! for the day of the LORD is at hand…. Blow ye the trumpet in Zion, and sound an alarm in my holy mountain: let all the inhabitants of the land tremble: for the day of the LORD cometh, for it is nigh at hand.
>
> And the LORD shall utter his voice… for the day of the LORD is great and very terrible; and who can abide it?

Therefore… saith the LORD, turn ye even to me with all your heart, and with fasting, and with weeping, and with mourning: And rend your heart, and not your garments….” (Joel 1:13-15, 2:1-17).

"Every Eye Shall See Him!"

Human imagination, enshrouded in a mysterious cloud of "business-as-usual" thinking, pre-conceived notions couched in religious and philosophical isms, and various levels of dis-belief and unbelief, seem either unable or unwilling to comprehend the shocking-to-our-human sensibilities event soon to wrap up history as we know it.

Whether or not you, I, or we believe it is irrelevant in that it is decreed by a divine Creator, unveiling the divinely-ordained plan for destiny, resulting in either eternal bliss or eternal damnation, depending solely upon our willingness to choose. Consequences will flow inevitably from our choices which ultimately will be based not on feelings but on true and convincing faith, culminating either in joyful hope or unprecedented horror.

Here, then, is what we should expect as the end of time is manifested in the "unveiling of the mystery of the ages." Here is a clear presentation of the unprecedented revelation of the Prince of Peace to a persistently rebellious planet.

1. **HE WILL COME IN DUE SEASON**

   A season is neither a day nor an hour but a broader, yet observable and definable period of time. The ancient prophets spoke with varying levels of specificity regarding the "season" of the Messiah's appearance. Yet there was little discernment among Israel's trusted religious leaders, either as to the season or identifying marks of the prophesied Mashiach because of pre-conceived expectations. When tested as to signs from heaven verifying the Messiah's coming, Yeshua responded to both the Pharisees and Sadducees, marveling that they could "not discern the signs of the times" (Matt. 16:1-4). Jesus wept over Jerusalem because spiritual blindness had "hid from thine eyes" the reality of the messianic presence in their midst, stating that their viewpoint enshrouded their perceptions so that "thou knewest not the time of thy visitation" by Messiah (Luke 19:41-44).

Revelation, however, was not lacking to those Jews having intimately witnessed Yeshua's ministry and the concurring events following His resurrection. Here are but a few setting the identity of the season, not for a first coming but for a second coming of the Mashiach.

A. Matt. 24:14 – The end shall come when the "gospel of the kingdom" is preached throughout the world as a witness, which has now been accomplished.

B. Rom. 11:25 – The mystery will be revealed when "the fulness of the Gentiles" is completed, only then will the "blindness in part that is happened to Israel" be unveiled.

C. Gal. 4:4 – Just as God sent forth his Son, Yeshua, in "the fulness of time," even so will the Son return in His glory in *the fulness of time.*

D. Mal. 4:1-6 – Just as HaShem sent forth John the Baptist to prepare the way so prophesied by Isaiah 40:3 before Yeshua's first coming as Israel's Messiah, even so will HaShem, as a just God, send forth another in the spirit of Elijah to prepare the way for Yeshua's Second Coming so that all, both Jew and Gentile, will be forewarned to prepare so as to escape "the great and dreadful day of the LORD" when Messiah comes to "judge the world with righteousness, and the people with his truth" (Psa. 96:13; Psa. 98:9; Acts 17:31).

2. **HE WILL COME ROYALLY**

The book of the Unveiling (Apocalypse) declares that upon Mashiach's return He will come (not as servant and shepherd as at the first) but rather as a reigning royalty with "a name written, KING OF KINGS, and LORD OF LORDS." He came first on a donkey as prophesied in Zechariah 9:9, but returns on "a white horse" to "judge and make war" against the unrighteousness of all nations and against the reigning beast empire and its counterfeit christ (Rev. 19:11-21).

3. HE WILL COME SUDDENLY

The planet and its people have been given not less that two millennia to prepare, because God is just and has always given due process through His servants the prophets. But the heavenly court is about to be seated and the time to make ready is rapidly waning. As Yeshua passionately warned:

> Watch therefore: for ye know not what hour your Lord doth come.
>
> Therefore be ye also ready: for in such an hour as ye think not the Son of man cometh (Matt. 24:42-44).

4. HE WILL COME UNSUSPECTINGLY

One would reasonably think that after nearly 2700 plus years of prophetic wooing and warning that seemingly otherwise intelligent people would seriously prepare their lives for such a momentous and forewarned moment of Messiah's unveiling, but a veil has somehow blinded the eyes, minds and hearts of the masses, both Jew and Gentile. "As it was in the days of Noah," Jesus warned, "so shall it be also in the days of the Son of man" (Luke 17:26). It will be business as usual, until suddenly the unveiling explodes in unfathomable and fearful glory before their terrified eyes.

5. HE WILL COME VISIBLY AND BODILY

Messiah's coming will not be a matter of virtual reality nor a figment of the imagination. On the contrary, the physical descendants of Abraham, Isaac and Jacob "shall look upon me whom they have pierced," declared the Lord (Zech. 12:10). In fact,

> Every eye shall see him, and they also which pierced him: and all kindreds of the earth shall wail because of him [because they were unprepared] (Rev. 1:7).

Messiah shall "come in like manner" as his disciples watched Him ascend to heaven from the Mt. of Olives many days after his resurrection. Such return was poignantly foretold by the Hebrew prophet Zechariah, declaring, "Behold, the day of the LORD cometh," and "his feet shall stand in that day upon the mount of Olives" and "the mount of Olives shall cleave in the midst thereof" forming a great valley (Zech. 14:1-4).

6. HE WILL COME DRAMATICALLY

The high drama experienced by Israel at Mt. Sinai at the giving by God of the "Ten Words" or *Ten Commandments* will be re-enacted with even greater drama at the coming/ return of the Living Word – Mashiach. As it is written by Rabbi Shaul...

> For the Lord himself shall descend from heaven with a shout, with the voice of the archangel, and with the trump [divine shofar] of God... (I Thess. 4:16).

As disclosed in the *Apocalypse* – the final and indisputable Unveiling – unequalled drama will disclose the decisive conclusion, resolving for time and eternity the "mystery of the ages."

> And I saw heaven opened, and behold a white horse; and he that sat upon him was called

Faithful and True… and his name is called The
Word of God.

And he hath on his vesture and on his thigh
a name written, KING OF KINGS, AND
LORD OF LORDS (Rev. 19:11-16).

What Then Should We Do?

This is the question posed by the Jewish seekers who came to
hear "the voice of one crying in the wilderness" to prepare for the
first coming of the one called Yeshua (Jesus) who was sent to "save his
people from their sins" (Matt. 1:21; Luke 3:3-17). The prophet Isaiah
had foretold of this "Elijah that was to come" for the express purpose
to "Prepare the way of the LORD," calling the people to "make straight
in the desert a highway for our God" (Isa. 40:3-5). He further foretold
of the Messiah's Second Coming, declaring…

And the glory of the LORD shall be revealed, and **all flesh
shall see it together:** for the mouth of the LORD hath
spoken it (Isa. 40:5 – emphasis added).

But when John the Baptist, as the one who came in the spirit
and power of Elijah, called the people to "Prepare ye the way of the
Lord," they failed to comprehend in their spiritual blindness what
their response should be, so they cried out…

"What shall we do then? (Luke 3:10)?

This Hebrew (Jewish) prophet boldly proclaimed the message of
HaShem's expectation for the people, to begin first in Israel:

"Repent ye: for the kingdom of heaven is at hand" (Matt. 3:2).

This call to repentance was attitude and behavior specific. It
required a change of mind and heart out of which their ways would

become pleasing to God. He warned that rabbinic practices and religious traditions were actually frustrating the faith God desired, warning both the Pharisees and Sadducees to forget about merely claiming a heritage through Abraham but to live holy themselves and to "bring forth therefore fruits meet for repentance" (Matt. 3:7-9). It was time for broken-hearted confession of sin and turning from it in genuine repentance (Matt. 3:6).

This same John [the one coming in prophetic fulfillment of the "Elijah" that was to come] made clear to those coming to repent and be baptized that he was not the Christ [Messiah] but merely a forerunner to prepare the way for the one Jesus (Yeshua) whom he declared to be "the Lamb of God, which taketh away the sins of the world" (John 1:29). When Yeshua came also to be baptized (to fulfill all righteousness), John proclaimed that he witnessed the Spirit of God descend upon Yeshua in the form of a dove, coupled with a voice from heaven, saying, "This is my beloved Son, in whom I am well pleased," thus confirming the messianic anointing proclaimed by the Psalmist (Psa. 2:7), further proclaiming for all time…

"Blessed are all they that put their trust in him" (Psa. 2:12).

Yeshua then came preaching "the gospel [good news] of the kingdom of God…" (Mark 1:14). His message was not informational but rather transformational. He need not talk theoretically or didactically about the Torah or the word of God because he was the living Torah, transformed into human flesh so as to "flesh out" God's true meaning and intent. Thus, the people were astonished, "for he taught them as one that had authority, and not as the scribes" (Mark 1:22).

The message made manifest over the two millennia last passed has never changed. It is a message calling all peoples to repent of unbelief, disbelief and rejection of Messiah and His call to righteousness. The cry of the Father echoes down through time – "Today, if you will hear my voice, harden not your heart."

"Repent and believe the gospel" cried Yeshua and his Jewish disciples (Mark 1:15). The heart of the gospel is that Yeshua is the long-awaited Messiah, and if we would have the hope of salvation from the sin that besets us, we must confess our sin before Him, accept His blood as the sole and final sacrifice, repent from our sinful ways, and place our full trust and confidence in Him, whether we be Jew or Gentile.

Time is fleeting and the moment of truth lies straight ahead in the valley of decision. Soon, the trumpet will sound, and time will be no more. Messiah came once to save us from our sin. When He comes again, He will judge us in and for our sin.

The Apocalypse – the Book of the Unveiling – the Book of Revelation brings to us a crescendo of divine plea for our precipitous moment on the near edge of Messiah's Second Coming. The word *repent* occurs seven times from Revelation 1 through Revelation 22 amid the final Unveiling. He that hath ears to hear, let him or her hear. Repentance begins with humbly receiving Yeshua (Jesus) as Messiah, trusting Him for salvation, and conducting your life in trusting obedience to His Word, His Will and His Ways. Are you ready for THE THIRD DAY?

> Multitudes, multitudes [are] in the valley of decision: for the day of the LORD is near in the valley of decision (Joel 3:14).

Endnotes

Chapter 2

1. Richard C. Lewontin, "Billions and Billions of Demons" review of *The Demon-Haunted World* by Carl Sagan, January 9, 1997.

Chapter 3

1. Maimonides, *Mishneh Torah* (Melachim uMilchamot, Chapter 11).

Chapter 5

1. "Messiah Where?", Herb Keinon, The *Jerusalem Post International Edition*, August 10, 1997, pp. 20-22.
2. "Chief Rabbi Sees Imminent Coming of Messiah," *WorldNetDaily.com*, August 12, 2005.
3. "Two Messiahs," jewishroots.net/library/messiah/twomessiahs, January 19, 2021.
4. Hasidic Judaism," Wikipedia.org/wiki/Hasidic. February 7, 2021.
5. Ibid.
6. Ibid.
7. Ibid.
8. "Rabbi Reveals Name of Messiah," *israeltoday.co.il*, April 30, 2007.
9. "Zion Needs the Messiah," Yosef ben Shlomo Hakohen, *Arutz Sheva* (Israel National News), israelnationalnews.com, March 1, 2009.

Chapter 6

1. "The Age of Aquarius 2020: Now is the Time For Revelation," Sara Shipman, starcrazypie.com/2020/07/25/the-age-of-acquarius-2020, January 19, 2021.
2. Ibid.

3. "2020 The Start of New World Order! The Dawn of the Age of Aquarius," blog.spirituality.com/2020-the-start-of-the-new-world-order, January 19, 2021.

4. Op. cit., "The Age of Aquarius 2020…."

5. Op. cit., "The Age of Aquarius 2020…."

6. Op. cit., "2020 The Start of New World Order!…"

7. "John Kerry: Biden presidency opens door to globalist 'Great Reset,'" Art Moore, wnd.com/2020/4871642.

8. Ibid.

9. Ibid.

10. Ibid.

11. Ibid.

12. Op. cit., "The Age of Aquarius 2020…"

13. John A Steinbacher, *Senator Robert Francis Kennedy, the Man, the Mysticism, the Murder,* pg. 29, quoting Helena Petrona Blavatsky.

14. H.P. Blavatsky, *The Secret Doctrine Vol. II, Anthropogenesis,* Blavatsky Collected Writings 1888, The Theosophical University Press, Pasadena, CA, 1988, p. 513.

15. *An Abridgment of the Secret Doctrine,* edited by Elizabeth Preston and Christmas Humphreys, Quest Books, The Theosophical Publishing House, 1966, p. 38.

16. Ibid, p. 38.

17. Gary H. Kah, *The New World Religion,* Hope International Publishing, Inc, 1999, p. 29.

18. Ibid, p. 30.

19. Ibid, p. 30.

20. Ibid, p. 46.

Chapter 7

1. *All About Spirituality,* allaboutspirituality.org/new-age.

2. New Age Religions; Major Religions of the World, majorreligions.com/ new_age, (as of February 16, 2021).

3. Is President Lorenzo Snow's oft-repeated statement – "As man now is, God once was; as God now is, man may be"—accepted as official doctrine by the Church?, https://www.churchofjesuschrist.org/study/

ensign/1982/02/i-have-a-question/is-president-snows-statement-as-man-now-is-god-once-was-as-god-now-is-man-may-be-accepted-as-official-doctrine?lang=eng. (as of February 24, 2021).

4. Gary H Kah, *The New World Religions*, Hope International Publishing, Inc., Noblesville, Indiana, 1999, p. 20.

5. Ibid, p. 30.

6. Warren B. Smith, *False Christ Coming—Does Anybody Care?: What New Age Leaders Really Have in Store for America, The Church, and the World*, Mountain Stream Press, Magalia, CA, 2011, pp. 17-19.

7. Ibid, p. 20.

8. Ibid, pp. 20, 25-27.

9. Ibid, pp. 35-40.

10. Maitreya (Theosophy), www.wikipedia.org/wiki/Maitreya, (as of February 18, 2021).

11. Is Maitreya the antichrist?, www.gotquestions.org/Maitreya-antichrist, (as of February 18, 2021).

12. Op. cit., *False Christ Coming…*, p. 49.

13. Charles Crismier, *King of the Mountain*, Elijah Books (Richmond, VA), 2013, p. 109.

14. Ibid, pp. 111-112.

15. Ibid, p. 155.

16. Ibid, pp. 113-123.

17. "The Messiah Factor" – "Der Messias Faktor," *Der Spiegel*, Spiegel online, July 2008, cover story.

18. "Who Runs The World?" Wrestling for Influence," *The Economist*, internet edition, July 7, 2008, p.3.

19. Jerome Rifkin, "New Europe Shapes Its Version of Dream," *Richmond Times Dispatch*, November 7, 2004, p. E-1, from *The Washington Post*.

20. Jerome R. Corsi, "Bush OK's 'integration' with European Union," *worldnetdaily.com*, May 8, 2007.

21. Jerome R. Corsi, "7-year plan aligns with Europe's economy," *worldnetdaily.com*, January 16, 2008.

22. Ian Traynor, "love tops agenda as Sarkozy launches Mediterranean Union," *The Guardian, guardian.co.uk*, July 14, 2008.

23. Benita Ferrero-Waldner, "The Secret of Europe's Success," *Haaretz Israel News, haaretz.com*, May 9, 2007.

24. Kobi Nachomi, "The Sanhedrin's peace initiative," *ynetnews.com*, May 6, 2007.

25. Steve Watson, "Euro Globalists: Anyone Who Resists EU Is a Terrorist," *New Interviews, prisonplanet.com*, June 18, 2007.

26. Op. cit., *King of the Mountain*, pp. 113-123.

Chapter 8

1. Warren B Smith, *False Christ Coming*, Mountain Stream Press, Magalia CA, 2011, pp. 80-81.

2. Ibid, pp. 80-81.

3. Ibid, p. 76.

4. Charles Crismier, *King of the Mountain*, Elijah Books, Richmond VA, 2013, pp. 111-112.

5. Op. cit., *False Christ Coming*, p. 76

6. Ibid, p. 77.

7. Gary H. Kah, *The New World Religion*, Noblesville, Indiana: Hope International Publishing Inc, 1998.

8. Ibid, p. 77.

9. Ibid, p. 209.

10. Ibid, p. 203.

11. Ibid, p. 204.

12. Ibid, p. 65.

13. Ibid, p. 65.

14. Ibid, p. 65.

15. Ibid, p. 65.

16. Ibid, p. 206.

17. Ibid, p. 206.

18. Ibid, p. 216.

19. James A. Beverly, "Smorgasborg Spirituality," *Christianity Today*, January 10, 2000, p. 30.

20. "One World Religion on its way?", *worldnetdaily.com*, June 14, 2005.

21. Ibid.

22. John Dart, "Ecumenism's New Basis: testimony," *Christian Century*, August 21, 2007, p. 12.

23. Ibid.

24. Ibid, p. 13.

25. Mike Anton and William Lobdell, "Hold the Fire and Brimstone", *Los Angeles Times*, June 19, 2002.

26. Zachary Keyser, "House of Worship for Christians, Jews, Muslims being built in Berlin," https://www.jpost.com/diaspora/house-of-worship-for-christians-jews-muslims-being-built-in-berlin-660560, March 1, 2021.

27. Sergei Rzhevsky in Culture, Religion, Travel, "The Temple of All Religions in Kazan," https://russiatrek.org/blog/culture/the-temple-of-all-religions-in-kazan/, as of March 1, 2021.

28. Samuel B. Freedman, "A Church That Embraces All Religions and Rejects 'Us' vs. 'Them'," *The New York Times*, https://www.nytimes.com/2013/07/13/us/a-religion-that-embraces-all-religions.html.

29. Bahá'í Faith, *Wikipedia*, https://en.wikipedia.org/wiki/Bah%C3%A1%CA%BC%C3%AD_Faith.

30. "Pope Francis: Even Atheists can be Redeemed", heard on *Morning Edition* on NPR. https://www.npr.org/sections/parallels/2013/05/29/187009384/Pope-Francis-Even-Atheists-Can-Be-Redeemed

31. "Netanyahu: People of All Faiths Can Worship at Temple Mount", https://www.voanews.com/world-news/middle-east-dont-use/netanyahu-people-all-faiths-can-worship-temple-mount, November 2, 2014.

32. "United House of Prayer for All People," Wikepedia.org/united

33. Olive J. Hemmings, *The Emerging Church, Oprah Winfrey, and the Reshaping of American of American Conciousness*, Washington Adventist University, (Publishing date unknown, available via the internet)

34. Rav Berg, "What is Messiah?", *The Kabbalah Centre, Kabbalah Magazine Vol. 5*, Issue 1, 2000, Republished January 19, 2015.

35. Alan Rosebaum, "Kabbalah Book review: The fundamental ideas of Kabbalah," https://www.jpost.com/kabbalah/book-review-from-infinity-to-man-the-fundamental-ideas-of-kabbalah-634198, July 23, 2020.

36. Charles G. Finney, *The Character, Claims and Practical Workings Of Freemasonry*, 1869, later republished by JKI Publishing, Tyler, Texas, 1998.

37. Arnoldo M.A. Goncalves, "Freemasonry and Jewish Kabbalah: An Unusual Association," *Journal of Liberal Arts and Humanities*, April 2020, pp. 48-58.

38. Op. cit., Charles G. Finney, pp. 89-90.

39. Christopher Earnshaw, PhD 33d, *Freemasonry: Quest for Immortality, Book Reviews*, The Masonic Library and Museum of Pennsylvania, June 17, 2020.

40. Ibid.

Chapter 9

1. *Concise History of World Religions*, edited by Tim Cooke, National Geographic, Washington, DC, publication date unknown, p. 28.

2. "The Rise of Messianic Buddhism," https://taoofnewbuddhism. wordpress.com/2015/01/01/the-rise-of-messianic-buddhism/.

3. Op. cit., *Concise History of World Religions*, p. 43.

4. Op. cit., "The Rise of Messianic Buddhism."

5. Ibid, p. 25.

6. Prof. Johan Malan, Middleburg, South Africa, "Messianic Expectations in the Eastern Religions," https://bibleguidance.co.za/Engarticles/Eastern.htm, April 2007.

7. Ibid.

8. "What Do Hindus Believe About Jesus?", https://www.beliefnet.com/faiths/hinduism/2002/05/what-do-hindus-believe-about-jesus.aspx.

9. "Bahá'í Faith," https://en.wikipedia.org/wiki/Bah%C3%A1%CA%B-C%C3%AD_Faith.

Chapter 10

1. James Patterson and Peter Kim, *The Day America Told the Truth*, New York, Penguin, 1991, pg. 25.

2. *Forbes* Magazine, 75th Anniversary Issue, titled, "Why we feel so bad," September 1992.

3. "Stunning number of Americans don't hold a biblical worldview," Art Moore, https://www.wnd.com/2021/04/stunning-number-americans-dont-hold-biblical-worldview/.

4. "New Barna Poll: The Christian Church is Seriously Messed Up," https://pulpitandpen.org/2020/08/12/new-barna-poll-the-christian-church-is-seriously-messed-up/.

5. "Moralistic therapeutic deism," https://en.wikipedia.org/wiki/Moralistic_therapeutic_deism.

6. Ibid.

7. "Competing Worldviews Influence Today's Christians," https://www.barna.com/research/competing-worldviews-influence-todays-christians/.

8. "Moralistic Therapeutic Deism. What is it?—Roman Catholic Man," https://www.romancatholicman.com/moralistic-therapeutic-deism/.

Chapter 11

1. William J Federer (editor), *America's God and Country*, Fame Publishing, Inc., Coppell, Texas, 1994, pp. 10-11.

2. Ibid, pp. 701-702.

3. *Bahá'í Teachings for the New World Order*, compiled by Mouhebat Sobhani, Waldorf Enterprises, New York, NY, 1992.

4. David Langness, "The Bahá'í World Order," *bahaiteachings.org/bahai-world-order/*.

5. Ibid.

6. David Langess, "Globalization: welcome to the New World Order," *bahaiteachings.org/globalization-welcome-new-world-order/*.

7. Ibid.

8. Ibid.

Chapter 12

1. Dr. Hushidar Hugh Motlagh, *King of Kings* (ebook) on Amazon.com. Also, *King of Kings: Vol. III Prophecies of the Second Coming* (Paperback), December 18, 2020, Independently published.

2. "The World Order of Bahá ú lláh," https://www.bahai.org/library/authoritative-texts/shoghi-effendi/world-order-bahaullah/.

3. Ibid.

4. Ibid.

5. "The Bahá'í Faith and the UN," http://www.nwotoday.com/the-united-nations-is-world-government/the-baha-i-faith-and-the-united-nations.

6. Ibid.

7. Ibid.

8. Tim Hinchcliffe, "A Timeline of 'The Great Reset' Agenda," https://www.globalresearch.ca/timeline-great-reset-agenda-foundation-event-201-pandemic-2020/5745205 May 15, 2020 and June 6, 2021.

9. "The 'great reset' timeline, 2014 to 2021," https://www.worldtribune.com/the-great-reset-timeline-2014-to-2021/, May 17, 2021.

10. "GREAT RESET: 'By 2030 You'll Own Nothing And You'll Be Happy'," montana daily gazette.com/2021/06/30/

11. *Bahá'í Teachings for the New World Order*, compiled by Mouhebat Sobhani, Waldorf Enterprises, New York, NY, 1992.

12. Rachel Donadio and Laurie Goodstein, "Pope Urges Forming New World Economic Order to Work for the 'Common Good'," https://www.nytimes.com/2009/07/08/world/europe/08pope.html, July 8, 2009.

    Ethan A. Huff, "Pope calls for world government, 'New World Order'," https://www.naturalnews.com/038477_pope_world_government_new_order.html, December 27, 2012.

    "Pope Francis Calls for One World Government, Attacks Border Walls and National Sovereignty," https://pulpitandpen.org/?s=pope+francis+calls+for+one+world+government%2C+attacks+border+walls+and+national+sovereignty, May 3, 2019.

13. Op. cit. *Bahá'í Teachings for the New World Order*, p. 1.

14. "Full Text of Pope Francis' speech to United Nations," https://www.pbs.org/newshour/world/full-text-pope-francis-speech-united-nations, September 25, 2015

15. Ibid.

16. "Pope Francis Unveils Globalist New World Religion at Summit with United Nations' Leader," bigleaguepolitics.com/pope-francis-unveils-globalist-new-world-religion-at-summit-with-united-nations-leader/.

17. Rod Dreher, "Actually, the Pope wants global government too," https://www.theamericanconservative.com/dreher/pope-benedict-global-government-one-world-catholic/, October 25, 2011

18. Op. Cit., *Bahá'í Teachings for the New World Order*, p. 33.

19. Ibid, p. 49.

20. Ibid, p. 49.

21. Ibid, pp. 49-50.

22. Ibid, p. 51.

23. Ibid, pp. 51-52.

24. Baxter Dmitry, "Pope Francis Calls For 'One World Government' To 'Save Humanity'," newspunch.com/pope-francis-one-world-government/, June 23, 2017.

Chapter 13

1. Alex Knapp, "Jason Silva Muses on Humans Turning Into Gods," *Forbes*, August 5, 2011,

2. Proverbs 23:7, The *Bible*.

3. Gospel According to John, Chapter 1:1-14, The *Bible*.

4. "Transhumanism," *Wikipedia*, Wikipedia.org/wiki/transhumanism.

5. *TIME* Magazine cover title, "2045 – The Year Man Becomes Immortal," February 21, 2011 Feature article by Lev Grossman.

6. Op. cit., "Transhumanism," Wikipedia.

7. Sharon Begley, *TIME*, "Genome, Uncoding the Human Body," April 10, 2000.

8. "The most important map ever," "Human genome's mad map opens new era of evidence," Los Angeles Times/ Washington Post News Service, as reported by *Richmond Times Dispatch*, June 27, 2000, p. 1 and A6.

9. Ibid, "Public private ventures share major achievement."

10. "'Playing God': Cloning fans debate," *The Cincinnati Post*, February 25, 1997, p. 1 and 6A.

11. Sharon Begley, "Can We Clone Humans?", *Newsweek* cover, March 10, 1997, with cover story titled "Little Lamb, Who Made Thee?", pp. 53-59.

12. Kenneth L. Woodward, "Today the Sheep…," *Newsweek*, March 10, 1997, p. 60.

13. Ibid.

14. George Dvorsky, "9 Unexpected Outcomes of Human Cloning," https://gizmodo.com/9-unexpected-outcomes-of-human-cloning-1606556772, July 17, 2014.

15. Abby Tang, Michelle Yan Huong, and Victoria Barranco, "The real reason we still haven't cloned humans," https://www.businessinsider.

com/ethics-of-human-cloning-scientific-progress-2020-7?op=1, April 14, 2021.

16. Robert Wright, "Can Souls Be Xeroxed?", *TIME*, March 10, 1997, p. 73.

17. Kenneth L. Woodward, "A Question of Life or Death," *NEWSWEEK*, July 9, 2001, p. 31.

18. "Human farms?," *WORLD*, July 17, 1999, p. 11.

19. Roy Maynard, "Double Trouble," cover story for *WORLD*, March 7, 1998, pp. 12-15, pg. 14.

20. Melinda Beck, et. al., "How Far Should We Push Mother Nature?", *NEWSWEEK*, pp. 54-57, January 17, 1994.

21. Daniel Martin and Simon Caldwell, "150 human animal hybrids grown in UK labs: Embryos have been produced secretively for the past three years," https://www.dailymail.co.uk/sciencetech/article-2017818/Embryos-involving-genes-animals-mixed-humans-produced-secretively-past-years.html, July 22, 2011.

22. Michael D. Lemonick, "The Sperm that Never Dies," *TIME*, June 10, 1996, p. 69.

23. Dr. W. French Anderson, "A Cure That May Cost Us Ourselves," *NEWSWEEK*, January 1, 2000, pp. 75-76.

24. Kurt Schenker, "Frozen Solid, Immortal, and Thawed Again—The Illusion Continues!", *Midnight Call*, November 2019, pp. 24-25.

25. David Brinn, "Is it possible that death may not be a foregone conclusion to life?", https://www.jpost.com/israel-news/meet-the-israelis-who-dont-believe-that-death-is-the-end-of-life-660164, February 27, 2021.

26. Jeffrey Kluger, "Can We Stay Young?", *TIME*, November 25, 1996, (Cover Story), pp. 89-98, specifically pp. 93 and 94.

27. Joe Kovaks, "They want to live forever. They want to be gods," wnd.com, February 21, 2021.

28. Ibid.

29. 'Big Data is transforming humanity," Anthony LoBaido, https://www.wnd.com/2019/07/big-data-is-transforming-humanity/.

30. Steve Elwart, "Transhumanism: Man's new quest for immortality," https://www.wnd.com/2014/09/transhumanism-mans-new-quest-for-immortality/, September 21, 2014. In Diversions, Front Page, Health, U.S., World.

31. Patrick Wood, "Technocracy News and Trends, as republished by *vachristian.org* under the title: "The Siamese Twins of Technocracy and Transhumanism," April 17, 2021.

32. "Transhumanism," wikipedia.org/wiki/Transhumanism.

33. Ronald Bailey, "Transhumanism: The Most Dangerous Idea?", https://reason.com/2004/08/25/transhumanism-the-most-dangero/, August 25, 2004.

34. Op. cit., "Transhumanism," wikipedia.org.

35. "Transhumanism—AAPS | Association of American Physicians and Surgeons," *aapsonline.org*, AAPS news, April 2021.

36. Ibid, also tinyurl.com/26apce8m.

37. Ibid.

38. Ibid.

39. Op.cit., "The Siamese Twins of Technology and Transhumanism."

40. Ibid.

Chapter 14

1. Aida Besancon Spencer, et. al., *THE GODDESS REVIVAL*, Baker Books, Grand Rapids MI 49516, 1995, p. 27.

2. Ibid.

3. Ibid, pg. 28.

4. Ibid, p. 77.

5. Ibid, p. 82.

6. Naomi R Goldenberg, *Changing of the Gods: Feminism and the End of Traditional Religions*, listing on amazon.com, including review comments.

7. Berit Kjos, "How Feminist Spirituality is Changing the Church: And Betraying the Women It Promised to Heal," Book review of *A Twisted Faith*, https://www.cuttingedge.org/news/n1645.cfm.

8. Robert Nelson, "Environmentalism Has Become Primitive Religion," *Richmond Times Dispatch,* op.ed., Earth Day April 22, 2010, p. A13.

Chapter 15

1. Robert Nelson, "Environmentalism Has Become Primitive Religion," *Richmond Times Dispatch*, op.ed., April 22, 2010, p. A-13.

2. Ibid.

3. Ibid.

4. Gary H. Kah, *The New World Religion*, Hope International Publishing, 1999, p. 135.

5. Ibid, p. 142.

6. Ibid, p. 143

7. Jerome R. Corsi, "U.N. advances global governance with climate accord," https://www.wnd.com/2016/04/u-n-advances-global-governance-with-climate-accord/, April 22, 2016.

8. Andrew Alderson, "Global warning has reached a 'defining moment,' Prince Charles warns," https://www.telegraph.co.uk/news/earth/environment/climatechange/4980347/Global-warming-has-reached-a-defining-moment-Prince-Charles-warns.html, March 12, 2009.

9. James Kirkup and Louise Gray, "Copenhagen climate summit: Barack Obama says 'world running out of time'," https://www.telegraph.co.uk/news/earth/copenhagen-climate-change-confe/6839650/Copenhagen-climate-summit-Barack-Obama-says-world-running-out-of-time.html, December 18, 2009.

10. Marc Morano, "Flashback: Gore: U.S. Climate Bill Will Help Bring About 'Global Governance'," https://www.climatedepot.com/2009/07/10/flashback-gore-us-climate-bill-will-help-bring-about-global-governance-2/, July 10, 2009.

11. Ibid.

12. Op. cit., *The New World Religion*, p. 155.

13. "New York Times columnist: Now Democrats have only 1 year to save planet," https://www.wnd.com/2021/07/new-york-times-columnist-now-democrats-1-year-save-planet/, July 2, 2021.

14. Arthur Fabel and Donald St. John (editors), *Tielhard in the 21st Century*, Orbis Books, New York, 2003, cover subtitle and p. 1.

15. Ibid.

16. Ibid, p. 77.

17. Ibid, p. 77-85.

18. Op. cit., "New York Times columnist: Now Democrats have only 1 year to save planet."

19. Ibid.

20. Op. cit., "U.N. Advances Global Governance with Climate Accord."

21. "Global Cooling," wikepidia.org.

22. "Global Warming Industry is hiding Developing 'Cold Sun' Dark Winter Phase," Russ Winter, https://www.winterwatch.net/2021/02/global-warming-industry-is-hiding-impending-cold-sun-dark-winter-phase/, February 16, 2021.

23. Ibid.

24. Patrice Lewis, "The Church of Global Warming," https://www.wnd.com/2009/12/117968/, December 5, 2009.

25. Ibid.

26. Jonathan Manthrope, "Global Warming is the new religion of First World urban elite," *Vancouversun.com*, July 28, 2009.

27. Gary H. Kah, *The New World Religion*, Hope International Publishing Inc, Indiana, 1999, pp. 155-157.

28. Ibid, pp. 155-157.

29. Dave, "Agenda 2030: Preparing the Way for the Antichrist & the New World Order," https://www.cuttingedgechristianity.com/religionspirituality/agenda-2030-preparing-the-way-for-the-antichrist-the-new-world-order/, November 17, 2015.

30. Larry L. Rassmussen, *Earth Community Earth Ethics*, Orbis Books, Maryknoll, N.Y., 1996, pp. 177-179.

31. Ibid, p. 104.

32. Ibid, p. 98.

33. Ibid, p. 350.

34. Cabot Phillips, "'EcoSexual' students at SMC 'marry the ocean'," https://www.campusreform.org/?ID=7622, May 26, 2016.

35. John Follain, "Pope Summons Scientists to Shape Climate Change Debate," *newsmax.com*, April 28, 2015.

36. Jason Devaney, "NY Times: Vatican Continues to Push Climate Change Agenda," *newsmax.com*, April 27, 2015.

Chapter 16

1. Arthur Fabel and Donald St. John (editors), *Teilhard in the 21st Century*, Orbis Books, Maryknoll, NY, 2004, p. 2.

2. Ibid, p. 4.

3. Ibid, p. 4.

4. Ibid, p. 6.

5. Ibid, p. 6.

6. Ibid, p. 8.

7. Ibid, p. 7.

8. Ibid, pp. 10-11.

9. Jerry Adler, "Evolution of a Scientist," *NEWSWEEK*, November 28, 2005, Cover Story, pp. 51-58, p. 54.

10. Ibid, p. 55.

11. Henry Morris, *Steeling the Mind of America*, New Leaf Press, June 1995, pp. 205-206.

12. Sarah Cassidy, "World Scientists Unite to Attack Creationism," *The Independent*, Online Edition, June 22, 2006, p. 1.

13. David Rogers, news story posted by National Post and Can West News Service online at www.canada.com, October 24, 2006.

14. Ernst Mayer, "Darwin's Influence on Modern Thought," *Scientific American* (vol. 283, 2000), p. 83.

15. Richard Levontin, *Review of the Demon-Haunted World*, by Carl Sagan, in *New York Review of Books*, January 9, 1997.

16. Mark Singham, "Teaching and Propaganda," *Physics Today*, (vol. 53, June 2000), p. 54.

17. Julian Huxley, *Essays of a Humanist*, Harper and Row, New York, 1964, p. 222.

18. Ibid.

19. Henry Morris, *Steeling of the Mind of America*, New Leaf Press, June 1995, pp. 220-221.

20. *Humanist Manifesto II*, 1973.

21. Ernst Mayr, "Darwin's Influence on Modern Thought," *Scientific American* (vol. 283, July 2000), p. 83.

22. Scott C. Todd, "A View from Kansas on the Evolution Debates," *Nature* (vol. 401, September 30, 1999), p. 423.

23. Will Provine, No Free Will," in *Catching Up With the Vision*, ed. By Margaret W. Rossiter, Chicago, University of Chicago Press, 1999, p. S123.

24. Henry Morris, *Steeling the Mind of America*, New Leaf Press, June 1995, p. 215.

ENDNOTES

Chapter 17

1. Kevin B. Nolan (Editor), *Karl Marx: The Materialist Messiah*, The Mercer Press, Dublin and Cork, 1984, the cover.

2. Warren S. Goldstein, "Messianism and Marxism: Walter enjamin and Ernst Bloch's Dialectical Thesis of Secularization," https://journals. sagepub.com/doi/abs/10.1177/08969205010270020501?journal-Code=crsb&, March 1, 2001.

3. John Spargo, "The Influence of Karl Marx on Contemporary Socialism," *The American Journal of Sociology*, Volume 16, Number 1, July 1910, pp. 21-40.

4. Ludovico Lalli, "Karl Marx, the Messiah," https://www.researchgate.net/ publication/339141236_Karl_Marx_the_Messiah, February 2020.

5. Antonius Aquinas, "Pope Francis Calls Marxist Economic Summit," https://stateofthenation.co/?p=5173, January 22, 2020.

6. Hanne Nabintu Herland, "How the neo-Marxist movement is strangling America," *WND News Center*, https://www.wndnewscenter.org/ how-the-neo-marxist-movement-is-strangling-america/, July 28, 2021.

Chapter 18

1. "Freemasonry", *Encyclopedia Britannica*, https.britannica.com/topic/ order-of-Freemasons

2. "What is Freemasonry and what do Freemasons Believe?", gotquestions. org.

3. Edmond Ronayne, *Handbook of Freemasonry* (1943), Chicago: Powner Co, 1973, p. 45.

4. Printed in *The Proceedings of the United States Anti-Masonic Convention* held in Philadelphia, September 11, 1830, and in John Quincy Adams Letters on the Masonic Institution, 1846.

5. H.L. Haywood, *Supplement to Mackey's Encyclopedia of Freemasonry*, vol. 3 (Chicago: The Masonic History Co, 1946) p. 1159.

6. Charles G. Finney, *The Character, Claims and Practical Workings of Freemasonry*, Jon Kregel, Inc, dba JKI Publishing, Tyler, Texas, 1998, pp. 5-13.

7. Ibid, p. 98.

8. Ibid, p. 99.

9. Ibid, pp. 135-137.

10. Ibid, p. 140.

11. Ibid, pp. 141-145.

12. Ibid, pp. 164-166.

13. J. Edward Decker, *Freemasonry: Satan's Door to America?*, Issaquah, WA: Free the Masons Ministries.

14. Op. cit., Charles G. Finney, p. XV.

15. John Quincy Adams, *Letters On The Masonic Institution*, Boston: T.R. Marvin, 1847, (Note: Cited also in *Charles G Finney* op cit., p. XV.

16. Albert Pike, *Morals and Dogma* (1871: Richmond VA: L. Jenkins, 1942), pp. 741, 744-745).

17. Albert G. Mackey, *Mackey's Encyclopedia of Freemasonry, vol. 2* (Chicago: The Masonic History Co., 1946), pp. 1022-1023.

18. "Illuminati of Bavaria," Ibid, vol. 1.

19. Op. cit., Charles G. Finney, pp. lxvi-lxvii.

20. Ibid, p. lxvii.

21. Ibid, p. 190.

22. Ibid, pp. 190-191.

23. Paul A. Fisher, *Behind the Lodge Door* (Washington, D.D., Shield, 1968), p. 57).

24. Ibid, p. 57.

25. Op. cit., Albert G. Mackey, "Public Schools," vol. 2, pp. 817-818.

26. Op. cit., Paul A. Fisher, pp. 186-187.

27. Op. cit., Charles G. Finney, p. 90.

Chapter 19

1. "The Top 7 Differences Between Talmud and Torah and Its definitions," https://kabbalahcenter.net/torah-vs-talmud-definition-and-top-7-differences/.

2. "LAWS, NOACHIAN," by Isidore Singer, Julius H. Greenstone, https://www.jewishencyclopedia.com/articles/9679-laws-noachian.

3. Ibid.

4. "The Rebbe and President Ronald Reagan," compiled by Dovid Zaklikowski, https://www.chabad.org/therebbe/article_cdo/aid/142535/jewish/The-Rebbe-and-President-Reagan.htm.

5. *Laws of Kings and Wars*, Translated from Rambam's Mishne Torah, Reuven Brauner, 2012, http://halakhah.com/rst/kingsandwars.pdf, Chapter 8, 8.14, p. 25.

6. Ibid, Chapter 8, 8.13.

7. "Beware of the Noahide Laws!" http://bewareofthenoahidelaws.followersofyah.com/.

8. "Shabbos Parshas Tsav, 5747," *Sichos in English*, vol. 35, p. 75.

9. "Conquer the World with Torah—A Message to the Shluchim Convention," 5747, *Sichos in English*, vol. 33, p. 270.

10. "Anatomy of a One World Religion?" https://stellarhousepublishing.com/theocracy/, Truth Be Known Archives.

11. Newly Formed Sanhedrin Ascend to Temple Mount," *Arutz Sheva News*, December 14, 2004.

12. "Sanhedrin Recognizes Council to Teach Humanity 'Laws of Noah'," *Arutz Sheva News*, June 9, 2006.

13. Avodat Kochavim-Chapter Ten, by Rabbi Moshe ben Maimon ("Maimonides"), translated by Eliyahu Touger, https://www.chabad.org/library/article_cdo/aid/912369/jewish/Avodat-Kochavim-Chapter-Ten.htm.

14. "Anatomy of a One World Religion?" https://stellarhousepublishing.com/theocracy/, Truth Be Known Archives.

15. A group of non-Jewish delegates have come to Jerusalem to pledge their loyalty to the laws of Noah," Ezra HaLevi, *Arutz Sheva*, https://www.israelnationalnews.com/News/News.aspx/96347#.USnAPVcsy6U, January 10, 2006.

Chapter 26

1. James Finn, "God is Dead, and religion is dying," nytimes.com, article first published *New York Times*, April 19, 1970.

2. Ibid.

Chapter 28

1. "The Conservative Movement is no more – it has turned Reform", Op-ed by Rabbi Prof. Dov Fischer, 10/11/2021, https://www.israelnationalnews.com/news/316658

2. "Mashiach: Man or Movement?," Op-Ed by Yshai Amichai, 20/07/21, https://www.israelnationalnews.com/news/310214.

3. "Heaven's perfect timing," Rabbi Berel Wein, 02/12/21, https://www.israelnationalnews.com/news/317976.

Chapter 29

1. Holman Illustrated Bible Dictionary, Holman Bible Publishers, Nashville TN, 2003, p. 79 "Apocalyptic."

About the Author

FOR A VETERAN TRIAL ATTORNEY to be referred to as "a prophet for our time" is indeed unusual, but many who have heard Charles Crismier's daily radio broadcast, *VIEWPOINT*, believe just that. Now, in *MESSIAH*, his words, full of "passion and conviction," provide clear direction to both seekers and professing believers, both Jew and Gentile, increasingly drawn into the deceptive ways of the rapidly-developing new global order.

Crismier speaks from an unusual breadth of experience. After nine years as a public schoolteacher, he spent twenty years as a trial attorney, pleading causes before judge and jury. As a pastor's son, also serving in pastoral roles for 36 years, Crismier has been involved with ten distinct Protestant denominations – both mainline and otherwise, together with other independent and charismatic groups from coast to coast and from North to South – providing an enviable insider's view of American Christianity and life. Interestingly, his oldest daughter and lifelong assistant both reads and speaks Hebrew.

Deeply troubled by the direction of the nation, the world and Church he loves, this attorney left his lucrative Southern California law practice in 1992 to form SAVE AMERICA Ministries and was awarded the Valley Forge Freedom Foundation award for his contribution to the cause of "Rebuilding the Foundations of Faith and Freedom." "Chuck probes the heart and conscience with both a rare combination of insight, directness, urgency and compassion, and a message that desperately needs to be heard and heeded before it is too late."

From the birthplace of America – Richmond, Virginia – this former attorney speaks provocatively and prophetically on daily national radio as "a Voice to the Church," declaring "Vision for the Nation" in our world's greatest crisis hour, preparing the way of the Lord for history's final hour.

Charles Crismier can be contacted by writing or calling:

P.O. Box 70879
Richmond, VA 23255
(804) 754-1822
crismier@saveus.org

or through his website at
www.saveus.org

Other Life-Changing Books
by Charles Crismier

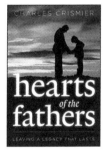

Hearts of the Fathers

Leaving a Legacy That Lasts! There is a fatherhood crisis in America. A serious "father problem" is at the core of nearly all social ills facing America today. Because fatherhood lies at the very root of a righteous relationship with the Creator Himself, the enemy of our souls desperately seeks to destroy that relationship. This book provides a "binocular" view of God's Word, exposing the deception all around us and illuminating the Heavenly Father's perfect prescription for both a temporal and eternal legacy.

$23

Lasting Love

Happily Ever After is the hope for most couples who proclaim their undying love by sacred vow. But is it a reasonable and attainable hope, or merely an illusion rooted in eros and emotion when we declare, "I DO?" The statistics of our time reveal a society tragically torn between the sacredness of a holy vow and the sorry state of marital bliss. In this small book, husband and wife will find marriage-transforming nuggets of truth passionately presented by Chuck and Kathie Crismier, whose 50 years of marriage are transparently translated so as to touch the life of every married couple.

$14

KING of the MOUNTAIN
The Eternal, Epic, End-Time Battle

All other issues and pursuits that consume the passions and purposes of mankind ultimately turn on the eternal question: "who will be king of the mountain?" This is the ultimate question of history which the power brokers and peoples of this planet must answer. Join this amazing journey from the Tower of Babel to the Temple Mount and from Creation to the Coming of Messiah.

$20

The SECRET of the LORD

God has a secret. It is a life-changing, destiny-determining secret. Yet it is a secret God desires to disclose to all who will seek it, unlocking all of the covenantal blessings and promises of God, both on earth and for eternity. Secrets are like mysteries. It remains a mystery until the right connections of fact are discerned, unveiling truth that sweeps away the shroud of "mystery." So it is with secrets. Once uncovered, the secret is no longer "secret" but becomes available for decision-making regarding life direction and eternal destiny.

$20

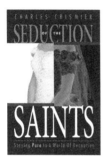

SEDUCTION of the SAINTS
Staying Pure in a World of Deception

"Take heed that no man deceive you," declared Jesus just before his crucifixion. His words were chilling! They cast a frame around life and eternity. In the final moments of his life on earth, Jesus chose to leave the disciples, with whom he had invested his life and ministry, a penetrating and haunting warning they would never forget... a warning that echoes through the centuries to all his disciples preparing for the end of the age.

$18

RENEWING the SOUL of AMERICA
(Endorsed by 38 National Christian Leaders)

"As a country and as individuals, we stand at a crossroads – to continue on the path to godlessness or to return to the way of righteousness." "Renewing the Soul of America is America's ONLY hope." But it must begin with you... one person at a time. Powerful inspiration for these difficult times.

$18

OUT of EGYPT
Building End-time Trust for End-time Trials.

Liberating... yet sobering. If Abraham, Moses, Israel, and... yes, Jesus had to "come out Egypt," how about us? The words "out of Egypt" or similar words appear over 400 times from Genesis to Revelation. Why has this theme been mentioned perhaps more than any other in the entire Bible? You will read... re-read this book!

$17

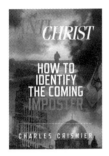